ENCYCLOPAEDIA OF
INDIAN GOVERNMENT:
PROGRAMMES AND POLICIES

ENCYCLOPAEDIA
OF
INDIAN GOVERNMENT: PROGRAMMES AND POLICIES

Vol. 40

Labour and Industrial Relations

Edited by

Satish Tiwari

ANMOL PUBLICATIONS PVT. LTD.
NEW DELHI - 110 002 (INDIA)

ANMOL PUBLICATIONS PVT. LTD.
4374/4B, Ansari Road, Daryaganj
New Delhi - 110 002

Encyclopaedia of Indian Government: Programmes and Policies

First Edition, 2000
ISBN 81-261-0515-1 (Set)

PRINTED IN INDIA

Published by J.L. Kumar for Anmol Publications Pvt. Ltd., New Delhi - 110 002 and Printed at Mehra Offset Press, Delhi.

Contents

Preface

Encyclopaedia of Indian Government: Programmes and Policies contains authoritative information on about fifty departmental policies and their future developmental programmes.

Organised to be completed in 40 volumes, this gigantic work covers Agriculture; Atomic Energy; Chemicals and Fertilizers; Coal; Commerce; Communication; Culture; Defence; Education; Environment and Forests; External Affairs; Finance; Food & Consumer Affairs; Food Processing Industries; Health and Family Welfare; Home Affairs and Internal Security; Human Resources; Industry; Information and Broadcasting; Labour; Law, Justice and Company Affairs; Non-conventional Energy Sources; Ocean Development; Parliamentary Affairs; Personnel, Public Grievances and Pensions; Petroleum and Natural Gas; Planning and Programme Implementation; Planning and Statistics; Posts and Telegraphs; Power; Rural Development; Science and Technology; Social Justice and Empowerment; Space; States Affairs; Steel; Steel and Mines; Sugar and Edible Oils; Surface Transport; Textiles; Tourism; Urban Development; Water Resources; Women and Child development etc.

Based on the information derived from authoritative sources, this work contains authentic facts and figures. I am deeply beholden to all the scholars whose writings are cited or substantially made use of in the present work. I am also thankful to Anmol Publications Pvt. Ltd. for undertaking publication of this encyclopaedia. I am solely responsible for shortcomings in presentation of matter.

Encyclopaedic in nature, this will prove a dependable reference work for scholars and academics besides those appearing for different competitive examinations.

—**Satish Tiwari**

1

Introduction

The Government has decided to setup Second National Labour Commission. The proposal for setting up of Second National Commission on Labour was first mooted by the Indian Labour Conference which made a recommendation to this effect in September, 1992. Various Central Employers and Trade Union Organisations also wrote to the Ministry of Labour from time to time suggesting the need to set up the Second National Commission on Labour.

The First National Commission on Labour was constituted in December, 1966 and the Commission submitted its report in August, 1969 after detailed examination of all aspects of labour problems both in the organised and unorganised sector.

The recommendations of the First Commission covered issues like recruitment agencies and practices, training and workers' education, working conditions, labour welfare, social security, industrial relations, employment of women and children, agricultural labour, Code of Discipline, grievance procedure, labour administration and India's relationship with the International Labour Organisation etc. The recommendations of the First National Commission have been fully implemented. Such implementation resulted in amendment of certain labour laws like the Workmens'

Compensation Act, 1923, Industrial Disputes Act, 1947, Employees State Insurance Act, 1948 and Employees Provident Fund (Miscellaneous Provisions) Act, 1952. Besides, certain new legislations were also enacted based on the recommendations of the National Commission. Thus, the Contract Labour (Regulation & Abolition) Act, 1970, Limestone and Dolomite Mines' Labour Welfare Fund Act, 1972, Equal Remuneration Act, 1976, Child Labour (Prohibition & Regulation) Act, 1986 etc., were enacted. Finally, in the areas of Wage Policy and Minimum Wages, employment services, vocational training, labour statistics and research the recommendations made by the Commission were taken into account and the policies, procedures and programmes were modified accordingly. The National Labour Institute, now known as V.V. Giri National Labour Institute was set up in 1972 in pursuance of the recommendations of the Commission.

Almost three decades have elapsed since the First National Commission on Labour made its recommendations. Many changes have taken place in the economic environment of the country, in recent years, necessitating corresponding change in the industrial policy and labour market. The large number of labour laws do not appear to be equipped to adequately and effectively deal with these complex situations and the challenges thrown up by them. It needs to be emphasised that review and revision of labour laws is a continuous process . However, during such reviews, these legislations, are considered in a piecemeal manner where the focus is generally very limited. Therefore, in order to have an indepth and critical review of labour welfare and related laws, the Government decided to set up the Second National Commission on Labour. The major tasks of the Commission would be :-

(a) to suggest rationalisation of existing laws relating to labour in the organised sector so as to make them more relevant and appropriate in the changing context of globalization and opening up of the Indian economy; and

(b) in the unorganised sector which constitute 92% of the total 320 million working population, the Commission would suggest an umbrella legislation so as to ensure a minimum level of protection to the workers. At present, various labour laws are applicable to the unorganised sector. These include laws like the Minimum Wages Act, the Payment of Wages Act, the Contract Labour (Regulation & Abolition) Act, Child Labour (Prohibition & Regulation Act, Beedi & Cigar Workers (Regulation of Employment & Conditions of Service) Act, the Bonded Labour System (Abolition) Act, Interstate Migrant Workmen (Regulation of Employment and Conditions of Service) Act, etc. However, these laws focus on a particular segment of the workers in the unorganised sector. The Commission would go into these aspects and try to suggest an umbrella legislation for the workers in the unorganised sector.

(c) in addition to the above, the commission would also review the implications of the recommendations made by the Jain Commission set up in May 1998 and Councils set up by the Prime Minister to review the various administrative laws. The Commission made recommendations on six important labour laws, viz., the Industrial Disputes Act, the Trade Unions Act, the Employees Provident

Funds (Miscellaneous Provisions) Act, the Employees State Insurance Act, the Contract Labour (Regulation & Abolition) Act and the Factories Act. A Committee has already been set up under the Chairmanship of the Chief Labour Commissioner (Central) to go into the implications of its recommendations and the National Commission would study these details and make suggestions: and

(d) the Commission will also study labour laws pertaining to Social Security, Occupational Safety and Health, Minimum Wages & Linking Wages with Productivity and safeguards and facilities required for women and disabled persons in employment.

The recommendations of the Second National Commission on Labour are also expected in formulation of the strategy for implementation of long term policies finalised for the Ninth Five year Plan of the Ministry of Labour. A Working Group on Labour Policy for the Ninth Plan was set up under the Chairmanship of Union Labour Secretary which identified major thrust areas as follows:

(i) reorientation of the role of employment exchanges from being mere registration and placement agencies to centres for compilation and dissemination of comprehensive market information, career counselling and vocational guidance;

(ii) improvement of economic and working conditions of the workers in the unorganised sector;

(iii) educational and training systems to be reoriented towards supplying requisite skills responsive to contemporary labour market changes;

(iv) abolition of child labour and rehabilitation of bonded labour.

In the above context, it may also be mentioned that Eighth Five Year Plan (1992-97) was initiated at a time when there were momentous changes in the global socio-economic arena. The Eighth Five Year Plan recognised the importance of the role of the market to ensure a balance between 'need' and 'supply'. The role of planning was seen as a means of overcoming the limitations of the market mechanism.

Human Development was the ultimate goal of the Eighth Five Year plan. The process of Liberalisation and globalisation which started in mid-1991 was meant to provide a competitive stimulus to Indian industry. The Eighth Plan sought to carry this process further, at the same time, ensuring a social safety net to the labour force to overcome the transitional adverse effects of liberalisation. Reaching full employment by the turn of the century was also a major objective of this Plan for which improvements in the quality of labour, productivity, skills and working conditions and welfare and social security measures for the unorganised labour were crucial. Hence, there was a lot of emphasis on skill formulation, strengthening of employment service, promotion of safety measures and worker's education and the pursuit of the goal of healthy industrial relations situation in the country. A National Child Labour Programme to withdraw children employed in hazardous industries/occupations/processes and secure their physical, economic and psychological rehabilitation through education, nutrition, check-up of health and skill training was also taken up, alongwith a continuous effort to eliminate and rehabilitate bonded labourers. Though a total outlay of Rs. 457.40 crores was provided, an amount of approximately Rs. 300 crores (excluding civil works) was spent during this Plan period.

However, to achieve the objectives set for the Ninth Five Year Plan, a total outlay of Rs.792.12 crores has been provided for the Ministry of Labour. It is expected that with the increased outlay made available to the Ministry of Labour, it would be possible to undertake Schemes for fulfilling the objectives set for the Ninth Five Year Plan and achieve increased welfare of the working class both in the organised as well as in the unorganised sector.

One of the items in the Agenda for discussion at the June, 1998 Session of the International Labour Conference at Geneva concerned adoption of a "Declaration of workers' fundamental rights at work and follow-up arrangments". The parameters of the follow-up were being discussed in the ILO for the past two years or so. As is known, member-countries of the ILO, on ratification of Conventions get duty bound to frame requisite legislation in their respective countries on lines and in terms with the requirements of the Conventions. Certain obligations also befall the countries once they become members of the ILO. It was apprehended by the Asia Pacific Group of countries that through the Declaration, an effort was being made to create new obligations for the member countries, such as additional 'supervisory mechanism. It was also apprehended that there was an attempt to link labour standards with international trade. The Asia-pacific Group, where India played an important part, adopted a united stand earlier in the November, 1997 Session of the Governing Body, when this item was discussed. Detailed discussions were held and ultimately many of the concerns expressed by the Asia Pacific Group and India were duly incorporated in the final text of the Declaration and follow-up. The text has reaffirmed that :-

(i) The ILO is the sole competant international organisation mandated to set and deal with labour standards;

(ii) The Declaration and follow up should be promotional and not complaint-based;

(iii) Technical assistance and advisory services will be a key element of the Declaration;

(iv) Labour Standards and the Declaration will not be issued for protectionist purposes; and

(v) The Declaration will focus on principles alongwith rights.

Considering the concerted efforts made by Workers! Group as well as some developed countries to adopt a binding Declaration and intrusive follow up, the final text of the Declaration and follow up is considered as a decisive achievement for the efforts made by the Asia-Pacific Group and Government of India.

Though the imminent danger has been averted through the united and concerted efforts of the developing countries, yet the problem remains. Efforts are continuing on the part of the developed countries to force the application of core labour standards' and to link them directly or indirectly with international trade. For instance, the European Union promulgated a legislation which tends to reward the exports from those developing countries which have ratified certain core labour standards. This indeed is a very dangerous trend and is expected to have adverse implications for the exports, from certain developing countries. When certain labour standards (Conventions) are adopted by the International Labour Conference it has nowhere been mentioned, either explicitly or implicitly that these can be used for adversely affecting the economic interests of certain member countries, who do not ratify these Conventions.

Therefore, this strategy on the part of developed countries is not in line with the objectives of the ILO. In case this strategy is continued to be adopted by certain developed countries, it may ultimately have adverse implications for the ILO, it-self. This aspect needs to be appreciated by one and all. At the same time, it needs to be emphasised that there is no denying the fact that the interests of the working class must be protected to the maximum extent possible. There is need to -ratify standards as adopted by the ILO to as large an extent as possible, so as to extend the benefits of these standards to the workers. Moreover, ratification of ILO's, Conventions/ Recommendations, itself depends on the economic and political situation obtaining in the member States. India has already ratified 38 Conventions and efforts are being made to ratify a few more Conventions in the near future.

This is a very encouraging trend particularly when it is seen in the perspective of ratification by other member States including certain developed countries. Therefore, while on the one hand, continuous efforts need to be made to promote the interests and welfare of the workers, through adoption and application of Labour standards, at the same time, attempts to harm the national economies in the name of the interest of the workers must be resisted and opposed. One of the terms of reference of the Second National Commission encompasses this aspect and it is hoped that the recommendation of the Commission will further help to delineate thinking and strategy on this aspect.

2

Organisational Structure and Functions

Labour jurisdiction

Constitutional status

Under the Constitution of India, Labour is a subject in the Concurrent List where both the Central & State Governments are competent to enact legislation subject to certain matters being reserved for the Centre.

Table

Labour Jurisdiction: Constitutional Status

Union List	*Concurrent List*
Entry No. 55: Regulation of Labour and Safety in mines and oil fields. Entry No. 61: Industrial disputes concerning Union employees Entry No. 65: Union agencies and institutions for "Vocational training . .".	Entry No. 22: Trade Unions; industries and labour disputes. Entry No. 23: Social Security and insurance, employment and unemployment. Entry No. 24: Welfare of labour including conditions of work, provident funds, employees' invalidity and old age pension and maternity benefit.

Personnel

Shri M.P. Veerendra Kumar continued to hold the charge of 'the Ministry of Labour till 19.03.1998. On 20.03.1998

Dr. Satyanarayan Jatiya took over the charge of the Ministry of Labour. Dr. Lakshmidhar Mishra continued to hold the charge of Secretary. On 19.01. 1998 Shri A.M. Nimbalkar, assumed the charge of the post of Additional Secretary. Shri S. Krishnan, continued to hold the charge of the post of Director General (Employment & Training). Shri R.K. Saini, and Smt. Padma Balasubramanian, continued to hold the charge of Joint Secretaries. Shri D.K. Trehan, contined to hold the charge of Labour and Employment Adviser. He also continued to hold the additional charge of the post of Economic Adviser (Assessor) in Wage Boards for Working Journalists and Non-Journalists Newspaper Employees. Smt. Chitra Chopra, assumed the charge of the post of Joint Secretary on 18.03.1998. Shri S.K. Das, continued as Joint Secretary and Director General of Labour Welfare. Shri Subhash Sharma, continued as Chief Labour Commissioner (Central).

Legend

Designation in ministry

JS – Joint Secretary

LEA – Labour & Employment Adviser

DGLW – Director General Labour Welfare

PGE – Protector General of Emigrants

FA – Financial Adviser

DIR – Director

DS – Deputy Secretary

WC – Welfare Commissioner

CA – Controller of Accounts

JD – Joint Director

US – Under Secretary

DD – Deputy Director

SA – Senior Analyst

Names of Sections/Desks/Units

AA – Anuvad Anubhag

ADM – Administration

AC – Audit Cell

B – Bank

B&A – Budget & Accounts

BL – Bonded Labour

C – Coal

C&WL – Child &Women Labour

CLS – Central Labour Service

CMT – Career Management &Training

COORD – Coordination

CR – Central Registry

DU – Departmental Undertaking

EMIG – Emigration

ESA – Economic & Statistical Analysis

FIN – Finance

ILAS – International Labour Affairs Section

IMP – Implementation

IR – Industrial Relations

ISH – Industrial Safety & Health

IWSU – Internal Work Study Unit

LC	–	Labour Conference
LDRC	–	Labour Documentation & Research Centre
LW	–	Labour Welfare
MISC	–	Miscellaneous
MMO	–	Meeting and Maintenance Officer
PAO	–	Pay & Accounts Off ice
PG	–	Policy General
PL	–	Policy Legal
PLG	–	Planning Unit
PU	–	Parliament Unit
RBN	–	Raj Bhasha Niti
RW	–	Rural Workers
SS	–	Social Security
TECH	–	Technical
W	–	Welfare
WB	–	Wage Board
WC	–	Wage Cell
(EPFO)	–	Employees' Provident Fund Organisation
(CBWE)	–	Central Board for Workers' Education
(ESIC)	–	Employees' State Insurance Corporation
(VVGNLI)	–	V.V. Giri National Labour Institute
(LB)	–	Labour Bureau

Names of Officers

JS(RKS)	–	Shri R.K. Saini
DGLW	–	Shri S.K. Das
LEA	–	Shri D.K. Trehan
JS(PB)	–	Smt. Padma Balasubramanian
JS(C)	–	Smt. Chitra Chopra
JS & FA	–	Smt. Praveen Tripathi
DIR(PMS)	–	Shri P.M. Sirajuddin
DIR(AB)	–	Shri A. Bhattacharya
DIR(PPM)	–	Shri P.P. Mitra
DIR(VK)	–	Smt. Vinita Kumar
DIR(RKR)	–	Shri R.K. Rang
DIR(PV)	–	Smt. Preet Verma
DIR(KK)	–	Shri K. Krishnamurthy
WC(HQ.)	–	Shri Y.P. Yajurvedi
DS(PK)	–	Dr. (Km.) Prafulla Kerkatta
DS(SS)	–	Shri Shingara Singh
CA	–	Smt. Anita Bansal
JD(GB)	–	Shri G. Bhujabal
JD(VP)	–	Shri V. Parameswaran,
US(JPS)	–	Shri J.P. Shukla
US(SVK)	–	Shri S.V. Krishnan
US(HS)	–	Shri Hari Singh
US(HG)	–	Shri H.C. Gupta
US(VG)	–	Shri S. Venugopalan

US(VDN)	–	Shri V.D. Nagar
US(TS)	–	Shri T.A. Srinivasan
US(CDB)	–	Shri C.D. Bhardwaj
US(KS)	–	Smt. Krishna Sharma
US(GS)	–	Shri Gopal Singh
US(PKR)	–	Shri P.K. Roy
US(KVB)	–	Shri K.V.B. Unny
US(SDK)	–	Shri S.D. Kashyap
US(RRS)	–	Shri R.R. Sharma
DD(D)	–	Shri O.P. Dahiya
DD(K)	–	Shri O.P. Kahol
DD(S)	–	Shri Mritunjay Singh
DD(LS)	–	Shri Lal Sengalur
DD(OL)	–	Shri K.N. Pandey
SA	–	Smt. Urmila Sharma
Dy.CA	–	Shri Rajesh Kumar

Table 2
Offices under the ministry of labour

Attached offices

- Directorate General, Employment and Training, New Delhi.
- Office of the Chief Labour Commissioner (Central), New Delhi.
- Labour Bureau, Chandigarh & Simla.
- Directorate General, Factory Advice Services and Labour Institutes, Mumbai.

Subordinate offices

- Directorate General, Mines Salary, Dhanbad.

- Offices of the Welfare Commissioner, Allahabad, Bangalore, Bhilwara, Bhubaneshwar, Calcutta, Hyderabad, Jabalpur, Karma (Bihar) and Nagpur.

Adjudicating bodies

- Central Government Industrial Tribunal-cum-Labour Court No. 1 Dhanbad (Bihar) and No. 1 Mumbai, No. 2 Dhanbad and No. 2 Mumbai and at Asansol, Calcutta, Jabalpur, New Delhi, Chandigarh, Kanpur, Bangalore and Jaipur.

Arbitration body

- Board of Arbitration (JCM), New Delhi

Autonomous orgnisations

- Employees' State Insurance Corporation, New Delhi.
- Employees' Provident Fund Organisation, New Delhi.
- V.V. Giri National Labour Institute, NOIDA (UP).
- Central Board for Workers' Education, Nagpur.

Table 3

Main subject

- Labour policy (including wage policy) and legislation;
- Safety, health and welfare of labour;
- Social security of Labour;
- Policy relating to special target groups such as women, child labour;
- Industrial relations and enforcement of labour laws in the Central sphere;
- Adjudication of industrial disputes through Central Government Industrial Tribunals Cum Labour Courts and National Industrial Tribunals;
- Workers' Education.
- Labour and Employment Statistics;
- Emigration of Labour employment abroad;
- Employment services and vocational training;

- Administration of Central Labour & Employment Services;
- International co-operation in labour and employment matters.

@ Refer to Appendix 1 for subjects allotted to Ministry of Labour as per Allocation of Business Rules.

Structure and formations

The Ministry has four attached offices and ten subordinate offices, four autonomous organisations, twelve adjudicating bodies and one arbitration body. (Box 2.2).

Attached offices

Directorate general of employment and training

This Office is responsible for laying down the policies, standards, norms and guidelines in the area of vocational training throughout the country and also for co-ordinating employment services.

Office of the chief labour commissioner (Central)

This Office is responsible for (a) prevention, investigation and settlement of industrial disputes in the Central sphere, (b) enforcement of awards and settlements, (c) implementation of Labour laws in industries and establishments in respect of which Central Government is the appropriate Government, (d) verification of membership of Unions affiliated to the Central Organisations of workers forgiving them representation on national and international conferences and committees and (e) fixation and revision of Dearness Allowance Component of minimum wages by notifications under the Minimum Wages Act, 1948 in scheduled employments.

Directorate general, factory advice service and labour institutes

This Office is concerned with the safety, health and welfare of workers in factories and docks. It is responsible for coordinating the implementation of the

Factories Act, 1948 by the State Governments and formulation of Model rules thereunder. It is also concerned with the administration of the Dock Workers (Safety, Health and Welfare) Act, 1986. It undertakes research in industrial safety, occupational health, industrial hygiene, industrial psychology and industrial physiology. It provides training mainly in the field of industrial safety and health including a diploma course of one year duration in industrial safety. The Diploma is an essential qualification for appointment of Safety Officers in factories. Regular in-servie training of Factory Inspectors is another important activity of this Organisation.

Labour bureau

This Off ice is responsible for collection, compilation and publication of statistical and other information regarding employment, wages, earnings, industrial relations, working conditions etc. It also compiles and publishes the Consumer Price Index Numbers for industrial and agricultural workers. The Bureau further necessary assistance to the States for conducting training programmes in Labour Statistics at State/District/Unit levels.

Subordinate offices

Directorate General of Mines Safety (DGMS)

This Office is entrusted with enforcement of the provisions of the Mines Act, 1952 and the Rules and Regulations framed thereunder. The provisions of the Indian Electricity Act, 1910 as applicable to mines and oil fields are also enforced by it.

Welfare commissioners

The nine Offices of Welfare Commissioners are responsible for providing welfare facilities to the workers employed in the mica, limestone and dolomite, iron ore, manganese and chrome ore mines and in the beedi and cinema industries.

Autonomous organisations

Employees' state insurance corporation

The Corporation is responsible for the implementation of the Employees' State Insurance Act, 1948 which provides for medical care and treatment to insured persons and their families. Assistance is given in terms of benefits during sickness and maternity, compensation for employment injury, pensions for dependents on the death of workers due to employment injury, etc.

The employees' provident fund organisation

This Organisation is responsible for administration of the Employees' Provident Funds and Miscellaneous Provisions Act, 1952. Schemes for Provident Fund, Family Pension and Deposit Linked Insurance are implemented by the Organisation for the benefit of the workers covered under the scheme. This Organisation is also responsible for administration of Employees' Pension Scheme, 1995 which has come into existence on 16.11.95.

Giri National Labour Institute

The Institute, a registered society, conducts action oriented research and provides training to grass-root level workers in the trade union movement, both in the urban and rural areas and also to Officers dealing with industrial relations, personnel management, labour welfare etc.

The central board for workers' education

The Board is a registered society dealing with schemes for training of workers in the techniques of trade unionism and in bringing about consciousness among workers about their rights, duties and responsibilities. The Board has also undertaken programmes for rural workers' education and functional adult education.

Adjudicating bodies

Central government industrial tribunals-cum-labour courts

Twelve Industrial Tribunal-cum-Labour Courts have been set up under the provisions of the Industrial Disputes Act, 1947 for adjudication of the industrial disputes in organisations for which the Central Government is the appropriate Government.

Arbitration body

The Board of arbitration

The Board, set up under the Scheme for Joint Consultative Machinery and Compulsory Arbitration is an institution for compulsory arbitration of disputes between the Government employees and the Government on pay and allowances, weekly hours of work and leave of a class or grade of employees.

Central labour service

The Central Labour Service (CLS) was constituted with effect from 3rd February, 1987 by merging Group 'A' posts belonging to (a) the Central Industrial Relations Machinery, (b) the Central Pool of Labour Officers and (c) the Welfare Organisation under the Ministry of Labour. The purpose behind the creation of the Service is to have an integrated structure of the existing functionaries in the area of industrial relations, labour law enforcement and labour welfare.

The sanctioned strength in different Grades of the Central Labour Service and their deployment is indicated in Box 2.4 and Box 2.5. Factories and mines employing 500 or more workers and plantations employing 300 or more workers are required to appoint a prescribed number of welfare officers under the relevant statutes. The Central Government establishments which come within the definition of "factory" under the Factories Act, 1948 including production units, hospitals, R&D Centres within the administrative control of various ministries appoint officers belonging to Central Labour Service as Asst. Labour Welfare Commissioner (C) and Dy. Labour Welfare Commissioner (C) for the purpose. These officers are supervised by Labour Welfare Commissioner (C). Apart from discharging statutory functions, they also advise and assist the management of the concerned establishments in the areas of industrial relations, safety, health and welfare, etc.

During the period from 1.1.98 to 31.12.98 these Officers handled 38333 grievances of which 36370 were settled. As such these Officers continued to play an important role in getting the grievances of workers settled thus preventing these grievances from turning into Industrial Disputes.

Table 4

Sanctioned Posts in the Central Labour Service in various Ministries/ Departments

Sl. No.	*Ministry/Department*	*Number of Asst. Lab. Wel. Comm. (C)*	*No. of Dy. Labour Welfare Comm.(C)*	*No. of Labour Welfare Comm. (C)*
1	*2*	*3*	*4*	*5*
1.	Ministry of Agriculture	–	1	–
2.	Ministry of Home Affairs (A & N Admn)	2	–	–
3.	Ministry of Communication	2	3	–
4.	Ministry of Defence	128	45	5
5.	Ministry of Finance	12	5	1
6.	Ministry of Health & Family Welfare	6	–	–
7.	Ministry of Science &Technology	1	–	–
8.	Ministry of Urban Development	17	8	

(Contd. . .)

9.	Ministry of Labour	2 (Asstt. Director)
10.	Office of the Chief Labour Commissioner (Central)	
	(a) Joint Chief Labour Commissioner (Central)	1
	(b) Chief Adviser (Labour Welfare)	1
	(c) Deputy Chief Labour Commissioner (Central)	6
	(d) Director (Training)	1
	(e) Regional Labour Commissioner (Central)	20
	(f) Regional Labour Commissioner (Central) (Training)	1
	(g) Assistant Labour Commissioner (Central)	75
11.	Office of Director General (Labour Welfare)	
	(a) Welfare Commissioner(C)	9
	(b) Assistant Welfare Commissioner(C)	5

Work study

During the yew 1998-99 (uptc 31st March, 1999), the Internal Work Study Unit has finalised/issued a number of reports of which the main ones are:-

(1) Report on maintenance of files in the Ministry of Labour

(2) Report on layout/space study conducted in Respect of Ministry of Labour, Main Secretariat.

(3) Draft study report in respect of Central Hospital, Joda and National Resource Centre VV Giri National Labour Institute, Noida.

(4) Final report of the work measurement study of

the (i) office of AWC, Cannanore, (ii) Library & Information centre and Hindi units of Labour Bureau, Simla and Chandigarh.

(5) Reports have also been prepared in respect of O&M Inspection and Record Management Study conducted at the office of RLC(C), Mumbai, CGIT-cum-Labour Court No. 1 & 2 Mumbai.

IWSU has also carried out work measurement study of (i) Welfare Commissioner's office at Allahabad including medical units at Varanasi, (ii) Welfare Administrator's Office at Dehradun, (iii) Central Board for Workers' Education at Calcutta, (iv) Protector of Emigrants, Calcutta, (v) Welfare Commissioner's office at Hyderabad, (vi) Asstt. Welfare Commissioner's office including Central Hospital, Elementary/High school at Kalichedu and Elementary/High school at Talcher. The other work measurement studies proposed to be conducted by March, 1999 are (i) Asstt. Welfare Commissioner's office at Madurai, (ii) Static-cum-mobile Dispensary at Chennai, (iii) Central Board for Worker's Education at Chennai, (iv) Welfare Commissioner's office including mobile unit at Bhubaneshwar (v) Asstt. Welfare Commissioner's office including mobile medical unit and mobile cinema unit at Barbil and (vi) Welfare Administrator, Rourkela. The 0 & M Inspections proposed to be conducted by March, 1999 are (i) POE, DGFASCL, CLI, CBWE, Mumbai and (ii) RLC, Inspectorate of Dock safety, CBWE & POE, Cochin.

The channel of submission of cases & final levels of disposal of various categories of cases is being reviewed again in the meeting being held by the Additional Secretary. The Brochure on the Organisation of the Ministry of Labour has been forwarded to Translation Bureau Deptt. of Official Language for translation into

Hindi.

O&M Inspection in respect of 80% Sections/Desks/Units in the Ministry (Main Secretariat) is expected to be completed by March, 1999.

Records management

To achieve better results in the disposal of cases/ records, the following special drives were launched:-

- Arrear clearance drive was conducted during the month of November, 1998.
- Special drive to review the work of records management was conducted during the month of October, 1998.
- Special drive to review contents of almirah was conducted during the month of January, 1999.

During the year 1998-99, recording of 4367 files, reviewing of 3938 files and weeding of 3674 files is expected to be done upto March, 1999.

Progressive use of hindi

Effective measures were taken for the progressive use of Hindi for official purposes. Efforts were made to ensure compliance of the Official Language Act/Rules as also the various orders/instructions issued by the Department of Official Language from time to time. Hindi Division, namely, Rajbhasha Niti Anubhag which looks after implementation work and 'Anuwad Anubhag' which attends to the translation needs of the Main Secretariat continued to function smoothly. Regular monitoring of the work in Hindi through quarterly reports was conducted. Offices were periodically inspected and instructions given for rectification of discrepancies pointed out during such inspections.

The Official Language Implementation Committee of the Ministry of Labour held meetings regularly. Follow-up action to implement the decisions of the Committee in the aforesaid meetings was also taken. Hindi Salahkar Samiti of Ministry of Labour is under reconstitution. For encouraging the use of Hindi in various attached and subordinate offices of the Ministry, Rajbhasha Shield Awards are given to the off ices located in Region 'A', and 'B' on the basis of regionwise competition held every year. On the Designation basis of work done in Hindi during 1996-97, office of Labour Bureau, Shimla and Central Labour Education Board, Nagpur are to be given Rajbhasha Officers Shield for Region 'A' and 'B' respectively.

During the Hindi fortnight special programmes were organised in the Ministry from 14.9.98 to 28.9.98. For encouraging use of Hindi in official work, as many as nine Hindi competitions were held during Hindi fortnight 108 employees enthusiastically participated in these competitions, out of which 40 employees were awarded. In order to give away the prizes to winners of various competitions, a prize distribution function was held on 2.11.98 which was presided over by Honourable Labour Minister. Shri Avanti Lal Ji Jain, Freedom Fighter and Journalist gave away the Cash Prizes and congratulated the winners. On the 50th Anniversary of Independence a Hindi Smarika was also published by the Ministry of Labour.

In addition to above a meeting was convened by the Union Labour Minister, during Hindi Fortnight, and a detailed discussion was held in connection with the progressive use of Hindi. Seven sections of the Ministry were specified to do their original official work in Hindi. In order to promote the use of Hindi in the Ministry on Computer, a meeting was convened which was attended by all officers conversant with computer work. A decision was also taken in the meeting to feed all the standard drafts in the computer. Most of the work relating to inspection, review, observation of Hindi Fortnight and quarterly report in respect of use of Hindi relating to Rajbhasha Niti Anubhag was done on the Computer. Under Hindi Training Scheme during 1997-98, five LDCs were trained in Hindi Typing and two Stenos were imparted training in Hindi Shorthand.

The requirement of documents to be issued bilingually (under Section 3(3) of the Official Languages Act) was complied with and all letters received in Hindi were replied to in Hindi. Position regarding office equipments (status of availability), skill level of functionaries and the targets and achievements relating to correspondence in Hindi as on 30.9.1998 is presented below:-

Progress of use of hindi in the ministry of labour, office equipment (status of availability)

	English	*Devnagari*	*Bilingual*
Typewriters	195	80	42
Telex Machines	01	–	01

Skill level of functionaries

Designation	*Total No. of employees Hindi*	*Employees with knowledge of Trg. in Hindi*	*Employees undergoing*
Officers	87	85	–
Employees	253	245	01
Total	340	330	01
* Typist	58	14	08
*Stenographers	48	19	11

*(included amongst employees)

Targets and achievements relating to correspondence in hindi

		Letters issued in hindi	*Letters issued in english*	*Targets laid down*
1.(a)	Letters sent to State Govts/Union Territory Admns etc. located in regions A & B and Persons in these regions.	5126 (60.00%)	3487	100%
(b)	Letters etc. sent to the Central Govt. offices located in regions A & B.	3927 (66.10%)	1872	100%
(c)	Letters etc. sent to Central Govt. offices located in regions 'C'.	1192 (60.00%)	818	65%
	Telegrams sent to regions A & B.	70 (72.00%)	188	100%

Career management and training

The main function of Career Management and Training (CMT) Unit is to organise training programmes on decentralised basis, for LDCs, UDCs and Stenographers etc. It also nominates Officers and members of staff of Ministry of Labour and its attached & subordinate offices and other autonomous organisations under it to the ISTM and other autonomous organisations for training on various courses.'

During the period from 1.1.98 to 15.9.98, 55 Officers and members of staff were sponsored for various training activities. One training programme was organised for UDCs. Five training courses on computer were also organised.

Finance wing

The Finance Wing is mainly responsible for scrutiny of all Plan Schemes and to give advice on all financial and allied proposals, preparation of budget and revised estimates related to services concerning the Ministry proper and the attached and subordinate offices, Performance Budget, expenditure control and financial review, work measurement studies, internal audit etc.

The accounting set up is headed by a Controller of Accounts, who is responsible for cash management.

The important tasks and activities of the Integrated Finance Division are :-

(i) to advise the Administrative Ministry on all matters falling within the field of delegated powers;

(ii) to screen all expenditure proposals required to be referred to the Finance Ministry for concurrence or comments;

(iii) to ensure that the schedule for preparation of Budget is adhered to by the Ministry and that the Budget is drawn up according to the instructions issued by the Ministry of Finance from time to time;

(iv) to scrutinise budget proposals thoroughly before sending them to the Ministry of Finance;

(v) to see that complete departmental accounts are maintained in accordance with the requirements under the General Financial Rules;

(vi) to keep itself closely associated with the formulation of Schemes and important expenditure proposals from their initial stages;

(vii) to associate itself with the evaluation of progress/performance in the case of projects and other continuing schemes and to see that the results of such evaluation studies are taken into account in the budget formulation;

(viii) to watch the settlement of audit objections, Inspection Reports, draft audit paras etc.; to ensure prompt action on Audit Reports and Appropriation Accounts, Reports of the Public Accounts Committee, Estimates Committee and Committee on Public Undertakings;

During the year 1998-99, all budget and accounts matters were attended to within the time schedule prescribed. By careful scrutiny of proposals, it was ensured that the expenditure conformed to budgetary appropriations, the rules and regulations prescribed by the Finance Ministry and that it was consistent with economy, efficiency and the objectives of the relevant schemes/programmes in connection with which it was being incurred. The guidelines with regard to fiscal prudence and austerity in Expenditure Management as prescribed by the Ministry of Finance, Department of Expenditure were also sought to be enforced and guidelines relating to effective cash management were also followed.

For the future, it is proposed to continue to see that an effective accounting system and internal controls are in place and also that a system of correct financial discipline consistent with efficiency, economy and effectiveness is maintained. It is also proposed to streamline and strengthen the functioning of the Internal Audit Wing and the Internal Work Study Unit which also function under the Integrated Financial Adviser.

3

Industrial Relations: Central Industrial Relations Machinery (CIRM)

CIRM headed by the Chief Labour Commissioner (Central) [CLC (C)], is entrusted with the task of maintaining good industrial relations in the Central sphere. At the headquarters, CIRM has a complement of 25 officers who perform line and staff functions. In the field, the machinery has a complement of 253 officers and their establishments are spread over different parts of the country with zonal, regional and unit level formations as presented in the organogram.

Functions of CIRM broadly consist of settlement of industrial disputes, enforcement of labour laws in Central sphere and verification of membership of trade unions.

During 1998, CIRM intervened in 445(P) cases of threatened strikes and its conciliatory efforts succeeded in averting 418 (p) strikes which represents a success rate of 90.70%.

Table

Specific functions of CIRM

- Prevention and settlement of industrial disputes in industries for which the Central Govt. is the appropriate Government' under the Industrial Disputes Act, 1947;
- Enforcement of Labour Laws in industries and

establishments in respect of which the Central Govt. is the appropriate Government';

- Verification of membership of Trade Unions under the Code of Discipline;
- Ad hoc verification of membership of trade unions in major ports;
- Verification of membership of registered trade unions;
- Enforcement of Awards and Settlements;
- Conduct of enquiry into the breaches of Code of Discipline;
- Formation of Works Committees and Workers' Participation in management;
- Collection of statistical information in the Central sphere pertaining to industrial disputes, work stoppages, wages, labour situation and labour regulations;
- Defence of court cases and writ petitions arising out of implementation of labour laws.

Enforcment of labour laws

The CIRM Officers focus special attention on the enforcement of beneficial labour legislation such as Payment of Wages Act, Minimum Wages Act, Contract labour (Regulation & Abolition) Act, Equal Remuneration Act, and Inter-State Migrant Workmen's (RE & CS) Act etc., with a view to securing benefits and facilities to the workers in the unorganised sector. In this regard, special drives for inspections under the Crash Programmes & Task Force inspections were organised during the year for extending coverage of labour laws like the Minimum Wages Act, Payment of Wages Act, Equal Remuneration Act & Contract Labour (Regulation & Abolition) Act to workers in the unorganised/ informal sector. A total No. 1074(P) inspections under the above enactments were carried out during the year 1998 as a result of which 15938(P) irregularities and 489(P) cases of short payments/ nonpayments were detected.

Quasi judicial work

The C.I.R.M. Officers from the level of ALC (C) up to the level of CLC (C) also perform certain Quasi Judicial functions. The ALC's (C) are controlling authorities under the Payment of Gratuity Act, authorities under the Equal Remuneration Act and Registering & Licencing Officers under CL (R&A) Act and ISMW (RE&CA) Act. The RLCs (C) have been appointed as authorities under the Minimum Wages Act for deciding claim cases, Certifying Officers under the Industrial Employment (Standing Orders) Act and appellate authorities under the P.G. Act, E.R. Act, CL (R&A) Act and ISMW (RE&CS) Act. The Dy. CLCs (C), Jt. CLC (C) and CLC (C) are appellate authorities under Industrial Employment (Standing Orders) Act. In addition, the CLC (C) is also a quasi judicial authority under Rule 25(2) (v) (a) & (b) of the CL (R&A) Central Rules. The cases decided by these officers under some of the enactments during the year 1997 are exhibited.

Labour officers

The Factories and Mines, employing 500 or more workers and Plantations employing 300 or more workers, are required to appoint a prescribed number of Welfare Officers under respective statutes. A large number of Central Government establishments coming under the definition of 'factory' appoint officers belonging to the Central Labour Service as Labour Officers and Senior Labour Officers. They function as Welfare Officers under Factories Act, 1948. Similarly, the officers of the Service are appointed in the Central Public Works Department for advising the administration of CPWD in the implementation of Labour laws applicable to that department. They are also appointed in hospitals and other units to ensure compliance with the provisions of the Industrial Disputes Act as also for securing implementation of non-statutory welfare measures. A number of posts of Deputy Adviser (Labour Welfare) have also been created in various Government Departments. The Labour Officers, the Senior Labour Officers and the Deputy Advisers are also to advise and assist the managements of establishments in areas of industrial relations, production and productivity, safety, health, welfare, recruitment, training and research. They help management of the establishments in the constitution of statutory and voluntary bipartite fora such as Works Committees, Unit level Joint Committees, Safety Committees, Canteen Managing Committees etc. and participate in the deliberations of these fora as ex-officio members or advisors. The Labour Officers play an important role in getting the grievances of the workers settled, thus preventing them from escalating into industrial disputes. About 94 percent of grievances handled by them during year 1998 wore settled.

Verificcation of trade union membership

The CIRM officers completed verification under the code of Discipline in respect of 7 establishments. All these conducted through secret ballot cations were conducted in establishments:

— Central warehouring corporation (M.P. Region).

— M/S Singareni Collieries.

— ONGC Ltd. (Bombay Regional Business Centre, Mumbai).

— Nuclear Fuel Complex, Hyderabad.

— India Govt. Mint, Hyderabd.

— Fruit &Vegetable Project, New Delhi.

— Heavy Water Plant (Manaugune) Hyderabad.

Statutory verification for the purpose of appointment of workmen directors in respect of one bank.,

— Allahabad Bank.

Adhoc verification of membership of unions for appointment of workers directors in Port Trust and Dock Labour Board during 1998 in the following establishments:

— Bombay Port.

— Calcutta Port.

General verification of trade unions

The representations of Centr al Trade Union Organisations (CTUOs) on national and international fora is determined on the basis of strength of membership of Trade Unions affiliated to Central Trade Union Organisations. The last general verification with December 31, 1989 as the date of reckoning was completed and the verification results were declared on 26.12.96. The verification results indicated that there are 8 Central Trade Union Organisations (CTUOs) which have a membership of at least 5 lakhs and a spreadover at least 4 states and 4 industries (including agriculture). The process of next General Verification has already started and the Union Labour Minister has held meetings in April 1998 and May 1998 with the Central Trade Union Organisations (CTUOs) to decide on the verification procedure, the -machinery for such verification and also the date of reckoning. As there are difference of opinion among the CTUOs on the date of reckoning and the verification procedure, the matter would be discussed further by the Ministry with the CTUOs so that a consensus could emerge. The process of next verification would be taken up after a consensus is reached among them.

Table

Settlement of grievances by labour officers/senior labour officrs during the year 1998(P)

(Figures in numbers)

		Handled	*Total Handled*	*Settled*	*Total*
(1)	Individual Grievances	26670	31154	24830	29794
(2)	Collective Grievances	5484		4964	
(3)	Grievances relating to terms and conditions of services etc.	20408	31154	9486	29794
(4)	Other Grievances (Private Domestic)	10746			10308
(5)	Percentage of success :		94.00%		

In pursunce of the LM/ Secretary (Labour)'s direction on the basis of advice received from Solicitor General of India and Order Consistiting a Standing Committee to determine the procedure for conducting verification of membership of trade unions affiliated to CTUOs for the purpose of determining the strength of CTUOs and to sortout the problems arising there under a standing committee has been constituted under the Chairmanship of CLC(C) on 20 July 1998. So far four meeting of the Standing Committee have taken place on 3.8.98, 11.9.98, 26.10.98 and 14.12.98 for finalising the darft procedure for verification. The next meeting of the Standing committee will be held on 12.1.99.

Works committees

Under Section 3 of the Industrial Disputes Act, 1947,

Works Committees are required to be constituted in industrial establishments employing one hundred and more workmen. Works Committees at the plant level promote measures for securing and preserving amity and good relations between employers and workmen and comment on matters of common interest in order to harmonise any difference of opinion between the employers and workmen in respect of such matters. Works

Committees consist of elected (both unionised as well a non-unionised workers in a proportionate manner).Elections are held once in every two years. The total number of representatives on the Works Committees is limited to 20, of which not less than half are workmen's representatives. (2) Information relating to the number of Works Committees to be formed and the number of the Works Committees actually formed in the central sphere establishments during 1998 is given in Table 3.5.

Table

(A)	*(B)*	*(C)*	*(D)*
No. of Works committees to be formed	*No. of workers under (A) format*	*No. of works committees actually*	*No. of workers covered under (C)*
11265(p)	1309691 (P)	870(P)	835512(P)

Major industrial relations events 1998 cntral sphere

Post and telegraph

The Director (S.R.), Department of Post, New Delhi informed that National Federation of Postal Employees and Federation of National Postal Federations had served a joint strike notice dated 25.12.97 on Secretary, Department of Post proposing one-day token strike on 6.1.98 in support of their demands relating to implementation of Justice Talwar Committee report.

RLC(C), Headquarters held conciliation proceedings on 5.1.98. and submitted FOC as no settlement could be arrived at and the strike could not be averted. The response to the strike was, however, partial.

National Federation of Postal Employees and Federation of National Postal Organisations; served a strike notice to the Secretary, Dept. of Post proposing to go on nation-wide indefinite strike. The main demands of the Federations/unions were implementation of Talwar Committee report on Extra-Departmental employees, improvement of pay scales, restructuring of cadres, finalisation of bonus formula, etc. The matter was seized in conciliation at the level of Dy.CLC(C), Headquarters. The conciliation proceedings were held on 29.6.98, 6.7.98 and 7.7.98. Nearly six lakh employees including ED employees went on strike from 9.7.98 which resulted in disruption of postal services throughout the country. However, following an assurance of a fair deal by the Government, the strike was called off on 16.7.98.

Major ports

About 2500 dock workers of Visakhapatnam Dock Labour Board under the aegis of Visakhapatnam Port Employees Union (HMS) and Visakhapatnam Harbour & Port Workers Union (AITUC) resorted to indefinite strike from 23.1.98 in support of their demands including revision of piece rate wage scheme and filling-up of vacancies, etc. When conciliatory efforts of ALC(C) Visakhapatnam failed, RLC(C), Hyderabad intervened and held discussions with the unions and the management on various dates. Subsequently the matter was taken up by the Chief Labour Commissioner (Central) with the Secretary; Ministry of Surface Transport and with announcement of ad hoc advance payment of Rs. 1 0,000/ to each worker by the management, the strike was called off and workers resumed duty from 1800 hrs on 3.2.98.

The Transport and Dock Workers' Union, Mumbai served a strike notice dated 21.5.98 on the Bombay Custom House Agents' Association proposing indefinite strike from any day after 10.6.98 over a 14-point charter of demands which includes revision of pay-scales, various allowances, etc. Dy.CLC(C), Mumbai intervened in the matter, and held conciliation proceedings on several days. The strike commenced on 12.6.98, but conciliatory efforts continued, and the strike at Custom House, Mumbai Port was called off following a settlement arrived on 18.6.98, About 4000 workers were benefitted by the settlement.

New Mangalore Port Trust: Karnataka Dock & General Workers Union (HMS) and Kanara Stevedoring Workers' Union (INTUC) operating in New Mangalore Port Trust struck work without notice with effect from 6.00 A.M. of 27.9.98 in protest against the decision of the management to mechanise cement cargo movement. Assistant Labour Coommissioner(C), Mangalore intervened and conciliation proceedings were initiated. As no amicable settlement could be arrived at during conciliation by the Assistant Labour Commissioner(C), the Regional Labour Commissioner(C), Bangalore intervened and the strike was called off with effect from 9,10.98. About 900 workers were involved in the strike.

Coal mines

Sreerampur Division of Singareni Collieries Co. Ltd. struck work from 7 a.m. of 4.2.98 demanding that all of them should be allowed to remain at surface till the alleged variations in the dimensions of newly procured tubs were clarified. Consequent upon the above alleged illegal strike, the management declared lockout for 105 workers (except essential staff) from 3 p.m. of 4.2,98. However, the strike was called off unconditionally from 7 a.m. of 5.2,98 and the management lifted the lockout.

About 65 workers of Mahaveerkhani Bellampalli

Division of Singareni Collieries in Andhra Pradesh truck work from 7.00 a.m. of 6.4.98 in support of Bandh call given by SIKAS (Sungreni Karmika Samakhya). The Management declared lockout for all other workmen except essential staff. The strike has been called off unconditionally from 7.00 A.M. on 7.4.98. The management also lifted the lockout, on the same day.

Joint Action Committee of five unions have served a strike notice on 18.4.98 on the management of Singareni Collieries. RLC(C), Hyderabad seized the matter into conciliation and advised the union not to resort to strike. The Chief Minister of A.P. has also intervened in the matter on 24.5.98. Before him the parties agreed to the following

(a) Payment of interim relief @ 12% w.e.f. 1.6.98.

(b) Temporary, Employment to the dependants in case of death or invalidation by Medical Board, etc.

(c) Election through secret ballot for, verification of trade union membership. Due to the killing of a union leader belonging to banned P.W.G. in police encounter, the situation became tense. Inspite of the agreement nearly one lakh workers went on strike w.e.f. 25.5.98. RLC(C), Hyderabad seized the matter in conciliation. Chief Minister of Andhra Pradesh also used his good offices in resolving the issues. The strike was called off from 22.6.98 following the agreement arrived at in presence of the Chief Minister, Andhra Pradesh.

On 9.9.98 secret ballot election was conducted by the RLC(C), Hyderabad for verification of membership of trade unions operating in Singareni Collieries, Andhra Pradesh. Nearly 1.25 lakh workers of Singareni Collieries spread over four districts of Andhra Pradesh took part in the election. It was completed peacefully. Singareni Collieries Workers Union affiliated to A.I.T.U.C. secured highest position with 33.24% of votes followed by Singareni Collieries Staff and Workers Union with 21.95% and Singareni Collieries Labour Union with 15.82% votes.

Departmental undertaking

The constituent trade unions of Joint Wage Negotiation Committee comprising of Bharat Electronics Employees Union (BEEU), Kamgar Congress (KC), ASCO Employees Union (ASCOEU), Bharat Electronics Limited Employees Union (BELU), BELTEX Employees Union (BELTEXEU), Bharat Electronics Workers Unity Forum (BEWUF), Bharat Electronics Workers' Union (BEWU), and BEL Head Office Staff Association (BELHOSA), operating in nine units of Bharat Electronics Limited situated in different states served a joint strike notice dated 17.1.98 on the Chairman-cum-Managing Director, BEL, proposing a one-day token strike in support of their demand for payment of 15% interim relief w.e.f. 1.1.97. On receipt of this strike notice, Dy. CLC(C) Bangalore was asked to intervene and hold conciliation proceedings. Despite his conciliatory intervention, the strike could not be averted. The response to strike was near total. The Dy.CLC(C), Bangalore has submitted failure of conciliation report to Ministry of Labour.

Hospitals

Delhi Nurses Union, served strike notice proposing indefinite strike from 5.5.98 for their demands viz. revised pay scales, time bound promotions, Nursing allowance 025% of basic pay in lieu of NPA, family accomodation and filling up of vacant posts etc. Conciliation proceedings held by ALC(C), New Delhi ended in failure.

Group C & D employees of all the government hospitals/local hospitals in Delhi gave a strike notice. Immediately, the matter was seized into conciliation by the

RLC(C), New Delhi. The main demands of the unions were relating to pay and allowances, restructuring of staff structure, privatisation of certain hospital services, etc. There presentatives of the Directorate General of Health Services pointed out that most of the demands raised by the employees were beyond- their purview and they involved policy decision by Government. Nearly 6000 employees resorted to strike with effect from 20.7.98, thus seriously affecting the working of hospitals and dispensaries. The RLC(C), New Delhi continued his conciliatory effort and submitted his Failure of Conciliation report on 27.7.98 to the Government. The strike was called off with effect from 28.7.98 following an agreement between the Directorate General of Health Services, Ministry of Health & Family Welfare and unions which allowed increase in patient care allowance to the extent of Rs. 620/- per month per employee, washing allowance to uncommon categories of hospital employees, etc.

Banks

Syndicate Bank Employees Union (AIBEA), Hyderabad proposed to go on one-day strike on 16.5.98 besides resorting to agitational programme, as the Bank Management is effecting the transfers of sub-staff cadres without consulting the Union. The ALC(C), Hyderabad held conciliation proceedings on 15.5.98 and advised the Union not to resort to strike. However, about 2018 staff in the Andhra Pradesh went on one-day strike on 16.5.98 in support of their demand.

Regional rural banks: All India Gramin Bank Workers Organisation and All India Gramin Bank Officers Orgnisation issued notice dated 12.6.98 proposing one-day nation wide strike on 22.9.98 over a 17-point charter of demands which pertains to policy decision, service matter and parity of wages and allowances between the employees of nationalised banks and the employees of

Regional Rural Banks. Regarding pay and allowances, Ministry of Finance have set up a committee known as Mahalik Committee to look into the matter and suggest further action. However, at the intervention of Union Minister of Labour, the proposed strike was withdrawn.

An all-India strike call on 13.9.98 was given by the United Forum of Bank Unions for securing expeditious comprehensive wage settlement at the industry level. RLC(C), Mumbai intervened in the matter. After prolonged discussions, the Indian Bank Association and United Forum of Bank Unions agreed to start negotiations forthwith with an open mind to come to an , amicable, settlement. Hence the proposed strike was withdrawn by the United Forum of Bank Unions.

Oil fields

The Cochin Refineries Workers Association served a strike notice dated 22.7.98 on the Management of Cochin Refineries Ltd. to go on one ay token strike on 18.8.98 over a charter of 5 demands viz. settling of Promotion Policy, Wage Anomaly, Denial of Privilege leave, enhancement of man power and House Lease facility. The RLC(C), Cochin held conciliation proceedings on 14.8.98 and 18.8.98 and averted the proposed strike through his timely intervention.

Atomic energy

Verification of membership of unions operating in Nuclear Fuel Complex was conducted on 31.10.98, through secret ballot, under the supervision of RLC(C), Hyderabad. Nuclear Fuel Complex Employees Association Regn. No. A. 86 secured 60% votes and emerged as majority union. Election was peaceful.

Miscellaneous

All India strike

Nation-wide strike call was given by the major Central Trade Unions on 11.12.98 in support of charter of demands.

Regional Labour Commissioners (Central) were advised to hold conciliation proceedings in respect of strike notices pertaining to establishments in Central sphere, received by them. The Union Labour Minister also issued an appeal to the Central Trade Unions urging them to refrain from going on the proposed strike. The over all picture which emerged on 11.12.98 was that all Indian Airlines flights except flights bound for eastern sector were on schedule, Railway and State Bank of India functioned normally. By and large, Public Sector Undertakings functioned normally. The strike in Banks and Insurance was partial except in West Bengal, Bihar and Uttar Pradesh where the strike in Banks and Insurance was nearly total. The strike in Coal Mines was partial except in West Bengal. The strike in Coal Mines was partial except in West Bengal. The strike in Major Ports was partial except in Calcutta, Mumbai and Cochin.

All India radio and doordarshan

It was reported in "Hindustan Times" dated 8 * 12.98 that the Programme Staff Association of All India Radio and Doordarshan had decided to go on indefinite strike with effect from the morning of 10.12.98 if their demands relating to parity in wages and filling up the vacancies are not met. RLC(C), New Delhi was asked to intervene and the matter was seized in conciliation. The RLC(C), New Delhi appealed to the 24 union not to resort to strike. Union Minister of I&B also assured the unions that their demands would be looked into. It has been reported that the strike was partial on 10 and 11. 12.98 and the normal functioning of the All India Radio and Doordarshan was not affected.

Verification of trade unions

The Ministry of Labour issued orders for conducting Verification of membership of Unions in 27 Industrial Establishments and recommended grant of recognition in favour of trade unions in 7 establishments on the basis of verifications conducted earlier. In 30 cases, advice was rendered to Central Ministries, State Governments, Managements and Trade Unions, Verification Procedure & Rights and Privileges of Recognised and Registered unions etc.

The representations of Central Trade Union Organisations (CTUOs) on national and international forums is determined on the basis of strength of membership of Trade Unions affiliated to Central Trade Union Organisations. The last General Verification with December 31, 1989 as the-date of reckoning was completed and the verification results were declared on 26.12.1996. The verification results indicated that there are 12 Central Trade Union Organisations (CTUOs) which have a membership of at least 5 lakhs and a spreadover at least states and 4 industries (including agriculture). The process of next General Verification has already started under the Chairmanship of Chief Labour Commissioner (C).

Screening of appeals against awards

The system evolved in August, 1969 for Screening of proposals for filing by the Central Public Sector Undertakings against Awards of Labour Courts in respect of Industrial Dispute continued to be in operation. The objective of this system is to avoid unnecessary litigation and delay in settlement of disputes, During the year 1998-99 the Ministry of . Labour Screened and granted approval to 50 requests of various Public Sector Undertakings for seeking permission to challenge the awards of Labour Courts and Industrial Tribunals. Out of these, 46 cases related to the Department of Banking one each case to Department of Coal, Ministry of Power and Ministry of Chemical & Fertilisers.

Adjudication

There are 12 Central Government Industrial Tribunals-cum-Labour Courts constituted by the Labour Ministry dealing with industrial disputes in respect of which the Central Government is the 'appropriate Government. Of these 12 CGITs, two each are located in Bombay and Dhanbad, and one each at Asansol, Bangalore, Calcutta, Chandigarh, Jabalpur, Jaipur, Kanpur and Now Delhi. Two new CGIT-cum-Labour Courts, one each at Nagpur and Lucknow have been sanctioned. It is also proposed to set-up three more CGIT-cum-Labour Courts during 1998-99.

The Industrial Tribunals and Labour Courts set up by the State Governments and Union Territory Administrations are also utilised by the Central Government for adjudication of industrial disputes and disposal of applications under Section 33C(2) of the Industrial Disputes Act, 1947 in the Central Sphere. According to information available with the Ministry the number of Industrial Tribunals and Labour Courts set up by the State Governments and the Administrations of the Union Territories as* on 31.10.1997 was 331. (Table 3.6)

Data on the number of cases and applications handled by the Central Government Industrial Tribunals-cum-Labour Courts during the year 1998 (as on 31.10.1998) are furnished in Table 3.7.

Table

State labour courts-cum-industrial tribunals

The number of labour courts (LCs), industrial tribunals (ITs) and labour court-cum-industrial tribunals (LC & IT) set up by state governments & union territory administrations as on 31.10.1997.

Sl.	*Name of states/ union territory*	*No. of labour courts*	*No. of industrial tribunals (IT)*	*No. of labour courts-cum-industrial tribunals (LC & IT)*	*Total*
1.	Andaman & Nicobar	1	1	0	2

2.	Andhra Pradesh	6	2	3	11
3.	Arunachal Pradesh	0	0	0	0
4.	Assam	2	3	0	5
5.	Bihar	14	3	0	17
6.	Chandigarh	6	0	1	7
7.	Dadra & N.H.	1	0	0	1
8.	Daman & Diu	1	0	0	1
9.	Delhi	10	3	0	13
10.	Goa	1	0	1	2
11.	Gujarat	40	16	0	56
12.	Himachal Pradesh	0	0	1	1
13.	Haryana	0	0	7	7
14.	Jammu & Kashmir	0	0	1	1
15.	Kerala	4	5	0	9
16.	Karnataka	12	4	0	16
17.	Lckshadeep	0	0	0	0
18.	Meghalaya	1	0	1	2
19.	Maharashtra	41	27	0	68
20.	Manipur	0	1	0	1
23.	Madhya Pradesh	26	5	0	31
22.	Mizoram	0	1	0	1
23.	Nagaland	1	1	0	2
24.	Orissa	3	1	0	4
26.	Punjab	6	1	0	7
26.	Pondicherry	3	1	0	4
27.	Rajasthan	1	1	7	9
28.	Sikkim	0	0	0	0
29.	Tripura	3	3	0	6
30.	Tamil Nadu	10	1	0	11
31.	Uttar Pradesh	19	6	0	25
32.	West Bengal	2	9	0	11
	Total	214	95	22	331

Employees' participation in management

The Participation of workers in management bill, 1990

The rationale of labour participation in management lies not merely in raising productivity and promoting industrial peace but more importantly in creating a sense of involvement of the workers in the enterprise. In 1975, the Constitution was amended and Article 43(A) was inserted in the Directive Principles of State Policy to encourage and secure the participation of workers in management. The Participation of Workers in Management Bill, 1990 has been referred to the newly constituted Parliamentary Standing Committee on Labour & Welfare. First sifting of the newly constituted Committee was held on 14.8.98. The Committee desired that the comments may be invited fresh from the employers and trade unions on the Bill and amendment notices. Comments from employers and trade unions, have been received and are under process. After finalisation, the Committee will be apprised of the position.

Plan scheme for education and training to promote workers participation in management

During the year 1998-99, Central Board for Workers Education, Nagpur will conduct 26 training courses to promote Workers Participation in Management (Two courses at National level and 24 courses at Regional level)' the National level courses will be conducted at the Indian Institute of Workers' Education, Mumbai and Regional level courses at their Regional Centres. The total proposed cost of the project is Rs. 1.98 lakhs.

Trade unions (Amendment) bill, 1998

The Government has approved certain amendments to the Trade Unions Act, 1926. The objective of these amendments, in brief, is to ensure organised growth of trade unions and reduce multiplicity of trade unions.

Industrial disputes act, 1947

Draft amendments proposals have been formulated and are under consideration of the Government.

Monitoring of industrial relations

The Labour Relations Monitoring Unit set up in the Ministry of Labour continued to perform its function of monitoring industrial relations with the objective of analysing the trend, incidence, nature and impact of strikes, lockouts, layoffs, retrenchment, closures, etc. throughout the country. A computerised data bank on labour unrest has been developed based on monthly / quarterly returns from the Labour Bureau. The Daily Summary of Information on strikes/ lockouts/work stoppages, brought out by the Ministry of Home Affairs are also analysed with a view to taking timely action on threatened agitations.

According to information available from the Labour Bureau the number of strikes and lockouts, workers involved and the resulting loss of mandays has shown a steady decline during the nineties. It is possible that the Government's proactive role through timely and effective conciliation and involvement of social partners in the tripartite fora in formulation and implementation of labour and industrial relations policies and programmes has achieved some success in harmonising the interests of employers and workers. This has resulted in a change of attitude from confirmation to One of collaboration in bipartite and tripartite discussions. A statement indicating the number of strikes and lockouts, workers effected therein and mandays lost during 1992-1998. Number of establishments affecting closures, lay-off and retrenchment and workers affected as a result of this are given in Tables.

In addition to collection, compilation and analysis of industrial relations data, the Monitoring Unit has, also been studying the process of restructuring in the economy and has been giving views from time to time on proposals of closure and rehabilitation of sick Central Public Sector Undertakings (CPSUs), disinvestment proposals, amendment of Bills directly related to interests / welfare of organised labour, etc.

With a aim of tackling the problem of non-payment of statutory dues of workers employed in CPSUs, the Ministry of labour has started monitoring the status of these defaults on a quarterly basis. The concerned administrative ministries/departments controlling the CPSUs are required to send quarterly reports on the amount of dues outstanding against workers. In addition, the Ministry has also been holding inter-ministerial meetings in order to find out the reasons for defaults and to evolve a strategy for liquidation of these arrears within a given time frame.

Re-constitution of special tripartite committee/ industrial tripartite committees

A Special Tripartite Committee was constituted by the Ministry in 1992 to discuss the impact on labour of economic reforms and restructuring of industries. The first meeting of the Special Tripartite Committee took place on 13.5.98. to discuss issues such as non-payment of statutory dues of workers employed in Central Public Sector Undertakings (CPSUs), problem -of industrial sickness, increasing contractualisation of labour force, the Voluntary Retirement Scheme, etc. The Committee was re-constituted on 22nd September 1998.

With a view to deliberating upon problems of labour in specific industries, the following Industrial Tripartite Committees were re-constituted:

Name of the committee	*Constituted on*	*Reconstituted on*
Tripartite Industrial Committee on Sugar	3.10.97	18.9.98

Tripartite Industrial Committee on Cotton Textile Industry	11.3.1992	18.9.1998
Tripartite Industrial Committee on Jute Industry	24.3.1992	18.9.1998
Tripartite Industrial Committee on Engineering Industry	9.5.1992	18.9.1998
Tripartite Industrial Committee on Chemical Industry	23.3.1992	21.9.1999
Tripartite Industrial Committee on Electricity Generation and Distribution	31.3.1992	6.10.1998
Tripartite Industrial Committee on. Road Transport Industry	6.4.1992	21.9.1998

The meetings of the above Industrial Tripartite Committees are to be convened in the coming months.

Reference of labour disputes to industrial tribunals

The Central Government is the appropriate Government for industrial disputes relating industries owned or controlled by the Central Government, railways, statutory corporations, banking and insurance, mines, oil fields, major ports, etc. If a dispute is not settled by negotiations or conciliation, the Government may, at its discretion refer the dispute for adjudication to a Labour Court or Industrial/National Tribunal.

The Industrial Desks provide the second tier in settlement of industrial disputes. If the Conciliation Officer of the Industrial Relations Machinery fails to settle the dispute, he submits a Failure of Conciliation Report (FOC) to the appropriate Government. The FOC Reports are then processed in the IR Desks for referring the dispute to the

Tribunal or for declining reference. If, on the basis of the information available in the FOC Report a prima facie case for reference to Industrial Tribunal / Labour Court exists, and if the dispute pertains to an establishment in the Central Sphere as defined in the ID Act, it is mandatory to consult the administrative Ministry concerned before making a reference to the Tribunal. The terms of reference of the dispute have also to be clearly defined.

The Government may decline reference in certain cases. However, reason for declining is to be communicated by the speaking order to the concerned parties. If the petitioner challenges the powers of the Government or the vires of the ID Act, such petitions are contested by filing replies in Court.

The IR Desks are also to notify reference of disputes for Arbitration if both parties have mutually agreed to this as provided under Section 10 A of the ID Act. The notification is to be made in the Official Gazette within one month of receipt of reference. Awards of the Tribunal given in the case of industrial disputes referred to them are also to be notified by the IR Desks within 30 days of receipt,

During the period January to October 1998, 4159 industrial disputes were received and 3907 disputes were disposed of. During the same period, 791 awards were notified. As part of a plan to modernise the IR Desks, all the FOC reports are now being computerised with the help of a special software developed by NIC. The objective of the computerisation drive launched in January 1998 is to further expedite the disposal of cases as well as to develop a data base on industrial disputes.

Permission for closure, retrenchment and lay-off

The Industrial Relations Desks are also required to process applications received for closure, retrenchment and lay-off under provisions of the ID Act. A hearing is held in which the affected parties are represented. The fact.,, of each case are examined in depth and a decision is taken on merits of the case. Prominent among the cases handled was the one regarding closure, of HCL's Mosaboni mines in Bihar involving retrenchment of 201,9 workers. The order of the Ministry was challenged in the Ranchi Bench of the Patna High Court and the Divisional Bench of the Calcutta High Court. The Divisional Bench of the Calcutta High Court upheld the decision of the Ministry.

Between January to October 1998, 6 applications were returned as non-maintainable and permission was not granted in respect of 4 applications. During the calendar year 1997 60 applications were received for retrenchment/lay-of/closure out of which 39 wore returned as non-maintainable. Permission was granted in 6 cases and refused in 15 cases.

Table
Number of Strikes and Lockouts

Year	*Central Sphere*	*State Sphere*	*Public Sector*	*Private Sector*	*Strike*	*Lock-out*	*Total*
1992(P)	514	1200	617	1097	1011	703	1714
1993(P)	272	1121	359	1034	914	479	1393
1994(P)	249	952	316	885	808	393	1201
1995(P)	285	781	343	723	732	334	1066
1996(P)	316	850	381	785	763	403	1166
1997(P)	384	921	448	857	793	512	1305
1998 (Jan-Sep.) (P)	119	482	136	465	350	251	601

Table

Workers involved in strikes & lockouts (in thousands)

Year	Central Sphere	State Sphere	Public Sector	Private Sector	Strike	Lock-out	Total
1992(P)	498	754	566	686	767	485	1252
1993(P)	513	441	565	389	672	282	954
1994(P)	490	356	523	323	626	220	846
1995(P)	700	289	725	264	683	307	990
1996(P)	478	461	606	333	609	331	939
1997(P)	624	358	618	363	637	344	981
1998 (Jan-Sep.) (P)	278	154	303	129	338	94	432

Table

Mandays lost due to strikes & lockouts (in millions)

Year	Central Sphere	State Sphere	Public Sector	Private Sector	Strike	Lock-out	Total
1992(P)	0.77	30.49	1.92	29.33	15.13	16.13	31.26
1993(P)	1.20	19.10	2.29	18.01	5.61	14.69	20.30
1994(P)	0.59	20.40	1.32	19.67	6.65	14.33	20.98
1995(P)	3.86	12.43	4.79	11.50	5.72	10.57	16.29
1996(P)	1.20	19.09	3.15	17.13	7.82	12.47	20.28
1997(P)	1.41	15.62	2.18	14.85	6.30	10.74	17.03
1998 (Jan-Sep.)(P)	1.63	6.34	1.76	6.10	3.86	4.01	7.87

Table

Number of closures and workers affected therein during 1985-86 by spheres

	Closures					
	Central Sphere		*State Sphere*		*Total*	
Year	*A*	*B*	*A*	*B*	*A*	*B*
1985	4	821	180	19638	184	20259
1986	2	21	234	28006	236	28027
1987	3	3400	195	15749	198	19149
1988	4	1568	255	12518	259	14086
1989 (P)	–	–	239	6921	239	6921
1990 (P)	–	–	164	4967	154	4967
1991(P)	3	537	235	20902	238	21439
1992(P)	–	–	187	12422	187	12422
1993 (P)	3	79	490	25579	493	25658
1994 (P)	–	–	228	21394	228	21394
1995 (P)	–	–	183	14495	183	14495
1996(P)	1	102	203	11288	204	11390
1997(P)	2	150	152	12794	154	12944
1998(Jan-Sep)(P)	–	–	49	2192	49	2192

Table 11

Number of Units effecting lay off and workers laid off during 1988-98 spheres

	Central Sphere		*State Sphere*		*Total*	
Year	*A*	*B*	*A*	*B*	*A*	*B*
1988 (P)	37	9061	540	96048	577	105109
1989 (P)	64	22749	474	47904	538	70653
1990 (P)	56	13907	386	50173	442	64080

(Contd..)

1991 (P)	46	10791	415	60269	461	71060
1992 (P)	101	49979	3776	59633	477	107612
1993 (P)	52	19212	373	46416	425	65628
1994 (P)	60	177806	282	40261	342	58067
1995 (P)	21	8176	263	53810	284	61986
1996 (P)	54	14291	253	47046	307	61337
1997 (P)	52	21601	255	43564	307	65165
1998 (P) (Jan-Sep)	49	7960	132	15848	181	23808

Table

Number of units efecting retremchment and workers retrenched therein during 1985-98 by spheres

	Central Sphere		State Sphere		Total	
Year	*A*	*B*	*A*	*B*	*A*	*B*
1985	49	5098	404	6182	453	11280
1986	19	3194	461	6010	480	9204
1987	18	1020	338	4182	356	5202
1988	14	475	365	4539	379	5014
1989 (P)	3	73	171	3185	174	3258
1990 (P)	1	8	267	3029	268	3037
1991 (P)	2	54	233	4342	235	4396
1992 (P)	2	85	220	3751	222	3836
1993 (P)	3	178	186	2713	189	2891
1994 (P)	–	–	135	2192	135	2192
1995 (P)	–	–	94	1792	94	1792
1996 (P)	4	285	775	20877	79	2372
1997 (P)	10	526	151	2716	161	3242
1998 (P) (Jan-Sep)	1	1	775	1067	76	1068

Arbitration body

Board of arbitration (JCM)

The Government of India had introduced in 1966 a Scheme for Joint Consultative Machinery and Compulsory Arbitration for resolving differences between the Government, as an employer and the general body of its employees.

The Scheme provides for compulsory arbitration on pay and allowances, weekly hours of work and leave of a class or grade of employees.

Under the Scheme, the board of Arbitration (JCM) was set up in July, 1968. The Board consists of a Chairman and two other members. The Chairman is a whole time person. The other two members are appointed by the Ministry of Labour at the time of referring the dispute to the Board out of a panel of members both from the staff side as well as from the official side maintained by it.

Till 31st December, 1998, 241 cases had been referred to the Board and the Board had given its Awards (disposed of) in 223 cases.

4

Productivity

The term productivity implies production per unit of the input factor. It is considered to be one of the key indicators of economic and technological progress. It is a measure of efficiency with which resources both human and material are converted into goods and services. Faster rate of economic growth can be ensured through accelerated production and higher productivity in all branches of economic activity. It has been admitted that no real advance in the workers standard of living is possible without a steady increase in productivity. Higher productivity can be ensured by adopting technological innovations and making optimum utilisation of the human resources.

Comparison of Productivity Indices of Asian countries for the period 1986 to 1995 (on base 1986) reveals that the rate of growth in productivity in 1995 has been the highest in the Republic of China, followed by the Republic of Korea, Singapore, Hongkong, Malaysia, Nepal, Sri Lanka, India, Pakistan, Japan, Philippines and Islamic Republic of Iran. India stands 8th among the 18 Asian countries. It may be seen that Productivity Indices compare unfavourably even with the neighbouring Asian countries and are lower than that of Singapore, Malaysia, Nepal and Sri Lanka. However productivity in India has been increasing during all these years during the year

1992. Labour productivity indices in India are not strictly comparable with those of other countries as while calculating productivity indices in India, only the organised sector has been taken into account.

Labour Productivity Indices derived from GDP Index and Labour Index in various sector of Indian Economy with base 1986 = 100. Inter sectoral comparison shows that during 1995 the Labour Productivity was highest in the Transport and Communication Sector followed by Electricity, Gas and Water, Manufacturing, Agriculture, Construction, Trade, Mining and Finance Sector.

During the period from 1987 to 1993-94 the Labour Productivity has shown maximum increase in the Basic Metal and Alloys Industries followed by the Manufacturing Industries viz. Motor Vehicles, Wool, Silk and Man Made Fibre Textiles, Aluminium Manufacturing, Textile Products and Leather & Fur Products.

Although it is comforting to note that Indian Productivity has kept up a rising trend, it has not been sufficiently high to make Indian Products compete successfully in the International Market. This is a cause of concern in view of globalisation of the Indian Economy. According to Asian Productivity Organisation Report the South Asia Region which was considered as relatively behind the vibrant growth of Asian Countries has shown an impressive sign of economic recovery and development from 1986 to 1995. During this period average economic growth of Bangala Desh was 4.1 %, India 4.1 %, Nepal 4.7% and Pakistan 4.9%. The figures reveal that the economic growth in India is less than that of the adjoining Countries.

Prime Minister's Shram Awards

To give recognition to outstanding contribution towards production and productivity, technological innovations, cost saving, import substitution, saving of foreign exchange and for showing exemplary zeal and enthusiasm in the discharge of duties, the Ministry of Labour administers a scheme entitled "Prime Minister's Shram Awards" to workmen (as defined in Industrial Dispute Act, 1947) employed in departmental/public sector undertakings of the Central/State Governments. Only those workmen sre eligible for the Award, who are engaged in manufacturing and productive processes and whose performance is assessable. These Awards are announced every year on the eve of Independence Day. The Awards in the order of precedence are Shram Ratna, Shram Bhushan, Shrarn Vir and Shrarn Shri/Devi. From the year 1997, the amount of cash prize for these awards has been doubled. It is now as in table

Table

The amount of cash prize and the number of awards given during 1997

Name of Award	*Amount of Cash Prize (fig. in Rupees)*	*No. of Awards*
Shrarn Ratna	2,00,000	1
Shrarn Bhushan	1,00,000	2
Shram Vir	60,000	6
Shram Shri/Devi	40,000	8
Total		17

On the eve of independence day 1998, the Prime Minister's Shram Awards for the year 1998 were announced. Since there were some joint winners, 31 workers were selected for the 17 Awards.

The Awards for the year 1997 were presented by the Prime Minister in a function held on 14.10.1998 at New Delhi.

Table
Industry wise index labour productivity in India in manufacturing 1987–88=100

Sl.	Name of Industry	1988-89	1989-90	1990-91	1991-92	1992-93	1993-94
1	**2**	**3**	**4**	**5**	**6**	**7**	**8**
1.	Food products	122	137	123	124	115	144
2.	Refining of Sugar	141	144	110	1177	124	150
3.	Hydrogenated Oils/ Vanaspati	82	75	84	80	60	66
4.	Beverages Tobacco and Tobacco Products	115	93	106	112	108	130
5.	Cotton Textiles	106	124	136	118	117	126
6.	Wool, Silk & Manmade Fibre Textiles	114	155	183	165	178	220
7.	Jute, Hemp & Mesta Textiles	100	87	89	97	102	109
8.	Textiles Products	118	126	138	163	162	195
9.	Wood & Wood Products, Furniture & Fixture	117	111	165	165	86	96
10.	Paper & Paper Products, Printing etc.	110	127	138	128	117	142
11.	Pulp Paper & Paper Board	124	163	174	147	126	130
12.	Leather and Fur Products	82	91	108	122	135	193
13.	Rubber, Plastic, Petroleum & Coal Products	103	105	118	103	135	154
14.	Chemical & Chemical Products	109	130	147	142	168	182
15.	Basic & Industrial Chemicals & Gases	131	102	114	124	106	127
16.	Fertilizers and Pesticides	115	123	152	163	164	153

(Contd. . .)

1	2	3	4	5	6	7	8
17.	Paints and Vamishes	83	124	128	158	122	117
18.	Drugs and Medicines	109	118	128	145	149	176
19.	Non-metallic Minera Products	110	125	149	1771	137	53
20.	Structure Clay Products	103	95	105	106	107	142
21.	Glass & Glass Plaster	114	169	147	202	170	188
22.	Cement Lime & Plaster	113	127	1773	215	136	117
23.	Basic Meta & Alloys Industries	135	133	160	127	157	329
24.	Iron & Steel in Primary/ Self Finished Forms	145	137	172	139	161	192
25.	Foundry For Casting & Forging	108	140	171	150	170	176
26.	Ferro Alloys	97	91	71	64	170	24
27.	Copper Manufacturing	67	155	207	191	73	26
28.	Zinc Manufacturing	97	137	141	156	275	78
29.	Zinc Manufacturing	161	217	143	173	193	209
30.	Meta Products and Parts	105	85	83	92	86	109
31.	Machine Tools & Parts	98	114	120	142	147	149
32.	Agriculture Machinery	86	108	138	133	113	113
33.	Prime Movers, Boilers	113	116	111	102	94	75
34.	Industrial Machinery for Food and Textiles	103	139	149	160	159	148
35.	Industrial Machinery other than Food and Textiles	97	101	95	100	103	115
36.	Refrigeration & AC	110	141	113	116	164	162
37.	Machine Tools and Parts	83	79	81	74	81	77
38.	Electrical Machinery	106	121	141	129	135	146
39.	Electrical Industry Machinery	98	117	134	118	123	111

(Contd. . .)

1	2	3	4	5	6	7	8
40.	Transport Equipment	106	121	141	129	135	146
41.	Locomotive Parts	109	128	89	77	120	75
42.	Railways Wagons	68	111	111	86	91	86
43.	Motor Vehicles	109	112	125	119	117	275
44.	Motor Cycle, Scooter	105	100	148	164	155	181
45.	Bicycle Parts	106	95	149	119	135	151
46.	Other Manufacturing Industries	90	115	108	138	148	233
	All Industries	111	119	130	126	139	158

5

Wages

There is no uniform wage policy for all sectors of the economy. Wages in the organised sector are determined through negotiations and settlements. In the case of Central Public Sector Enterprises, the Department of Public Enterprises issues guidelines and permits negotiations for wage revision. During the Eighth Five Year Plan, the Government permitted the fifth round of negotiations and issued guidelines for new wage settlements under which managements were free to negotiate the wage structure consistent with generation of resources/profits by individual enterprise/unit & provided there was no increase in labour cost per unit of output. The period of the wage settlement was to be five years. The Department of Public Enterprises also issued guidelines on 19th July, 1995 introducing a slab system of payment of Dearness Allowance for the employees of Central Public Sector Enterprises. The matter regarding guidelines for the sixth round of Wage Negotiations between the managements of public Enterprises and the Workers' Unions to come into effect from Jan., 1997 for a period of 5 years is presently under active consideration of the Government.

Wageboards

In the 1950s and 60s, when the organised labour sector was at a nascenet stage of its development without adequate unionisation or with trade unions without adequate bargaining power, Government in appreciation of the problems which arise in the arena of wage fixation due to absence of such bargaining power, constituted various Wage Boards. The Wage Boards are tripartite in character in which representatives of workers, employers and independent members participate and finalise the recommendations. The utility and contribution of such boards in the present context are not beyond question. Except for the Wage Boards for Journalists & Non-Journalists Newspaper and News-agency Employees, which are statutory Wage Board, all other Wage Boards are non-statutory in nature. Therefore recommendations made by these Wage Boards are not enforceable under Law.

The importance of the non-statutory Wage Boards, has consequently declined over a period of time and no non-statutory Wage Board has ' been set up after 1966, except for sugar industry, where last such Wage Board was constituted in 1985. The trade unions, having grown in strength in these industries, -are themselves able to negotiate their wages with the management. This trend is likely to continue in future.

Tripartite industrial committee for sugar industry

The recommendation of the last Wage Board for Sugar Industry notified in December, 1989 were made operative for a period of 5 years i.e. upto December, 1994. After expiry of this period, the various Trade Unions started representing the Government for setting up of Another Wage Board for Sugar workers. In this connection, a special meeting was held on 4.10.96 under the Chairmanship of Labour Minister to discuss the specific problems of workers in Sugar Industry. It was decided in principle to constitute a compact group to look into the various issues and demands of sugar workers raised by trade unions. It was also decided that before constituting such a group, major sugar producing States shall be consulted. Accordingly, the Ministry started the process of consulting the sugar producing States. In a further meeting held on 4.7.97 in which both employees and employers organisations took part, the demand for setting up of a Wage Board was again raised. But later on the Unions changed their demand to the setting up of a tripartite committee to go into the issue relating to Sugar workers. The Government has accordingly constituted a Tripartite Industrial Committee on 3.10.97 to took into the problems of Sugar Industry. 4 The Committee will, inter-alia, examine the issues of wage structure of the sugar workers.

Wage board for newspaper employees

The Working Journalists and other Newspaper Employees (conditions of Service) and Miscellaneous Provisions Act, 1955 regulates conditions of service of Working Journalists and other persons employed in Newspaper establishments. The Act provides for the setting up of Wage Boards for fixation and revision of rates of wages in respect of Working Journalists and non-journalist newspaper/news-agency employees.

In the past the Wage Boards for such employees were set up in the years 1956,1963, 1975 and 1985. The Wage Board set up in the year 1985 under the chairmanship of Justice U.N Bachawat submitted its final report in May, 1989. The Government accepted the recommendations of Bachawat Wage Boards on Pay Scales, D.A. etc. vide Notification dated 31.8.89. The rates of HRA and CCA were notified on 22.1.90. The State Governments were requested to implement the recommendations and also advised to establish tripartite committees/special cells at the state level in this regard. As per information received from the State Governments as on 31.3.98 out of 1710 newspaper establishments 622 have fully, and 28 partially implemented the recommendations of Bachawat Wage Boards. Efforts are continuing to pursue the state Governments for more effective implementation. State wise position of implementation of the Bachawat Wage Board recommendations are given in table.

On persistent demands from the working journalists and other newspaper employees for the setting up of new Wage Boards to consider wage revisions, the Government , in September, 1994, constituted two Wage Boards, for the Working Journalists and for the non-journalists newspaper and news-agency employees respectively under the common chairmanship of Retired Chief Justice Rajkumar Manisana Singh. The Wage Boards submitted Interim Report on the Interim Rates of Wages recommending enhancement by 15% of the basic wages with effect from 20.4.95. The Government examined this recommendation of the Board and decided to grant interim enhancement of wages at the rate of 20% of basic wage and an additional amount of Rs. 100%-per month, to be effective from 20.4.95.

After the setting up of the Wage Boards on 2.9.94, there were also demand from newspaper employees and employers' organisations for increasing the number of representatives on the Boards. The Government, agreeing to provide a wider representations on these Boards, introduced a Bill in the Parliament, for increasing one representative each for employers, employees, and independent members. The Bill was passed by both houses of Parliament and the Working Journalists and other Newspaper Employees (Conditions of Service) and Miscellaneous Provisions (Amendment) Act, 1996 was notified on 28.9.96. Now the matter regarding filling up of additional seat in the Wage Boards is under consideration of Government. On the other hand, the task of finalising the recommendations by the Manisana Wage Board is in progress and is expected to be completed by the end of 1998.

Minimum wages

The Minimum Wages Act, 1948 which is applicable to workers in the unorganised sector, empowers both Central and State Governments to fix/ revise the minimum rates of wages for the scheduled employments under their respective jurisdiction. The Act also provide for the setting up of enforcement machinery to seek compliance with the provisions of the Act.

The Central Government is responsible for fixation and revision of minimum wages in 44 Scheduled employments. Out of 44 scheduled employments, the following four scheduled employments have been added in the Central sphere recently.

Table

Scheduled employments for which central government has fixed minimum wages under the minimum wages act, 1948

Sl. No.	*Name of Employment*	*Date of lost Revision*	*Minimum wage* to the lowest paid worker*
1	2	3	4
1.	Agriculture	12.08.92	Rs. 68.40
2.	Construction or maintenance of roads or building operations.	12.07.94	Rs. 42.02
3.	Stone breaking or stone crushing.		
4.	Maintenance of buildings.	–do–	–do–
5.	Construction and Maintenance of Runways.	–do–	–do–
6.	Gypsum mines.	–do–	–do–
7.	Barytes mines.	–do–	–do–
8.	Bauxite mines.	–do–	–do–
9.	Manganese mines.	–do–	–do–
10.	China Clay mines.	–do–	–do–

(Contd. . .)

11.	Kyanite mines.	–do–	–do–
12.	Copper mines.	–do–	–do–
13.	Clay mines.	–do–	–do–
14.	Stone mines.	–do–	–do–
15.	White clay mines.	–do–	–do–
16.	Ochre mines	–do–	–do–
17.	Fire Clay mines	–do–	–do–
18.	Steatite (Soapstone and Talc) mines	–do–	–do–
19.	Asbestos mines	–do–	–do–
20.	Chromite mines	–do–	–do–
21.	Quartzite mines.	–do–	–do–
22.	Quartz mines	–do–	–do–
23.	Silica mines	–do–	–do–
24.	Magnesite mines	–do–	–do–
25.	Graphite mines	–do–	–do–
26.	Felspar mines	–do–	–do–
27.	Redoxide mines	–do–	–do–
28.	Laterite mines	–do–	–do–
29.	Dolomite mines	–do–	–do–
30.	Iron Ore mines	–do–	–do–
31.	Granite mines	–do–	–do–
32.	Wolfram mines	–do–	–do–
33.	Magnetite mines	–do–	–do–
34.	Rockphosphate mines	–do–	–do–
35.	Hematite mines	–do–	–do–
36.	Loading, unloading in Railways' good shed	–do–	–do–
37.	Ash Pit Cleaning in Railways	–do–	Rs. 43.31

38. Marble and Calcite mines	–do–	Rs. 43.31
39. Uranium mines	–do–	Rs. 42.02
40. Mica mines	–do–	–do–
41. Employment in Lignite Mines**	–do–	–do–
42. Employment in Gravel Mines**	–do–	–do–
43. Employment in laying down of underground electric, Wireless, radio, television, telephone, telegraph and overseas communication cables and similar other underground cabling work.**		
44. Employment in the Slate Mines.**		

Table

Minimum rates of wages and variable special allowances per day revised with effect from 1.10.98

(Amount in Rs.)

Category of worker	*Basic Wage*	*Spl. All.*	*Total Wage*	*Basic Wage*	*Spl All.*	*Total Wage*	*Basic Wage*	*Spl All.*	*Total Wage*
1	**2**	**3**	**4**	**5**	**6**	**7**	**8**	**9**	**10**
	I. Construction								
"A"	Area "B"	Area "C"	Area						
Unskilled	36.00	17.13	53.13	34.00	17.13	51.13	28.00	14.02	42.02
Semi-skilled	43.00	20.23	63.23	41.00	20.23	61.23	34.00	17.13	51.13
Unskilled Supervisory Skilled/	57.00	24.91	81.91	51.00	24.91	75.91	43.00	21.80	64.80
Clerical Highly Skilled	65.00	31.16	96.16	63.00	31.16	94.16	51.00	24.91	75.91
II. Agriculture									

(Contd. . .)

Category of worker	Area "A"	Area "B"	Area "C"						
Unskilled	33.00	42.40	75.40	28.00	42.40	70.40	26.00	42.40	68.40
Semi-skilled/	41.00	42.40	83.40	35.00	42.40	77.40	29.00	42.40	71.40
Unskilled/ Supervis-									
ory Skilled/ Clerical	48.00	42.40	90.40	41.00	42.40	83.40	34.00	42.40	76.40
Highly Skilled	58.00	42.40	100.40	50.00	42.40	92.40	41.00	42.40	83.40

III. Leading/ Unloading and Ash Pit Cleaning in Railway

	Area "A"			Area "B"			Area "C"		
Unskilled	42.00	20.55	62.55	33.00	16.20	49.20	29.00	14.31	43.31
Wage Spl. All.	Basic sed	Revi- Wage	Total Wage Spl. All.	Basic sed	Revi- Wage	Total			

IV. Mining

1	2	3	4	5	6	7
Category of worker	**Above Ground**			**Below Ground**		
Unskilled	28.00	14.02	42.02	34.00	17.13	51.13
Semi-skilled/	34.00	17.13	51.13	41.00	20.27	61.27

1	2	3	4	5	6	7
Unskilled Supervis-ory Skilled	41.00	20.27	61.27	50.00	24.91	74.91
Clerical	41.00	20.27	61.27			
Highly Skilled	50.00	24.91	74.91	60.00	29.60	89.60

Table

State-wise details of minimum wages

Central/State Government/ Union Territory		No. of employments for which minimum wages have been fixed/ revised	@ Range of Minimum Wages per day (in Rs.)	
			Mini-mum	Maxi-mum As on 1.10.98
1		2	3	4
I.	Central Government	40	42.02	75.40
II.	State			
1.	Andhra Pradesh	58	25.96	62.85
2.	Arunachal Pradesh	16	21.00	24.00
3.	Assam	57	32.80	49.10
4.	Bihar	61	27.30	44.23
5.	Goa	17	15.00	93.00
6.	Gujarat	50	34.00	77.80
7.	Haryana	50	63.12	64.12
8.	Himachal Pradesh	24	26.00	45.75
9.	Jammu & Kashmir	35	30.00	30.00
10.	Karnataka	58	26.00	62.88
11.	Kerala	36	30.00	114.16
12.	Madhya Pradesh	36	26.46	62.96
13.	Maharashtra	63	8.46	101.50
14.	Manipur	5	27.35	56.88
15.	Meghalaya	22	35.00	35.00
16.	Mizoram	2	45.00	45.00

17. Nagaland	37	25.00	25.00
18. Orissa	82	30.00	30.00
19. Punjab	60	60.95	63.50
20. Rajasthan	39	44.00	42.29
21. Sikkim Minimum Wages Act 1948 is yet to be extended and enforced			
22. Tamil Nadu	58	22.40	79.00
23. Tripura	11	26.63	46.15
24. Uttar Pradesh	65	42.02	64.21
25. West Bengal	39	31.88	96.17
III. Union Territories			
26. A & N Islands	8	50.00	86.77
27. Chandigarh	44	65.27	65.27
28. Dadar & Nagar Haveli	43	35.00	40.00
29. Daman & Diu	39	35.00	35.00
30. Delhi	29	74.50	74.50
31. Lakshadweep	4	41.46	41.46
32. Pondicherry	2	19.25	40.20

Table

Enforcement of provisions of wage laws by central industrial relations Machinery (CIRM) during 1997

Sl.	*Name of the law tions done*	*No. of insp- es Re- ctified*	*Irregu- lariti- ions laun- ched*	*Pros- ecut- obtai- ned*	*Convi- ctions*	*Claims field*
1	2	3	4	5	6	7
1.	Payment of Wages Act, 1936					

(Contd. . .)

(i) Mines	4721	58343	1717	1422	12
(ii) Railway	1747	10758	–	1	–
(iii) Air Transport Service	151	1491	5084	3270	1909
2. Minimum Wages Act, 1948	12340*	134183	5084	3270	1909
3. Contract Labour (R&A) Act, 1970	4186	67733	3216	2155	–
4. Equal Remuneration Act, 1976	4403	4375	1173	605	–
5. Payment of Bonus Act, 1965	816	968	31	42	–
6. Child Labour (P & R) Act, 1986	2016	2069	25	5	–

Table

Comparative statement of variations in consumer price indices (CPI) for industrial workers (IW) and agricultural labourers (AL)

Year	*CPI(I)*	*Percentage variation (Anually)*	*CPI (AL)*	*Percentage variation (Anually)*
1	2	3	4	5
1984-85	582	6.40	521	0.19
1985-86	620	6.53	516	4.80
1986-87	674	8.71	572	4.76
1987-88	736	9.20	629	9.97
1988-89	802	8.977	7708	12.56
1989-90	853	6.36	746	5.377
1990-91	951	11.49	803	7.64
1991-92	1080	13.56	958	19.30

(Contd. . .)

1992-93	1183	9.54	1076	12.32
1993-94	1272	7.52	1114	3.53
1994-95	1400	10.06	1247	11.94
1995-96	1543	10.21	1381	10.75
1996-97	1686	9.27	1508	9.20
1997-98	1803	6.94	1558	3.32

(1) Lignite Mines

(2) Gravel Mines

(3) Slate Mines

(4) Laying of underground electric, wireless, radio, television, telephone, telegraph and overseas communication cables and similar other underground cables, electric lines, water supply lines and sewerage pipe lines.

The Central govt. revised the minimum rates of wages for the 39 scheduled employments relating to mining, construction and railway sectors in the central sphere w.e.f. 12.7.94. The minimum wages for agriculture were revised on 12.8.92. The minimum rates of wages in respect of newly added employments are being fixed shortly. A list of scheduled employments under central sphere, the date of revision and the minimum wage for the lowest unskilled workers is given in table.

There is also a provision of Special Allowance -as part of the Minimum Wages in all the scheduled employments in the Central Sphere. The Special Allowance is linked to the Consumer' Price Index numbers and is revised every 6 months commencing on the 1st April and 1st October of each year. The rate of minimum wages alongwith special allowance for different scheduled employments in Central sphere as on 01. 10.98.

The government has now initiated the process of

revision of minimum rates of wages for the employment in agriculture and a preliminary notification indicating the proposed rates of wages was issued on 29.9.97. The government vide notification dated 1.8.97 have also revised the piece rate wages for various activities including stone breaking or stone crushing in the employment in stone mines. The piece rate wages for the activity of stone breaking have been fixed for the first time according to the size of stone to be broken. These rates vary from Rs. 167 per 200 cubic feet of broken stone to Rs.407 per 200 cubic feet of broken stone.

Number of employments by States covered under the Act (as on 1. 10. 1998) for which minimum wages have been fixed/revised and the range of wages for the unskilled category of workers in various States is given in Table 5.4.

National minimum wage

The subject of national minimum wage has been considered by several bodies and fora in the past. The National Commission on Labour (1969) was of the view that such a wage in the sense of uniform minimum monetary renumeration for the country as a whole is neither feasible nor desirable. The 28th Indian Labour Conference (1985) also discussed the need for national minimum wage. It was felt that till such time the national minimum wage is feasible, it would be desirable to have regional minimum wage in regard to which the Central Government may lay down the guidelines.

Regional minimum wages advisory committees

As a follow up of the above recommendations of the Indian Labour Conference, 1985, the Central Government set up six, Regional Minimum Wages Advisory Committees in 1987. The scope and function of these committees have since been broadened to cover all subjects of importance to labour and have been renamed as

Regional Labour Ministers' Conferences. These conferences have held three rounds of meetings so far. The third round was held during 1996. The conference for Western region was held in May 98 in which implementation of Minimum Wages Act was reviewed amongst other subjects and the States were requested to reduce regional disparities in the minimum wages for different scheduled employments. As per one of the decisions taken in this Conference, the floor level minimum wage (basic subsistence level wage) was increased in August 98 to Rs.40/- per day from Rs. 35/- per day in view of rising price level. The conference for Northern region was held in October 98. Though these conferences could not come to any conclusion on the fixation of uniform minimum wages for any employment in any region, after revision of floor level minimum wage to Rs.40/- per day in Aug. 98, all States/Uts were urged at the level of Prime Minister to ensure minimum wages not below Rs.40/- per day.

Enforcement of minimum wages

Enforcement of the Minimum Wages Act, 1948 in the Central Sphere is secured through the officers of the Central Industrial Relations Machinery (CIRM), (Table-5.5). In respect of employments within the jurisdiction of the State Government, the enforcement of the Act is ensured by the State machinery.

Workers awareness

Workers awareness with regard to the provisions of the Minimum Wages Act, 1948 is sought to be enhanced through publicity in the media. The Central Board for Workers Education also gives wide publicity to the provisions of the Act through their various educational programmes for rural and unorganised workers. The Labour Bureau conducts special studies on implementation of minimum wages in various sectors.

Cost of living

Movement of Consumer Price Index Numbers determines

the nearest approximation of the changes in cost of living of the workers and these indices are used for wage indexation. On the basis of measurement of relative change in costs at retail prices, of baskets of goods and services consumed by the Working Class Families of Industrial Workers and Rural Labour Households, the Labour Bureau, Shimla compiles Consumer Price Indices for Industrial Workers and Agricultural and Rural Labourers respectively. The consumption pattern of Industrial Workers is determined on the basis of Family Income and Expenditure Surveys conducted by the Labour Bureau and that of Agricultural and Rural Labour on the basis of data thrown up by quinquennial survey of Consumer Expenditure of the N.S.S.O. The All India Consumer Pride Index Numbers for Industrial Workers on base 1982=100 are compiled on the basis of price data collected from 226 markets of 70 industrial centres spread over the country. The Consumer Price Index Numbers for Agricultural and Rural Labourers on base 1986-87=100 are computed with the help of price data obtained from 600 villages spread over 20 States (w.e.f. November 1995).

The rate of growth in both the Consumer Price Indices for Industrial Workers (CPI-IW) and Consumer Price Indices for Agricultural Labourers (CPI-AL) which had been decelerating since 1991-92, has showed an upward trend during 1994-95. The annual percentage variation in CPI-IW had declined from 13.56 in 1991-92 to 7.52 in 1993-94, increased to 10.21 in 1995-96 and again declined to 6.94 in 1997-98 (Table 5.6). The annual percentage variation in CPI-AL had declined from 19.30 in 1991-92 to 3.53 in 1993-94, but increased to 11.94 in 1994-95. It, however, registered a downward trend thereafter reaching a level of 3.32 during 1997-98 (Table 5.6). Tables 5.7 and 5.8 present the monthly variations in the Consumer Price Indices for Industrial and Agricultural workers respectively. The monthly percentage variation in

CPI-IW for the 79 months period from April, 1992 to October 1998 varies from a low of(-) 1.25 to a peak of 3.23 points with a range of 4.48 while the monthly percentage variation in CPI-AL for the same period varies from a low of (-) 1.66 to a peak of 3.74 with a range of 5.40 points.

The inflation rate based on CPI(IW) which was decelerating since August, 1992, showed an accelerating trend from August, 1993 and attained a peak of 11.39 in July, 1995 and again declined to 8.46 in October, 1996 recording a steepfall to a level of 4.66 during August 1997. Thereafter it started increasing and reached a level of 9.71 in January, 1998. However it declined to 8.19 in April 1998 and again showed an upward trend to a level of 18.63 in October 1998. (Table 5.9). The CPI (AL) showed a similar trend in inflation rate, accelerating since September, 1993 and attaining a peak of 14.53 in July 1995 and again declined to 6.84 in February, 1996. It again increased to 11.44 points in February 1997 and then started declining to a level of 3.80 points in Feb, 1 998. Thereafter it started increasing and reached a level of 15.59 in October 1998. The Tables 5.9 and 5. 10 present the annual rate of inflation for Industrial workers and Agricultural Labourers computed monthly on point to point basis.

Average labour cost

Labour Cost comprises of various components like wages and salaries, all types of bonus, contribution to Provident &other funds and workman & staff welfare expenses. Latest statistics on Labour Cost under the Census Sector of the Annual Survey of Industries (ASI), which represents a major sphere of the factory sector in terms of employment, is available for the year 1994-95. Table 5.11 presents a comparative picture of Labour Cost in 1992-93, 1993-94 and 1994-95 rounds of the ASI.

The average labour cost per manday worked at all India level was found to be the highest in the industry division 36 "Manufacture of Electrical Machinery, Apparatus, Appliances and Supplies parts" (Rs. 248.41) and the lowest in the industry division 22 "Manufacture of Beverages, Tobacco and Related Products" (Rs. 55.29) during ASI 1994-95. Statistics show an increase in the labour cost per manday worked in a number of industries during ASI 1994-95 over 1993-94. Maximum increase (28.5%) in the Labour Cost per manday worked was observed to be in the industry group 43 "Non Conventional Energy Generation and Distribution". The increase at all India level has been observed at 13.8% in 1994-95 over 1993-94.

Payment of bonus act, 1966

The Payment of Bonus Act, 1965 provides for payment of bonus to employees as defined under the Act. According to Section 2 (133#) of the Act, "employees" means any person (other than an apprentice) employed on a salary or wage not exceeding three thousand and five hundred rupees per mensem in any industry to do any skilled or unskilled, manual, supervisory, managerial, administrative, technical or clerical work for hire or reward. However according to Section 12 of the Act, the bonus payable to an employee, whose salary or wage exceeds two thousand and five hundred rupees per mensem, has to be calculated as if his salary or wage were two thousand and five hundred rupees per mensem. The above wage ceilings under Section 2(13) and Section 12 of the Act respectively were last revised vide Payment of Bonus (Amendment) Ordinance, 1995 promulgated on 9.7.95 and made effective from 1.4.93. After the amendment of the Payment of Bonus Act, a number of establishments challenged the retrospective affect of the amendment of the Act by filing writ petitions in various High Courts in India. The Government decided to contest all such cases and in two cases filed at the High Court of Jaipur the action of Government of India with regard to the retrospectivity of the notification has been upheld by the hon'ble court.

The Government is now again considering proposals for review/abolition of wage ceilings prescribed under Payment of Bonus Act. Presently th views of the concerned departments of the Central Government, State Governments/Union Territories Employees and Employers organisations have been invited on the subject. After receipt of their views the matter of raising the bonus ceiling will be examined further.

6

Social Security

Social security refers to protection which society provides for its members through a series of public measures against the economic and social distress caused by stoppage or substantial reduction of earnings resulting from sickness, maternity, employment injury; unemployment, invalidity, old age and death and to provide for medical care and to subsidise such medical care for families with children. Social security programmes are designed to provide benefits, both in cash and kind, on occurrence of such contigencies. Under the Constitution of India social security in its broad sense is envisaged in terms of the Directive Principles of state policy. Though India has not ratified all the ILO Conventions relating to social security, there are national ,laws which provide for certain mandatory benefits in respect of certain employments. These include medical care and sickness benefits, invalidity and survivors' benefits, employment injury benefits and maternity benefits. There are also laws enacted and Schemes established by the Central/State Governments providing for social security and welfare of specific categories of working people.

Table
Constitutional Provisions

(Directive Principles of State Policy)

- Right to an adequate means of livelihood (Article 39(a).

- The State shall within the limits of its economic capacity and development, make effective provision for securing public assistance in case of unemployment, old age, sickness, disablement and other cases of undeserved wants". (Article 41).
- "The State shall endeavour to secure to all workers agricultural, industrial or others-wise, a living wage, conditions of work ensuring a decent standard of life." (Article 43).

Soccial security laws

The principal social security laws enacted centrally are the following:

- The Workmen's Compensation Act, 1923: (W.C. Act).
- The Employees' State Insurance Act, 1948: (ESI Act).
- The Employees' Provident Funds & Miscellaneous Provisions Act, 1952; (EPF Act). (Separate Provident fund legislations exist for workers employed in Coal mines and Tea Plantations in the State of Assam and for Seamen).
- The Maternity Benefit Act, 1961: (M.B. Act).
- The Payment of Gratuity Act, 1972: (P.G. Act).

Table

Social seccurity conventions of ILO ratified by India

Convention No. 18:	Workmen's Compensation (Occupational-Diseases) 1925
Convention No. 19:	Equality of treatment (Accident Compensation) 1925
Convention No. 42:	Workmen's Compensation

	(Occupational Diseases) Convention (Revised) 1934
Convention No. 118:	Equality of Treatment (Social Security) 1962.

Administration of social security acts

The EPF & MP Act is administered exclusively by the Government of India through the EPFO. The cash benefits under the ESI Act are administered by the Central Government through the Employees State Insurance Corporation (ESIC), whereas medical care under the ESI Act is being administered by the State Governments and Union Territory Administrations. The Payment of Gratuity Act is administered by the Central Government in establishments under its control, establishments having branches in more than one State, major ports, mines, oil fields and the Railways and by the State Governments and Union Territory Administrations in all other cases. In mines and circus industry, the provisions of the Maternity Benefit Act are being administered by the Central Government through the Chief Labour Commissioner (Central) and by the State Governments in factories, plantations and other establishments. The provisions of the W.C. Act are being administered exclusively by State Govts.

The employees' provident funds and misccellaneous provisions acts, 1952

The EPF& MP Act, 1952 enacted by Parliament came into force with effect from 14th March, 1952. Presently the following three Schemes are in operation under the Act.

- The Employees' Provident Funds Scheme, 1952:
- The Employees' Deposit-Linked Insurance Scheme, 1976:
- The Employees' Pension Scheme, 1995:

Coverage

The EPF Act initially applied to factories/ establishments falling within 6 specified industries which had completed 3 years of existence and employed 50 or more workers. The Act is now applicable to factories/establishments engaged in 177 industries/classes of establishments employing 20 or more workers. The wage ceiling for coverage under the Employees' Provident Funds Scheme has been enhanced from Rs. 3,500/- to Rs. 5,000/ per month with effect from 1-10-1994. At the end of March, 1998, 2.99 lakh establishments with 21.22 million subscribers were covered under the Employees' Provident Funds Scheme. There may be some establishments which, though coverable, may be evading their coverage under the Act on one or the other pretext. Efforts are, therefore, being made to ensure that all coverable establishments are brought within the preview of the Act immediately after such establishments are detected.

Administration

The three Provident Fund related Schemes mentioned above are administered by the Central Board of Trustees. The Central Board is a tripartite body consisting of a Chairman, a Vice Chairman, representatives of the Central Government, State Governments, employers' and employees' organisations appointed by the Central Government.

Table

Central board of trustees-employees provident fund

- A Chairman (Minister for Labour)
- A Vice-Chairman, (Secretary, Ministry of Labour)
- 5 Representatives of Central Government.
- 15 Representatives of State Governments.
- 10 Representatives from the Employers' Organisations.
- 10 Representatives from the Employees' Organisation.

- Central Provident Fund Commissioner Ex-Officio.

The Central Provident Fund Commissioner is the thief Executive Officer of the Employees' Provident Fund Organisation and is Ex-Officio member of the Board.

The Employees' Provident Fund Organisation apart from the Central Office located at Delhi, has 256 field offices through-out the Country.

Table
E.P.F.O. Offices

- 17 Regional Offices
- 73 Sub-Regional Offices and Sub-Accounts Offices
- 166 Inspectorate Offices/ Service Centres;

Cost of administration

The cost of administration of Provident Fund Scheme and 84% of the administrative cost of the Employees' Pension Scheme is met out of the administrative charges received from the employers of unexempted establishments and inspection charges from the employers of exempted establishments. 16% cost of administration of the Employees' Pension Scheme is borne by the Pension Fund. The administrative cost of the Employees Deposit Linked Insurance Scheme is borne by th employers of the covered establishments,

Contribution

The normal rate of contribution to the provident fund by the employees and the employers prescribed under the Act which was earlier 8.33% has since been raised to 10% of the wage of the employees w.e.f.. 22.9.97. The Act also empowers the Central Government to enhance, if deemed fit, the rate of contribution now to 12% (earlier 10%) of wage in respect of any industry or class of establishments. The Central Government has so for enhanced the rate of contribution to 12% in respect of 172 categories of establishments. Investment and rate of interest

The Provident Fund Contributions are invested as per the pattern of investment prescribed by the Central Government from time to time.

As on 31.3.98 the total investment amounted to Rs. 62303.56 crores, out of which Rs.35597.51 crore pertained to unexempted establishments. The Government of India, on the recommendation of the Central Board of Trustees, has approved crediting of interest at 12% in the members' accounts on monthly running balances. Arrangements have been made, after consultation with the Ministry of Finance, to get the investments handled by the State Bank of India.

Employees provident fund arrears

The Provident Fund arrears as on 31.3.98 were of the order of Rs.463.07 crore. Out of this the amount immediately realisable was Rs.69.82 crore. The Employees' Provident Fund Organisation recovers outstanding dues from defaulting employers under Section 8 of the EPF Act. The Organisation also launches prosecution against the defaulting employers under Section 14 of the EPF Act. Further, the organisation prosecutes employers who deduct employees' share of contribution but do not remit the same to the Fund under Section 406/409 of the Indian Penal Code.

During 1997-98, arrears amounting Rs. 193.65 crores were recovered as against recovery of Rs. 105.23 crores in the previous year.

Table

Pattern of investment of P.F. monies from 1.4.1998

(i)	(a) Central Government Securities	25 Percent

	(b) State Government Securities	15 Percent
(ii)	(a) Bonds/Securities of Public Financial Institutions	40 Percent
	(b) Certificates of deposit issued by a Public Sector Bank	
(iii)	To be invested in any of the above categories as may be decided by the Board of Trustees	20 Percent
(iv)	Bonds/Securities in private sector having credit rating at least from two credit rating agencies	upto 10% out of the amount given in category

Employees' deposit linked insurance scheme, 1976

This Scheme came into force with effect from August 1, 1976. All the employees who are members of the Provident Fund are members of this Scheme also.

Contribution

While the employee - members are not required to contribute to the Insurance Fund, the employers are required to pay contribution to the Insurance Fund at the rate of 0.5% of the pay of the employees-

Investment and rate of interest

Contributions received in the *Insurance Fund" till 31.3.1997 are kept in the Public Account of the Government of India. The rate of interest on such accumulations in the Public Account is 8 5%. A sum of Rs. 1977.79 crore was lying invested at the end of 199798. The contributions received in the Insurance Fund from 1.4.1997 onward are being invested as per the pattern prescribed for the Provident Fund.

Benefits under the scheme

On the death of an employee, who is a member, while in service, the persons entitled to receive the provident fund accumulations are paid an additional amount equal to the provident fund in the account of the deceased subject to the maximum of Rs.35000/-.

During 1997-98, there were 24058 claims settled and an amount of Rs. 36.12 crore disbursed.

The employees' pension scheme, 1995

Coverage

The Employee's Pension Scheme is compulsory for all the persons who were members of the Family Pension Scheme 1971. It is also compulsory for the persons who have become members of the Provident Fund from 16.11.1995 i.e. the date of introduction of the Scheme. The PF subscribers who were not members of the Family Pension Scheme, have an option to join the pension Scheme. The Scheme came into operation w.e.f. 16.11.1995, but the employees, including those covered under the Voluntary Retirement Scheme have an option to join the scheme w.e.f. 1.4.1993.

Eligibility

Minimum 10 year's contributory service is required for entitlement to pension. Normal superannuation pension is payable on attaining the age of 68 years. Pension on a discounted rate is also payable on attaining the age of 50 years. Where pensionable service is less than 10 years, the member has an option to remain covered for pensionary benefits till 58 years of age or claim return of contribution/withdrawal benefits.

Benefit

The Scheme provides for payment of monthly pension in the following contingencies:-

(a) Superannuation on attaining the age of 58

(b) Retirement

(c) Permanent total disablement

(d) Death during service

(e) Death after retirement/superannuation/permanent total disablement

(f) Children Pension

(g) Orphan pension

(ii) The amount of monthly pension will vary from member to member depending upon his pensionable salary and pensionable service. The formula for calculation of monthly member's pension is as under:-

$$\text{Member's Pension} = \frac{\text{*Pensionable Salary} \times (\text{Pensionable service} + 2)}{70}$$

To illustrate, if the contributory service is 33 years and pensionable salary is Rs.5000/- per month, the above formula operates as given below:

$$\text{Member's Pension} = \frac{\text{*Rs. } 500 \times (33 + 2)}{70} = \text{Rs. } 2500/- \text{ p.m.}$$

*Pensionable salary will be average of last 12 months' pay.

Family pension

(a) The rate of minimum widow pension is Rs. 450/- p.m. The maximum may go upto Rs. 2500/- p.m. payable as normal member's pension on completion of nearly 33 years' service. Family pension upto Rs.1,750/- p.m. is also payable to the widow of the member who has contributed only for one month to the pension fund.

(b) In addition to the widow pension, the family is also entitled to children pension. The rate of children pension is 25% of widow pension for each child subject to a minimum of Rs. 115/- p.m. per child payable upto two children at a time till they attain the age of 25 years.

(c) If there are no parents alive, the scheme provides for orphan pension 0 75% of the widow pension payable to orphans subject to the minimum of Rs. 170/- p.m. per orphan.

Option for return of capital

Under the Pension Scheme, the employees have an option to accept the admissible pension or reduced pension with return of capital. In the case of the employee opting for 10% less pension than the actual entitlement, the scheme provides for return of capital equivalent to 100 times of the original pension in the event of death of the pensioner. For example, if the monthly pension is Rs. 2000/- p.m. and the employee opts for reduced pension of Rs. 1800/ -, the family will have refund of the capital amounting to Rs. 2,00,000/- on death of the pensioner. In addition, the widow and two children will continue to get pension for life or upto the age of 25 years, as the case may be.

Finance

(i) Under the Scheme, neither the employer nor the employee is required to make any additional contribution. A Pension Fund has been set up and from 16.11.95 the employees share of PF contribution representing 8.33% of the wage is being diverted to the said Fund. All accumulations of the ceased Family Pension Fund have been merged in the Pension Fund. The Central Government is also contributing to the Pension Fund at the rate of 1. 16% of the wage of the employees. The invested corpus of Pension Fund as on 31.3.1998 was Rs.14693.48 crore.

Investment of pension fund

It has been decided to invest the pension fund as per the pattern indicated below:-

(i) Family Pension corpus as on 15.11.95 and the Central Governments' contribution from 16.11.95 onward are invested in the public account of the Government of India.

(ii) Other accretions to the Pension Fund are being invested as per the pattern prescribed by the Ministry of Finance from time to time.

Pension beneficiaries

The beneficiaries of the ceased Family Pension Scheme continue to get benefits under the new pension scheme. As on 15.11.98, there were 2,30,562 widows, 76632 children, 986 orphans and 184653 retired persons getting pension under the scheme. Total amount disbursed among the pensioners during the year was 271.55 crore. Pension is being disbursed through Nationalised Banks.

The Pension Fund is required to be evaluated through a qualified Actuary on annual basis. Based on valuation result, the benefit quantum could be revised. First actuarial valuation which became due on 15.11.1996 has been got done. Based on valuation recommendation, the Central Government has allowed 4% relief on pension in payment w.e.f. 15.11.1996 to the existing pensioners.

Computerisation

The process of computerisation in the EPF organisation was started in the year 1989 with introduction of one PC-XL Computer System at one of the Regional Office, Maharashtra primarily to clear the accumulated pendency in issue of Annual Statement of accounts to the Members.

Electronic Data Process Centres have been set up with fully operational Computer Centres at 85 field offices' of the Organisation. Effective steps to remove bottlenecks towards smooth computerisation were taken. Hardware systems were upgraded with latest model computer machines. In the software development area, implementation of the Employees' Pension Scheme was taken up through computer. Inner-connectivity through NICNET for better information/data exchange was successfully attempted. Plans are in hand to streamline computer operations to address the long term needs by developing integrated software systems. Steps to introduce Electronic Mail Facility in he Organisation through NICNET connectivity obtained through National

Informatic Centre have been taken. It is now possible for the field offices and Head Office to communicate between themselves using networking set up in the Organisation.

Public grievances

Redressal of grievances of the members as also the claimants became an area of higher priority for the Organisation. Efforts were put in by the Organisation in this area and mechanism was built up to acknowledge and settle the grievances of the members and claimants. A computerised public Grievances Handling System has been is introduced in all the field formations. Facilitation Centres also have been set up at all offices of EPF Organisation to redress the public grievandes.

Lok adalats

Lok Adalats are being organised on loth of every month for on the spot redressal of Grievances in all Regional/ Sub- Regional Offices.

Payment of gratuity act, 1972

The Payment of Gratuity Act 1972 applies to factories and other establishments employing 10 or more persons. On completion of five years service the employees are entitled to payment of gratuity @ 15 days wages for every completed year of service or part thereof in excess of six months subject to the maximum of Rs. 3.50 lakh. The current maximum limit is applicable from 24.9.1997. The wage ceiling for coverage under the Act has since been removed w.e.f. 24.5.94.

Provident fund scheme for tea p antation for Assam

Separate PF, Family Pension & EDLI schemes are in operation for tea plantation workers in the state of Assam. These schemes provide social security benefits as admissible to the workers covered under the EPF & MP Act, 1952 except that the Family Pension scheme modelled on the pattern of the ceased Family Pension Scheme 1971 is still continuing. During 1998-99 the Central Government contributed an amount of Rs.7.82 crore towards the Family Pension Scheme and amount of Rs. 1.95 crore towards the EDLI Scheme for workers in the state of Assam.

The employees' state insurance scheme coverage

The ESI Act provides for health care and cash benefit payment in the cases of sickness, maternity and employment injury. It is applicable to non-seasonal factories using power and employing 10 or more persons and non-power using factories and certain other establishments employing 20 or more persons. The Act is being implemented area-wise in a phased manner. The ESI Scheme is operated in 640 centres situated in 22 states/ union territories. As on 31.3.98 there are 8.36 million employees and 35.29 million beneficiaries covered under the Scheme.

Administration

The ESI Scheme is administered by a statutory body called the Employees' State Insurance Corporation (ESIC), which has members representing employers, employees, the Central Government, State Governments, medical profession and the Parliament. The Union Minister for Labour is the Chairman of the ESIC. A Standing Committee constituted from among the members of the Corporation acts as the Executive Body for administration of the Scheme and is chaired by Secretary to the Government of India in the Ministry of Labour. There is also a Medical Benefit Council to advise the Corporation on matters connected with provisions of medical benefit. There is a provision for setting up of the Regional Boards and Local Committees at the grass root level. There are 21 Regional Boards and 310 Local Committees in existence. The General Purposes Sub-Committee of the Corporation visits various states and union territories from time to time with a view to assessing the quality of medical care being provided and making suggestions for further improvement in the delivery system.

The Director General (ESIC) is the Chief Executive Officer of the Corporation and is Ex-officio Member of the Corporation.

The ESI Corporation apart from the Hqrs. office located at Delhi has a number of field offices throughout the country. The Corporation has 17 Regional off ices, 5 Sub-Regional off ices 793 cash off ices and 310 inspection offices all over the country for administration of the Scheme.

Funding and operation of the scheme

The ESI Scheme is mainly financed by contributions from the employers and the employees. Till, 31.12.96 the employers' contribution was equal to 4% of the wages payable to an employee. The employees" contribution was at the rate of 1.5%. With effect from 1.1.97 the rates of the employers' and the employees' contribution have been raised to from 4% to 4.75% and from 1.5% to 1.75% of the monthly wage respectively. The State Governments' share of the expenditure on the provision of medical care is to the extent of 12.5% (1/3th). The Corporation has prescribed a ceiling on the shareable expenditure on medical care. In order to improve medical care under the ESI Scheme, the expenditure on medical care has been enhanced from Rs. 410/- to Rs. 500/- per Insured Person Family Unit per annum with effect B from 1.4.1997. Out of this per capita ceiling amount of Rs. 165/- is earmarked for drugs and dressings. However, certain specific hems of expenditure are provided for outside the ceiling and shared in the same proportion. All capital expenditure on construction of ESI buildings including maintenance is borne exclusively by the Corporation.

Investment and rate of interest

All contributions received under the ESI Act and all other

moneys belonging to the fund which are not immediately required for defraying day to day expenses are invested in the manner prescribed statutorily. As on 30.9.98, the total investment of funds was Rs. 4222.38 crore. Out of this, an amount of Rs.2694.25 crore was invested in the Special Deposit account of the Govt. of India and the balance of Rs. 1508.13 crore was invested in fixed deposits with nationalised banks, financial institutions etc. Interest earned on the fund invested in the Special Deposit Account is 12% per annum.

Arears of ESI dues

A sum of Rs. 381 .01 crores was arrears on account of default by the employers of covered establishments. Out of this, an amount of Rs. 209.68 crores was locked up due to various reasons such as enterprises having gone into liquidation, enterprises being declared sick by the Board for Industrial and Financial Reconstruction (BIFR), enterprises being under Rehabilitation scheme sanctioned by BIFR, recovery being disputed in Courts etc. The balance amounting to Rs. 171.33 crores represented the effective arrears. The Corporation has been taking necessary legal and penal action under various provisions of the ESI Act and under the Indian Penal Code for recovery of ESI dues. The Corporation has also set up its own recovery machinery, in all the implemented states. During 1997-98, the Corporation realised Rs.37.31 crore from the defaulters through its own recovery machinery.

Health benefits

The medical care under the Scheme is administered by the State government who have the statutory responsibility in this regard, except in the National Capital Region of Delhi and NOIDA area in Uttar Pradesh. Besides, ESI Hospital in K.K. Nagar at Chennai, MGM Hospital Mumbai and Thakurpukur Hospital at Calcutta are also being run directly by the Corporation. The ESI Corporation commissioned 2 new hospitals (upto 31.10.1998) and 7 new dispensaries during the year.

Table

ESI Infrastructure (As on 31.3M)

ESI Hospitals (nos.)	129
ESI Annexes (nos.)	43
Beds in ESI run Hospital (nos.)	18985
Beds in ESI Annexes	867
Reserved beds in State Govt. hospitals	3840
ESI dispensaries	1450
Insurance Medical Officers	6059
Panel Clinics	2885

ESI performance status (1997-98)

- During 1997-98, the Scheme was implemented in new geographical areas covering 29 additional centres and 30,500 employees.
- There was a marked increase in the number of insured women covered Under the Scheme during 1997-98. It went up from 14.14 lakh in 199697 to 15.24 lakh by the end of March, 1998.
- The number of factories and establishments covered under the Scheme, as on 31st March 1998 was the highest ever at 2.13 lakh as against 2.00 lakh during 1996-97.
- The emphasis on development of new infrastructural facilities for extension of health care facilities to ESI beneficiaries resulted in commissioning of 2 new hospitals and 7 service dispensaries.
- The rate of payment of Extended Sickness Benefit which was increased from 125 percent to

140 percent of the Standard Benefit Rate with effect from 1st April 1994, continued to be operative during 1997-98 also.

- During 1997-98, the total amount paid on account of cash and other benefits was Rs.323.69 crore.
- The number of claimants for Permanent Disablement Benefit. (monthly cash compensation for physical disability) had increased from 103989 in 1996-97 to 113504 by the end of March, 1998.
- During 1997-98 as many as 352,998 patients were admitted to ESI Hospitals whereas, 1374451 cases were referred for specialist investigation. The total attendance recorded at ESI Dispensaries and panel clinics was about 500 lakhs.
- Provision of super-specialist facilities to insured persons and their dependants through the country's most advanced medical institutions is a unique feature of the ESI Scheme. During 1997-98, over 1000 cases, most of these requiring open heart surgery, kidney transplant or advanced treatment for cancer etc. were referred to these institutions across the country.
- Against a total contribution income of Rs.604.51 crores during 1996-97, the contribution income during 1997-98 was Rs. 1187.32 crores. The total expenditure on provision of medical benefits, (Corporation's share) cash benefit, administration etc. amounted to Rs.932.38 crores.
- The number of dependants; of deceased insured persons in receipt of Dependants Benefit (Family pension) had increased from 54698 in 199697 to 56503 by the end of March, 1998.

Other social security schemes

For workers of poor families not covered under any insurance scheme or any law/statute, the Central Government has introduced a Scheme of Personal Accident Insurance -Social Security Scheme. The Scheme is applicable to all persons in the age group of 18 to 55 who are earning members of poor families and meet with fatal accidents such as drowning, snake bite etc. The quantum of benefit is Rs. 3,000/- in each case. The scheme is implemented through the General Insurance Corporation (GIC).

International social security association

The Government of India and the Employees' Provident Fund Organisation are Associate Members of the International Social Security Association (ISSA), Geneva, while the Employees, State Insurance Corporation is an affiliate member. During 1998, India participated in the following important events of ISSA:-

- 75th Meeting of ISSA Bureau held in Geneva on 27-28.4.98.
- Meeting of the General Body Assembly of ISSA held at Marrakech, Morocco from 25th to 31st October, 1998.
- 16th ISSA Regional Training Course held in New Delhi from 17th to 27th November, 1998.

Maternity benefit act, 1961

The Act regulates employment of Women before and after child birth and provides 12 weeks maternity leave, medical bonus and certain other benefits. The Act is not applicable to the employees covered under the ESI Act.

Workmens' ccompensation act, 1923

The objectives of the Workmens' Compensation Act, 1923 is to provide compensation to workmen or their survivors in cases of industrial accidents and occupational diseases resulting in disablement or death. The compensation in the cases of death ranges from Rs. 50,000!- to 2,28,000/- and in the cases of permanent total disablement, it ranges from Rs. 60,000/- to Rs. 2,74,000. In the case of temporary disablement 50% of the monthly wages are payable as compensation for a maximum period of 5 years.

7

Labour Welfare

While the provision of social security to workers in the organised sector is sought to be ensured through the legal framework and institutional infrastructure created under the Employees' State Insurance Act, 1948 and the Employees Provident Fund and Miscellaneous Provisions Act, 1952, providing the same to the workers in the unorganised sector who Constitute more than 90% of the total workforce of 314 million has been a daunting problem. Since workers In the unorganised sector in general suffer from low earnings, lack of stability & durability of employment including its migratory nature in many cases, frequent changes in the employer and nature of employment, it has not been possible to extend to them the benefits of a contribution oriented or, employers' liability oriented social security scheme enjoyed by their counterparts In the organised sector, except to a small section of beedi workers and that too on a limited scale in respect of provident fund. The concept of labour welfare has been evolved in order to extend a measure of social assistance to workers in the unorganised sector. Towards this end, separate legislations have been enacted by Parliament to set up five Welfare Funds to be administered by Ministry of Labour to provide housing, medical care, educational and recreational facilities to workers employed in beedi industry, certain non-coal mines and cine workers. Efforts are afoot to substantially expand the Welfare Fund approach to cover more categories & subcategories of workers in the unorganised sector.

The scheme of Welfare Funds is outside the framework of specific employer and employee relationship in as much as the resources are raised by the Government on a non-contributory basis and delivery of welfare services effected without linkage to individual worker's contribution. Apart from the Welfare Funds set up by the Central government, various State Governments have also formulated and are implementing welfare programmes through the Fund approach for certain categories of unorganised labour. In fact, the State of Kerala Is a pioneer in the welfare fund approach and has set up as many as 35 Welfare Funds for the unoorganised workers working in different industries. Welfare Funds have also been created for the welfare of different categories of workers by the Government of Maharashtra, Orissa, Madhya Pradesh, Goa and Gujarat. Welfare funds which follow a sectorial approach are in addition to a large number of poverty alleviation and employment Generation programmes like IRDP, IAY, JRY, EAS, EGS, TRYSEM, DWACRA, tribal sub-plan, special component programme for SCs etc., which follow a regional approach and for which most of these workers are also eligible.

A Social Security Fund was created in 198889 by the Central Government to extend the insurance benefits to Economically Weaker Section of Society in the unorganised sector. This fund is being maintained by Life Insurance Corporation of India. The Life Insurance Corporation of India has been of late operating Group Insurance Schemes for the benefit of workers in 24 occupations. These occupations are beedi workers, brick-kiln workers, carpenters, cobblers, fishermen, harnals, handicraft-artisans, handloom weavers, handloom and khadi weavers, lady tailors, leather and tannery workers, papad workers attached to SEWA, physically handicapped self-employed persons, primary milk producers, rickshaw pullers/auto drivers, safai karamcharies, salt growers, tendu leaf collectors, scheme for urban poor, forest workers, sericulturists, toddy tappers, powerloom workers and women in remote rural hilly areas. About 50 lakhs workers were covered under Social Security Group Insurance Scheme as on 31.3.98. A Group Insurance Scheme for cine workers has also been introduced w.e.f. 1.4.1997. The, premiurn per workers under the scheme is fully paid out of the Cine Workers Welfare Fund. The National Social Assistance Scheme (NSAS) which was launched on 15.8.1995 by the Central Government also benefits a large number of workers in the unorganised sector. The scheme has the following components :-

(i) National Old Age Pension Scheme (NOAPS) under which pension at the rate of Rs. 75/- per month is available to destitutes over 65 years of age (estimated expenditure over Rs.484 crore benefiting over 53 lakh persons).

(ii) National Family Benefit Scheme (NFBS) under which lump sum benefit of Rs.5,000/- in the case of natural death and Rs. 10,000/- in the case of death due to accident of the primary bread winner of the family is available to the households below poverty line (estimated expenditure Rs. 190 crore benefiting over 3.5 lakh households).

(iii) National Maternity Benefit scheme (NMBS) under which lump sum benefit of Rs.300/ - would be available for the first two live births to women belonging to households below the poverty line (estimated expenditure Rs.136 crore benefiting over 45 lakh women).

Labour welfare funds

The Ministry of Labour is administering five Welfare Funds for beedi, cine and certain categories of non-coal mine workers. The Funds have been set up under the following Acts of Parliament for the welfare of these workers :

(1) The Mica Mines Labour Welfare Fund Act, 1946;

(2) The Limestone and Dolomite Mines Labour Welfare Fund Act, 1972;

(3) The Iron Ore, Manganese Ore and Chrome Ore Mines Labour Welfare Fund Act, 1976;

(4) The Beedi Workers' Welfare Fund Act, 1976; and

(5) The Cine Workers' Welfare Fund Act, 1981.

The above Acts provide that the fund maybe applied by the Central Government to meet the expenditure incurred in connection with measures and facilities which are necessary to provide the welfare of such workers and in particular: -

(a) to defray the cost of measures for benefit of such persons, directed towards the provision/and improvement of:

(i) public health and sanitation, medical facilities and the prevention of disease;

(ii) water supplies and facilities for washing;

(iii) educational facilities;

(iv) housing and recreational facilities including standards of living, nutrition and amelioration of social conditions;

(v) family welfare, including family planning, education and services;

(vi) transportation to and from place of work (for mine workers only); and

(vii) such other welfare measures and facilities as may be prescribed;

(b) to grant loan or subsidy to a State Government, a local authority or an employer, in aid of any scheme approved by the Central Government for the purpose connected with the welfare of workers engaged in beedi/cine/non-coal mine sector

(c) to pay annual grants-in-aid to a State Government/local authority/agency/owner of a mine which satisfies the prescribed criteria or to an employer who provides to the satisfaction of the Central Government welfare measures and facilities of the prescribed standard for the benefit of workers engaged in beedi/cine and non-coal mine sector

(d) to meet the allowances of the members to the State Advisory Committees and the Central Advisory Committees

(e) any other expenditure which the Central Government may direct to be defrayed from the Fund.

In order to give effect to the above objectives laid down in the above Acts, various welfare schemes in the field of health, education, housing, recreation and water supply have been formulated and are under operation. The details of such schemes are given in table 1.

Table 1
List welfare schemes for beedi, cine & mine workers

A. Health

1. Static-cum-Mobile/Static Allopathic and Static Ayurvedic Dispensaries for beedi workers.

2. Scheme for Reservation of Beds in T.B. Hospitals for beedi and mines workers.
3. Scheme for Domiciliary Treatment of beedi/mine workers suffering from T.B.
4. Scheme for Treatment of Beedi, Cine & Mine Workers suffering from Cancer.
5. Scheme for Treatment of Beedi & Mine Workers suffering from Mental Diseases.
6. Scheme for Treatment of Beedi & Mine Workers (including Gharkhata Workers) suffering from Leprosy.
7. Grant of Financial Assistance to Beedi & Mine Workers for purchase of Spectacles.
8. Maternity Benefit Scheme for Female Beedi & Mine Workers.
9. Scheme for payment of Monetary Compensation for Sterilisation to Beedi & Mine Workers.
10. Re-imbursement of expenditure as financial assistance to Beedi, Mine & Cine Workers in respect of Heart Diseases.
11. Re-imbursement of expenditure as financial assistance to Beedi, Mine & Cine Workers in respect of Kidney Transplantation.
12. Scheme for providing artificial limbs to mine workers.
13. Grant-in-aid to Iron Ore and Limestone & Dolomite Mines Managements for purchase of Ambulance Vans.
14. Scheme for payment of compensation in case of Fatal and Serious accident to mine workers.

B. Social Security

1. Group Insurance Scheme for beedi and cine workers.

C. Housing

1. Financial assistance to mines management for construction of low cost type-I and type-II houses for mine workers near work site.
2. Build Your Own House Scheme for beedi & mine workers.
3. Housing Scheme for Economically Weaker Section of Beedi Workers.

4. Grant of subsidy to Co-operative Societies of Beedi Industry for construction of worksheds and godowns.
5. Group Housing Scheme for beedi workers.

D. Education

1. Award of scholarship to the children of beedi workers (including Gharkhata Beedi Workers) cine and mine workers.
2. Composite Scheme for financial assistance to the school going children of Beedi and Mine Workers for supply of one set of dress, slates, note books and text books.
3. Payment of incentives on passing final University/Board examinations from High School onwards.
4. Scheme to provide incentive/financial assistance of Re. 1/- to female children of Beedi, mine & cine Workers, on the basis of attendance in schools.
5. Mid-day meals scheme for mine workers.
6. Assistance to mine owners for running Central Library.
7. Assistance for purchase of School buses to the mine managements.
8. Assistance to the mine managements for maintenance of Libraries.
9. Grant-in-aid for recognised schools in the Iron Ore mining areas for purchase of furniture & equipment.

E. Recreation

1. Establishment of Audio-Visual Sets/Cinema Vans/Exhibition of Films.
2. Organising sports, games, social and cultural activities.
3. Holiday Home Scheme.
4. Supply of TV. Sets to the Beedi Workers Industrial Co-operative Societies.
5. Establishment of Community Hall in Beedi Workers Housing Colony with colour TV. Set.
6. Scheme to provide buses for transportation of mine workers.

7. Setting up of Multipurpose Institutes/Developed Multipurpose Institutes for mine workers.
8. Setting up of Welfare Centres for mine workers.
9. Grants to M.P.Is/D.M.P.Is/Welfare Centres for mine workers.
10. Sports Grounds for mine workers.
11. Supply of Colour T.V. for mine workers.

F. Water supply

1. Financial assistance to small mine owners for sinking of wells.
2. Financial assistance too small mine owners for execution of water supply scheme.
3. Financial assistance to big mines management for execution of water supply scheme.

The Labour Welfare Organisation which administers these Funds is headed by a Director General (Labour Welfare)/Joint Secretary. He is assisted by the Welfare Commissioner (Headquarters) and nine Regional Welfare Commissioners for the purpose of administration of these Funds in the States. The nine regional offices are located at Allahabad, Bangalore, Bhilwara, Bhubaneshwar, Calcutta, Hyderabad, Jabalpur, Karma and Nagpur. The jurisdiction of each Welfare Commissioner has been shown in. To advise the Central Government on matters related to administration of the above Funds, tripartite Central Advisory Committees have been set up under the respective Welfare Fund Acts. These Committees are headed by Union Labour Minister. Earlier the membership of C.A.C. was 36 representatives, 12 each from Central Government, Employers and Employees excluding Chairman and Secretary. Need was felt to reduce the size of the Committee on the grounds that functioning of such unusual large committees tends to become unwieldy, they also make the task of providing logistic support extremely difficult and are unmanageable from the point of communication. Apart from this, such committees also entail additional financial expenditure, as most of the members tend to ask for air fare. On initiation of Secretary (Labour), membership of CACs has been reduced-to 18, 6 each representing Central Government, Employers and Employees to make the meeting meaningful from transmission of effective communication among the members and management and economy point of view. State-wise tripartite Advisory Committees headed by the Labour Minister of the concerned State, have also been set up in the state of Andhra Pradesh, Bihar, Madhya Pradesh, Rajasthan, Orissa, West Bengal, Karnataka, Kerala, Tamil Nadu, Gujarat and Maharashtra under the Beedi Workers Welfare Fund. Under the Limestone & Dolomite Mines Labour Welfare Fund, SACs have been constituted in the States of Uttar Pradesh, Madhya Pradesh, Bihar, Maharashtra, Karnataka and Gujarat, Madhya Pradesh, Orissa, under Iron Ore, Manganese Ore & Chrome Ore Mines Labour Welfare Fund in the states of Madhya Pradesh, Bihar, Karnataka, Maharashtra, Goa and Andhra Pradesh, Mica Mines Labour Welfare Fund has SACs in the state of Rajasthan, Bihar and Andhra Pradesh and Cine Workers Welfare Fund has SACs in the states on Maharashtra, Andhra Pradesh, Kerala, Tamil Nadu, Karnataka and West Bengal. The State Advisory Committees in the States approve the budget under each Fund for the respective State.

The Funds mentioned are financed out of the proceeds of cess levied under respective Cess/Fund Acts on manufactured beedis, feature films, export of mica, consumption of limestone & dolomite and consumption and export of iron ore, manganese ore & chrome ore.

Table 2
Welfare commissioners and their jurisdiction

Sl. No.	*Name of Region*	*States Covered*
1.	Welfare Commissioner, Allahabad	Uttar Pradesh, Himachal Pradesh, Punjab, Jammu & Kashmir
2.	Welfare Commissioner, Bangalore	Karnataka & Kerala
3.	Welfare Commissioner, Bhilwara	Gujarat, Rajasthan & Haryana
4.	Welfare Commissioner, Bhubaneshwar	Orissa
5.	Welfare Commissioner, Calcutta	West Bengal, Assam, Tripura & Meghalaya
6.	Welfare Commissioner, Hyderabad	Tamil Nadu & Andhra Pradesh
7.	Welfare Commissioner, Jabalpur	Madhya Pradesh
8.	Welfare Commissioner, Karma	Bihar
9.	Welfare Commissioner, Nagpur	Maharashtra & Goa

Beedi Workers Welfare Cess Act, 1976 provides for levy of cess by way of excise duty on manufactured beedis from Re.1/- to Rs.5/- per thousand manufactured beedis. Earlier this rate was from 10 paise to 50 paise. The Beedi Workers Welfare Cess Act, 1976 was recently amended by the Parliament to enable the Government to levy the cess on beedis between Rs.l/- to Rs.5/- per thousand manufactured beedis. The rate of cess per thousand manufactured beedis was ten paise w.e.f. 1.1.1982 and 30 paise w.e.f. 1.3.1987. This was enhanced to 50 paise w.e.f. 17.10.1995. At present (w.e.f. 20. 10. 1998) rate of cess is Re. 1 per thousand manufactured beedis.

The Cine Workers Welfare Cess Act, 1981 provided for duty of excise, at such rate not being less than one thousand rupees and not exceeding twenty thousand rupees, or- every feature film submitted to the Chairman, Central Board of Film Certification. Prior to October, 1994, the rate of cess provided in the Act was Rs.1,000/- per feature film. As the earlier rate was found to be low which resulted in a meagre collection and did not permit taking up any substantial programme for the welfare of cine workers, the rate of cess on feature films has been enhanced with effect from 13th October, 1994. But the balances in the fund are still not encouraging and due to financial constraints, it has not been found possible to extend welfare facilities to cine workers on the same scale as those being provided to beedi & mine workers under respective welfare funds. The possibilities of bringing the T.V. Serials, Short films, Advertisement films and other types of films (except feature films) which require certification from CBFC within the ambit of the Cine Workers Welfare Cess Act, 1981 are being worked out so that the fund could further be augmented and new schemes or extension of existing scheme applicable to other categories of unorganised workers for welfare of cine workers and their dependants could be evolved.

The Iron Ore, Manganese Ore & Chrome Ore Mines Labour Welfare Cess Act, 1976 provides for levy and collection of cess on Iron Ore, Manganese Ore & Chrome Ore between paise 50 to Re.l/-, Re.l/- to Rs.6/'- and Rs.3/ - to Rs.6/ respectively. At present these rates are Re.l/-, Rs.2/- and Rs.4/- respectively. The Welfare and Cess Commissioners have been entrusted with the task of collection of cess on Iron Ore, Manganese Ore & Chrome Ore consumed internally i.e. from metallurgical factories. The Department of Customs collects cess on the exported Iron Ore, Manganese Ore & Chrome Ore and is paid 1 % of the proceeds as collection charges.

The Limestone and Mines Labour Welfare Fund Act, 1972 provides for the levy and collection of cess on Limestone and Dolomite as a duty of excise at such rate not exceeding one rupee per metric tonne of limestone & dolomite. Ever since the inception of the Limestone & Dolomite Mines Labour Welfare Fund, rate of the cess was 20 paise per metric tonne. However, vide notification No. S-23013/2/87-W. I I dated 22nd April, 1988, the rate of cess has been enhanced to 50 paise per metric tonne with effect from 1st May, 1988. Rate of cess on manufactured beedis, feature films, Iron Ore, Manganese Ore, Chrome Ore, Limestone & Dolomite and Mica at a glance is given in

Table 3
Cess rates under welfare funds-at a glance

1. Iron Ore	Re.1.00 per metric tonne on export/ internal consumption from August, 1990.
2. Manganese Ore	Rs.2.00 per metric tonne on export/ internal consumption from August, 1990.
3. Chrome Ore	Rs.4.00 per metric tonne on export/ internal consumption from August, 1990.
4. Mica	4.5% ad-valorem on export from November 1990.
5. Limestone & Dolomite	50 paise per metric tonne on internal consumption.
6. Cine	Rs.10,000 per Hindi Feature Film; Rs.5,000 per feature film in Tamil,
	Telgu, Kannada and Malayalam w.e.f. 13.10.1964;
	Rs.3,000 per Marathi and Bengali feature film w.e.f. 13.10.94 and

	Rs.2000/- per English feature film w.e.f. 20.11.1993; and
	Rs.2,000 per feature film in all other languages w.e.f. 13.10.1994.
7. Beedi	Rupee 1/- per 1000 manufactured beedis w.e.f. 20.10.1998

The average daily employment of workers in Iron Ore, Manganese, Ore, Chrome Ore, Mica, Limestone and Dolomite Mines during 1997-98 is 99,093. The State-wise details have been shown in the table.

Table 4

Average daily employement in mines (1997-98)

State	*Iron Ore*	*Manganese Ore*	*Chrome Ore*	*Mica Ore*	*Limestone*	*Dolomite*
1	*2*	*3*	*4*	*5*	*6*	*7*
Andhra Pradesh	112	1280	–	250	2780	250
Assam	–	–	–	–	356	27780
Bihar	5522	1110	–	562	2658	624
Goa	3965	548	–	–	–	–
Gujarat	–	–	–	–	4121	401
Haryana	47	–	–	–	–	–
Himachal Pradesh	–	–	–	–	–	1060
Jammu & Kashmir	–	–	–	–	48	–
Karnataka	6449	2698	1012	–	1811	107
Kerala	–	–	–	–	210	–
Madhya Pradesh	9179	4102	–	–	7152	2270

(Contd. . .)

Maharashtra	177	2133	43	–668	189	
Meghalaya	–	–	–	–	180	–
Manipur	–	–	32	–	–	–
Orissa	13226	5859	5850	–	2620	374
Rajasthan	17	–	–	72	1870	91
Tamil Nadu	–	–	–	–	49277	–
Uttar Pradesh	–	–	–	–	894	25
West Bengal	–	–	–	–	–	44
Total	38,694	16,730	6,937	1,002	31,355	4,375

The number of workers employed in the Cine Industry is 63,823. The State-wise breakup of the employment in Cine Industry has been given in the table.

With a view to widen the number of cine workers presently being covered under the welfare schemes, a proposal to amend the definition of Cine Workers is under active consideration of the Government to raise the maximum income ceiling limit for eligibility to avail of facilities under the welfare schemes from Rs.1,600/- per month and Rs.8,000/- on lump sum basis to Rs.3,500/- and Rs.42,000/- respectively. Group Insurance Scheme has also been extended to Cine Workers w.e.f. 1.4.1997.

Table 5
Cine workers

Name of the Region	*State*	*No. of Cine Workers*
Hyderabad	(i) Andhra Pradesh	10,171
	(ii) Tamil Nadu	24,270
Bangalore	(i) Karnataka	4,089
	(ii) Kerala	750
Bhilwara	Gujarat	2,000

Nagpur	Maharashtra	20,843
Bhubaneshwar	Orissa	500
Calcutta	West Bengal	1,200
	Total	63,823

An overwhelming majority of beedi workers, estimated to be around 4.4 million, are home workers. Therefore, identification of these workers is a must for effectively extending benefits under the welfare schemes to them. This has been taken up on priority. A monthly target for issue of 250 identity cards has been fixed in respect of every dispensary area. At the same time,, the State Governments also help in identifying and issuing cards to beedi workers.

The Welfare Commissioners of the Labour Welfare Organisation have been asked to get in touch with the State Labour Departments and the State Labour Commissioners for drawing up a joint programme for such a campaign and to render maximum help and co-operation as may be possible within the limited resources available with them. The number of identity cards issued by them in various States is given in table.

Table 6

Statement showing state-wise details of the total numbebr of beedi workers

Sl.	*Name of the state*	*Total no. of workers estimated at present*	*No. of identity cards issued till date*
1.	Andhra Pradesh	625000	499120
2.	Assam	7725	5349
3.	Bihar	391500	244847
4.	Gujarat	50000	46095

5.	Karnataka	360000	291007
6.	Kerala	136416	112768
7.	Madhya Pradesh	750000	700000
8.	Maharashtra	256000	191760
9.	Orissa	160000	113176
10.	Rajasthan	100000	699778
11.	Tripura	5000	4476
12	Tamil Nadu	621000	587564
13.	Uttar Pradesh	45000	216865
14.	West Bengal	487000	465167
	Total	43,99,644	35,48,172

Financial assistance for housing facilities

Shelter has been recognised as one of the basic needs and necessities for protection of all living beings from the vagaries of nature. Human habitation in a civilised society perceives certain basic and minimum standards of living. However, certain sections of our society which are at the lowest ebb of our economy are not able to meet this requirement and live with dignity. Highest priority has, therefore, been attached to the programme for construction of housing for beedi and mine workers under the various Welfare Fund Acts enacted for these sections of our society. The basic object of these schemes is to provide financial assistance to these workers for providing them houses. The details of various housing schemes formulated with this object in mind alongwith the amount of financial assistance being provided are given as under :-

(a) Type I housing scheme for mine workers

Under this Scheme, mine managements are granted subsidy at the rate of Rs.20,000/- inclusive of developmental charges or 75% of the actual cost of construction per tenement, whichever is less.

(b) Type II housing scheme for mine workers

Under this Scheme, mine managements are granted subsidy at the rate of Rs.30,000/- inclusive of developmental charges or 75% of the actual cost of construction per tenement, whichever is less.

(c) Bulld your own house scheme for beedi and mine workers

Under this scheme, subsidy of Rs.3,000/- and a loan of Rs.10,000/- is sanctioned by the Welfare Commissioners to the beedi/mine workers .. The loan is interest free and is recoverable in monthly instalments spread over 9 years. An additional subsidy of Rs. 1,700/- is also given to those workers who adopt small family norms.

(d) Group housing scheme for mine and beedi workers

A Housing Scheme entitled as 'Group Housing Scheme' for Mine & Beedi Workers has been approved by the Government. The Scheme is applicable to the workers covered by the Labour Welfare Funds viz. the workers employed in iron ore, manganese ore, chrome ore, mica, limestone & dolomite mines, beedi industry (including Gharkhata Beedi Workers). The new scheme aims at encouraging the workers to form Cooperative Group Housing Societies of at least 50 workers which would build tenements for their members with their own resources supplemented by financial assistance from the Government of India and other sources. It will be lawful for the society to negotiate a second mortgage, in addition to mortgage to Fund, of the tenements in favour of Financial Institution or any other person. The Government sanctions the loan and subsidy at the following rates :-

Loan : Rs.4,000/- for mine workers & Rs.6,000/- for beedi workers per house, and

Subsidy : Rs.1,000/- for beedi & mine workers per house.

(e) Housing scheme for economically weaker sections engaged in beedi industry

Under this Scheme the Central Government gives subsidy to the State Government @ 50% of actual cost of construction per tenement subject to a maximum of Rs.9,000/- per bonafide beedi worker. Development charges @ 50% of actual cost of development subject to a maximum of Rs.800/- and Rs. 1,000/- per house for ordinary and black cotton/ swelly soil area respectively are also payable. The ceiling cost per house is Rs. 25,000/-.

(f) Scheme for grant of subsidy to co-operative societies of beedi workers for construction of worksheds or godowns or both:

Under this scheme a cooperative society having a minimum of 100 members is given financial assistance upto 75% of the actual cost of construction of worksheds or godowns or both or Rs.75,000/- for each, whichever is less. At least 25% of the construction cost has to be borne by the society.

Subsidy and loan, under various housing schemes amounting to Rs.223.21 lakh was released during 1997-98 towards cost of construction and development charges. During the year 1998-99 upto 21.1.99, under EWS, Type-I & II Housing Schemes, 717 houses were sanctioned involving total financial implications of Rs.2.39 crores.

Representations have been received from various quarters for giving upward revision to the amount of financial assistance under the present schemes as the cost of construction has increased enormously over the last few years. The problem of paucity of funds under the Beedi Workers Welfare Fund has now been overcome by revising the rate of cess from Rs.0.50 to Rs.1.00 per thousand manufactured beedis w.e.f. 20.10.98. The Government is, therefore, actively considering proposals for amending the various welfare schemes including housing schemes for beedi as well as mine workers to provide for more financial assistance.

Financial assistance for housing for hamals

A new housing scheme for hamals was formulated and introduced as a pilot scheme during the year 1996-97 with a budget provision of Rs.5 crores for providing financial assistance for construction of houses for hamals in the States of Karnataka and Madhya Pradesh. As the responsibility for administering the scheme was passed on to this Ministry later in the year, the release of Central assistance of Rs.3.3 crores could only be made on 31st March, 1997. Out of this Rs.3.3 crores, Rs.2 crores were released to the Government of Karnataka and Rs.1.3 crores to the Government of Madhya Pradesh for constructing 2000 houses and 1300 houses respectively in these two, States. The scheme was approved for introduction as a pilot scheme and based on its success, was to be extended to the other States. All the State Governments have been requested to survey the situation of hamals and tell this Ministry the requirement of funds for providing them houses at the rate of Rs. 10,000/- per hamal. With a view to adopt this scheme as a regular scheme during the 9th Five Year Plan and to implement it in other States having large congregation of hamals, a feasibility study of the project is being undertaken through National Centre for Human Settlements and Environment.

Problems of beedi workers

The responsibility for implementation of the provisions of the Beedi and Cigar Workers (Conditions of Employment) Act, 1966 rests with the State Governments who are also responsible for notifying the minimum wages for beedi workers within their respective geographical jurisdiction. The minimum wages for beedi workers are fixed on piece-rate basis (number of beedis rolled), the traditional yardstick being 1000 beedis. Various problems affecting the beedi workers which continue to be a cause of concern were included as an agenda item for the Regional Labour Ministers' Conferences of Eastern and North Eastern, Southern, Northern and Central Regions held during 1994-95 who deliberated upon the various issue at length. On the question of minimum wage, the Regional Labour Ministers' Conferences have made the following recommendations:

> "The minimum basic wage for beedi workers should not be less than Rs.25/- for 1000 beedis considering that an average worker could roll only 800 beedis per day. There should be a degree of uniformity in minimum wage rates in adjoining States. The variation should not be more than Rs.3/-. It was, therefore, recommended that while reviewing basic rate of wages, each State should take into account the rates of wages prevailing in adjoining States to avoid shifting of industry. The wages should also be linked with CPI and VDA should also be revised every six months. Payment in lieu of Bonus, leave with wages, National and Festival Holidays should also be taken into account."

With regard to various mal-practices concerning rejection of finished products on the ground of not conforming to quality standards, issue of inadequate quantity and poor quality raw materials like tendu leaf, tobacco and thread etc. by the manufacturers or their contractors/agents, the Regional Labour Ministers' Conference endorsed the recommendations of the Ministry for the constitution of a Tripartite Standardisation Committee and district level Vigilance Committees. It also recommended that minimum quantity of raw material to be issued should be 800 grams of tendu leaf of standard average quality and 300 grams of tobacco for 1000 beedis of standard size. It further recommended that the wage loss due to rejection should not be more than 2.5% instead of 5%. Alternatively, the rejected beedis should be returned to workers after deducting proportionate cost of tendu leaf and tobacco issued to them at the rates to be fixed by the State Governments from time to time alongwith wages. Under direction from Secretary (Labour), the State Governments as well as Welfare Commissioners have been requested to give wide publicity to the statutory provisions of Beedi & Cigar Workers (Conditions of Employment) Act, 1966, pertaining to rejection of not more than 2.5% beedis of sub-standard quality and ensure that employer/contractor supplies good quality of tendu leaf of the optimum quality to the workers. A Conference of North Eastern Labour Ministers was also held at Shillong on 19/7/97 to resolve the problems of workers particularly beedi workers and also to remove the feeling of isolation haunting the people of that region and bring them to the main stream of national development.

Assistance for medical facilities

The Labour Welfare Organisation is directly running 12 hospitals having capacity of 515 beds and 274 dispensaries (including one chest clinic) at different places in the country to provide basic health care and family welfare services to beedi and mine workers. In addition, 51 new dispensaries have been sanctioned in various parts of the Country for the welfare of the beedi workers on 1.4.97. Most of the medical institutions have a mobile unit attached to them to increase their outreach. A statement showing details of these hospitals and dispensaries is at table.

Table 7
Statement showing the welfare fund hospitals and dispensaries

S. N.	*Name of welfare fund*	*Location*	*No. of hos-*	*No. of beds pitals*	*No. of dis-pen-sar-ies*
1.	Iron Ore, Manganese Ore & Chrome Ore Mines Labour Welfare Fund	Joda (Orissa)	1	50	
		Barajamada (Bihar)	1	50	
		Kariganur (Karnataka)	1	25	
		Tisca (Goa)	1	60	
		Balaghat (M.P.)	1	50	
		Total	5	235	21
2.	Mica Mines Labour Welfare Fund	Karma (Bihar)	1	100	
		Tisri (Bihar)	1	10	
		Kalichedu (A.P.)	1	30	
		Total	3	140	11
3.	Limestone & Dolomite Mines Labour Welfare Fund Gangapur (Rajasthan)	Gangapur (Rajasthan)	1	30	
		Total	1	30	34
4.	Beedi Workers Welfare Fund	Mysore (Karnataka) T B. Hospital	1	50	
		Kodarma (Bihar) Gursahaiganj (Uttar Pradesh)	1	10	
		Total	3	110	208
				(including Chest Clinic)	
		Grand Total	12	515	2741

Construction of a 50 bedded hospital for beedi workers at Dhuliyan (West Bengal) is in final stage of completion. It has also been decided to construct two more 30 bedded hospitals for beedi workers one each at Sagar (Madhya Pradesh) and at Mukkudal (Tamilnadu) . A piece of 12.85 acres of land for the hospital at Sagar has already been allotted by the State Government of Madhya Pradesh and detailed estimates of construction of hospital are being prepared by CPWD, Bhopal. The proposal for setting up of the hospital at Mukkudal (Tamil Nadu) is also being finalised. Since there is paucity of funds to meet expenditure on new projects, the Beedi Workers Welfare Cess Act has recently been amended to enable the Government to raise the rate of cess on manufactured beedis and a notification raising the rate of cess from 0.50 paise per thousand manufactured beedis to Rs.1.00 per thousand manufactured beedis has also been issued on 20.10.1998. A Statement showing the details of medical assistance being provided under Welfare Funds is at Box.7.5.

A Group Insurance Scheme has also been extended to Pine Workers w.e.f. 1-4-97 on the basis of a similar scheme inexistence for beedi workers. Under the Scheme, upon death of the beneficiary, his family will be paid Rs.5,000/- in case of death due to natural cause and Rs.10,000/- in case of death due to accident. This will benefit all the identified cine workers. No premium is being charged from/cine workers under the scheme and whole of the amount of the premium to be paid to LIC under the scheme is being borne out of the Cine Workers Welfare Fund.

All Welfare Commissioners have been requested to give wide publicity to the existing Welfare Schemes through various media like Doordarshan, A.I.R., Press, etc. The dispensaries/ hospitals set up for beedi and mine workers are also playing important role in this regard through display of posters, distribution of pamphlets and organising of Awareness Camps in remote and solated areas. The Director General, Factory Advice Service and Labour Institute has also been involved in the survey of - occupational diseases prevailing among the workers.

Table 8

Diversified medical assistance under welfare funds

Purpose	Nature of assistance
Ophthalmic Problems	Financial assistance of Rs.70/- for purchase of spectacles for beedi & mine workers.
Tuberculosis	Reservation of beds in T.B.Hospitals and domiciliary treatment for mine and beedi workers. Medical treatment charges not exceeding Rs.50/ p.m. and subsistence allowance not exceeding Rs.250/- p.m. is paid to mine and beedi workers.
Heart Diseases	Reimbursement of expenditure upto Rs. 10,000/- to mine, beedi and cine workers for treatment of Heart disorders.
Kidney Transplant	Reimbursement of expenditure upto Rs. 15,000/- to mine, beedi and cine workers for Kidney transplant.
Cancer	Reimbursement of actual expenditure on treatment, medicines ani diet charges incurred by mine, beedi and cine workers or their dependants. Subsistence allowance upto Rs.250/- is also admissible alongwith railway fare, daily allowance etc.
Mental Disease	Grant for treatment, diet charges and

(Contd. . .)

	railway fare and subsistence allowance to mine and beedi workers.
Leprosy	–do–
Orthopedic problems	Supply of artificial limbs for mine workers.
Maternity	Grant of Rs.250/- for delivery to a female beedi worker (for first two deliveries).
Family Welfare	Monetary incentive of Rs.50/- per head to the beedi workers for undergoing sterilisation.
Grant-in-aid to mine management	Grant-in-aid @ 50% of the actual cost of the Ambulance Van or @ 33.33 of the cost of Standard Matador (Cheapest make) whichever is less admissible. Grant-in-aid for maintaining and improving hospital dispensaries upto 50% of the actual expenditure.
Group Insurance Scheme for Beedi Workers	An amount of Rs.3,000/- in case of death due to natural cause and upto Rs.25,000/- in case of death/disability due to accident is paid to the beneficiaries and their families.
Group Insurance Scheme for Cine Workers	An amount of Rs.5,000/- in case of death due to natural cause and upto Rs.10,000/- in case of death due to accident is paid to the family beneficiaries.
Accident Benefits	An amount of Rs.500/- is admissible in case of permanent incapacitation; of mine workers. Besides, a sum of Rs.150/- p.m. for 5 years is a admissible to his widow.

Educational facilities

Among the priority areas, education for workers' children has been identified as one of the thrust areas for the welfare of labour under the various Labour Welfare Funds. An expenditure of Rs.833.69 lakh was incurred during 1997-98 under the ongoing schemes for giving scholarships and financial assistance for purchase of school uniforms, text books, slates and note books for the children of beedi and mine workers, and nearly 3.02 lakhs students have benefited as a result. Details of educational facilities and the financial assistance provided under the various Labour Welfare Funds are given in table 8. Under the Mid-day Meal Scheme, the children of mica mine workers are provided Mid-day meal @ Rs.2.50 per day per child. Special provision has been made in the scheme to take care of special needs of female/SC/ST children. For the students belonging to SC/ST, it has also been decided to make a reservation under these schemes on the basis of percentage of SC/ST population in the district concerned, subject to the condition that it should not be less than 15% for SC and 7.5% for ST. Efforts are made to enlarge the coverage of female students also ensuring that at least 50% of female students are covered overall. Similar efforts also made to cover all children belonging to ST who have passed the last qualifying examination.

With a view to further encouraging educational activities among children of beedi mine and cine workers and especially among female children, following two schemes introduced in the year 1995-96.

(a) Incentive scheme on passing final examination from high school onwards; and

(b) Incentive/financial assistance to female students studying in class V and onwards attending schools.

Recreational facilities

An amount of Rs.6.16 lakhs was spent under various schemes to provide recreational facilities to mines and beedi workers during 1997-98.

The Labour Welfare Organisation also provides the following recreational, educational and cultural facilities through Multi-Purpose Institutes (MPI), Development Multipurpose Institutes (DMPI) and Welfare Centers.

- education of children and adults
- sports and games for adults and children
- motivation of workers
- mid-day meals for children
- training for female dependants of miners in tailoring and embroidery.

Table 9
Recreational Facilities under welfare funds

Sl. Scheme	Assistance provided	Total Amount disbursed during 1997-98 (Rs. in lakhs)
1. Grant-in-aid for excursion-cum-study tours	Provided on matching basis to the mine managements subject to a maximum of RS. 10,000/- p.a.	0.11
2. Audio-visual sets and mobile cinema units film hire charges.	Reimbursement upto Rs.20,000/- p.a. for	3.44
3. Television Sets set and Rs.4,000/ per Black &Whits Set	Reimbursement of Rs.10,000/- per colour	0.80
4. Organisation of games and sports	Rs 10,000/- per tournament	1.81

(Contd. . .)

5. Buses for transportation of workers	Grants-in-aid of Rs.1.25 lakhs for normal bus	–
and Rs.60,000/- for mini bus.		
6. Buses for school going children of Workers	1/3rd of the prevailing cost of a cheapest mini	
bus in the market.		
	Total	6.16

Water supply

A scheme for financial assistance for implementing Water Supply Schemes in mica, iron ore, manganese ore, chrome ore, limestone and dolomite mines is in operation. Under the scheme, Government provides financial assistance not exceeding 50%. of the estimated cost of approved Water Supply Schemes. In case of small mine owners, financial assistance is provided upto the extent of 75% of the total estimated cost. Similarly, a separate scheme is in operation for sinking of wells in the mining areas.

Expenditure incurred under all welfare funds during thefinancial year 1997-98

An abstract of expenditure incurred under different sub-heads in respect of all the Welfare Funds administered by the Ministry of Labour during the financial year 1997-98 is given below (Table 11). Comparative figures of total expenditure incurred during the financial year 1996-97 in respect of these Funds are also indicated therein.

Table 10

Sttus of Welfare funds 1997-98

(Rs. in crores)

Name of the fund	Year of ince-ption	Comm-ulative expen-diture upto 1.4.98	Reser-ve on 1.4.98	Cess Col-lection 1998-99	Expen-diture during 1998-99 (Prov.)

1	2	3	4	5	6
Beedi Workers	1976	174.99	7.97	12.04(9/98)	10.57
Cine Workers	1984	0.55	1.39	0.22(10/98)	0.01
Iron Ore, Manganese Ore & Chrome Ore Mines Labour Welfare Fund	1978	68.96	72.87	7.87(10/98)	3.09
Limestone & Dolomite Mines Labour Welfare Fund	1973	32.83	21.99	2.84(10/98)	1.81
Mica Mines Labour Welfare Fund	1946	28.87	(-)0.59	0.50(10/98)	1.58
Total		296.25	103.63	23.47	17.06

Table 11

Abstracctof expenditure of 19?8-99 under all welfare funds

(Rs. in lakh)

Sl.	Sub-Head	Beedi	LSDM	IMC	Mica	Cine	Total
1.	Health	804.22	107.95	210.46	91.03	1.17	1294.83
2.	Education	2.47	0.79	28.58	40.98	–	72.82
3.	Housing						
	(i) Subsidy	4.79	8.63	6.94	–	–	20.36
	(ii) Loan	29.17	1.20	–	–	–	30.37
	(iii) GIA	–	–	–	–	–	–
4.	Recreation	7.85	15.04	10.01	3.39	–	36.29
5.	Construction of Godown/ Workshed	–	–	–	–	–	–
6.	Water Supply	–	–	–	0.98	–	0.98

(Contd. . .)

7.	Administration	128.87	47.33	53.22	21.55	0.04	251.01
	Total 1998-99	11057.37	180.93	309.21	157.93	1.21	1706.66 (upto 10/98)
	Total 1997-98	2614.98	413.17	562.14	2.33.84	13.07	3837.20

8

Unorganised Workers

The first National Commission on Labour (1966-69) defined unorganised labour as those who have not been able to organise themselves in pursuit of common objectives on account of constraints like casual nature of employment, ignorance and illiteracy, small and scattered size of establishments and position of power enjoyed by employers because of the nature of industry etc. Nearly 20 years later the National Commission on Rural Labour (NCRL: 1987-91) visualised the same scenario and the same contributory factors leading to the present status of unorganised rural labour in India.

According to the ILO Convention 141 and Recommendation 149 on Rural Workers' Organisations, organisation of the unorganised rural labour is essential to achieve the following objectives:-

- Eliminating obstacles to their establishment
- Promoting their growth and pursuit of their lawful activities
- Preventing legislative and administrative discrimination against rural workers' organisation
- Enabling the organisations to further the interests of their members to make effective contribution to economic and social development
- Ensuring organisation as a means of participation without discrimination in economic and social

development and for the benefits resulting from them.

On the basis of the 1991 census the enumeration of organised and unorganised workers is as indicated below:-

— Out of the 286 million (main workers) about 27 million are in the organised sector and 259 million are in the unorganised sector,

— In relative terms organised sector accounts for merely 9.4% of total workers whereas unorganised labour accounts for 90.6%.

— By necessary implication the focus of the trade union activity has been on about 9% of the organised workers whereas remaining 91 % of the unorganised workers do not receive sufficient attention from the trade unions.

— Out of 191 million workers engaged in agriculture, forestry, fishery and plantation, about 190 million (99.2%) are in the unorganised sector.

— Amongst the unorganised agricultural workers, about 111 million are cultivators (58.4%) and about 25 million are agricultural labourers (39.5%).

— Evidently, the task of organising 75 million agricultural labourers; who are largely unorganised and many of whom are also share croppers and landless is a stupendous one and needs the active consideration and attention of trade unions, social action groups and NGOs.

— Out of 28.9 million workers in the manufacturing sector only 25% (7.3 Million) are in the organised sector and the balance 75% (21.62 million) are in the unorganised sector.

— In building and construction sector, workers in the organised and unorganised sectors work out to 22% and 78% respectively.

— Out of total work force of 314 millions 286 million are main workers and 28 million are marginal workers.

— In trade and commerce, 98% of are the unorganised workers.

— In transport, storage and communications as against 38.5% workers in the organised sector (3.1 million) the unorganised sector accounts for 61.5% (4.9 million).

Agricultural workers

Agricultural workers constitute by far the largest segment of workers in the unorganised sector and their number according to 1991 Census was 74.6 million. In addition, a significant number of 110.7 million listed as cultivators and another 6 million listed as engaged in allied activities, particularly those having very small holdings (small/ marginal farmers) may also come under the definition of agricultural labourers.

Broadly, the problems of agricultural labourers can be classified into two groups viz., (i) social and (ii) economic problems. Their social problems emanate from the low status of agricultural labour in the rural hierarchy and the economic problems are due to inadequacy of employment opportunities, poor security of tenure, low income and inadequate diversification of economic activity in rural area. They are dispersed, unorganised and generally have poor bargaining power. Agricultural labour yields employment for less than six months in a year and they have often to migrate for alternative employment in other areas in construction, industry etc., particularly during off season, women generally receive only about 60% of the wages earned by men. Circumstances force many of them to borrow from time to time from private sources either for consumption purposes (even to maintain a subsistence level) or to meet social obligations (marriages etc.) and quite a few of them end up as bonded labourers.

Several measures have been taken to protect the interests of the working class and uplift the condition of agricultural workers. The very first legislation, the

Minimum Wages Act, 1948 was applied to the agricultural sector also. Subsequently, the Plantation Labour Act, 1951 was enacted to provide certain basic facilities to plantation workers. Many other existing Labour Laws are applicable or have direct bearing on agricultural labour.

The following Acts are at present applicable to Plantation labour and contain enabling provisions to extend them to agricultural workers :-

1. The Employees State Insurance Act, 1948.
2. The Maternity Benefit Act, 1961.
3. The Payment of Gratuity Act, 1972.
4. The Payment of Wages Act, 1936.
5. The Personal Injuries (Compensation Insurance) Act, 1973. In addition the Employees Provident Fund & Miscellaneous Provisions Act, 1952, besides containing a similar provision is already applicable to a section of agricultural workers as discussed above.

The problems of underemployment and poverty amongst agricultural labourers has been sought to be tackled through multi-dimensional course of action viz., improvement of infrastructural facilities, diversification to non-farm activities, skill improvement programmes, financial assistance to promote self-employment, optimising the use of land resources etc., through a variety of rural development, employment generation and poverty alleviation programmes like Integrated Rural Development Programme (IRDP), directed at giving financial assistance for acquiring income generating assets; National Rural Employment Programme (NREP) for generation of additional gainful employment and creation of productive community assets; Rural Landless Employment Guarantee Programme (RLEGP) for landless labourers, women, SC/STs both since merged into Jawahar Rojgar Yojna (JRY), Development of Women and Children in Rural Areas

(DWCRA) for economic and social upliftment of those categories living below poverty line and Training for Rural Youth for Self Employment (TRYSEM) and Community polytechnics for skill upgradation of rural artisans etc. Since 1977-78, the Central Board for Workers' Education (CBWE) has so far trained about 1 lakh workers and the rural educators through its 2 day rural awareness camps and one month's intensive training programmes respectively.

Table 1

List of labour legislations which are at present applicable to agricultural workers partly or wholly

1. *The Minimum Wages Act, 1948*: which provides for fixation of minimum wages for different categories of workers, including agricultural workers and their periodical revision by the respective State Governments.
2. *The Equal Remuneration Act, 1976:* which provides for equal remuneration for women workers.
3. *The Workmen's Compensation Act, 1923:* which provides for payment of compensation by certain classes of employers to their workmen for injury by accident. Agricultural workers employed in mechanised farming by tractors and other mechanical/electrical appliances and those engaged in tapping of palm trees, felling or logging of trees and transportation of timber by inland waters (Entries XXIII and XXIX in Schedule 11) are covered.
4. *The Employees Provident Fund and Miscellaneous Provisions Act, 1952:* which provides for institution of provident fund, family pension fund and deposit-linked insurance fund for employees in factories and other establishments. At present the benefits are extended to agricultural farms, orchards, botanical gardens and poultry farms (entries 36 and 46 Appendix 1) having 20 or more workers.
5. *The Inter State Migrant Workmen (Regulation of Employment and Conditions of Service) Act, 1979:* which seeks to regulate the employment of inter-state migrant workmen and provides **for**

regulation of conditions of service in all establishments employing five or more inter-state migrant workmen on any day during the preceding 12 months.

6. *The Child Labour (Prohibition and Regulation) Act, 1986:* which regulates the conditions of work of children in establishments other than those covered under Section 3 (prohibiting employment of children in certain dangerous and hazardous occupations and processes).
7. *The Bonded Labour System (Abolition) Act, 1976:* under which every bonded labourer stands freed and discharged from any obligation to render any bonded labour with effect from 25.10.1975.

Existing welfare schemes applicable to agricultural workers

1. Group Insurance Scheme for Landless Agricultural Labour operated by Insurance Division, Ministry of Finance.
2. Group Life Insurance Scheme for IRDP beneficiaries operated by Department of Rural Development.
3. Group Insurance Scheme for Landless Agricultural Labourers of the State of Gujarat.
4. Asha Kiran Scheme of the Government of Karnataka.
5. Insurance-cum-Retirement Benefit special Scheme for the workers in the Unorganised sector of Tamil Nadu Government.
6. Scheme for Financial assistance to Landless Women Agricultural Labourers during Pregnancy operated by Gujarat Govt.
7. Personal Accident Insurance Social Security Scheme for Poor Families.
8. Hut Insurance Scheme.
9. Kerala Agricultural Workers Pension Scheme.
10. Andhra Pradesh Landless Agricultural Workers Pension Scheme, 1984.
11. Old Age Pension (Destitute Agricultural labourer) Scheme of Tamil Nadu.

12. Old Age Pension Schemes by State/U.T. Governments.

Though the above mentioned Acts/welfare schemes are applicable to Agricultural workers, they have not been able to adequately protect their interests. This is partly on account of inadequate enforcement machinery which is handicapped in its mobility in relation to the well spread out vast extent of agricultural operations and partly on account of lack of bargaining power due to non-unionisation. Keeping in view the above broad perspective and also with the objective of creating a Welfare Fund so as to introduce various social amenities like education, health and medical care, housing, drinking water, group insurance etc. for them, the Ministry of Labour is considering to enact a comprehensive legislation for agricultural workers-which inter-alia provides for standard term and conditions of employment, hours of work, rest period, overtime, harvesting wage and for giving preference for employment to such workers as have worked on a land in the previous season. It is also proposed to make a provision for minimum wage and its periodical revision, & creation of Agricultural Workers Welfare Fund at District level. The Fund will undertake various welfare/social security schemes including immediate financial assistance in case of death or injury, payment of group insurance premia, health, maternity benefits, old age pension, housing, education etc. There is also special provision for women workers prohibiting their employment after sunset, ensuring payment of equal wages, maternity benefits etc. and representation on Welfare Fund in view of their high proportion among agricultural workers.

Construction workers

There are about 8.5 million building and construction workers in India. The industry employing construction workers covers a vast field of activity in the engineering, mechanical and civil processes. In all the developmental activities, the industry has a great role to play. A large number of multinational, national and local companies employing lacs of workers and equally large number of self-employed individuals are engaged in actual construction works and allied activities like white washing, painting, plumbing and fixing of mechanical or electrical fixtures. The environment of construction is subjected to vagaries of nature such as rains, floods, elevations and depressions, uncertainities of geological and soil conditions and exposure to extreme temperature and weather. Construction jobs are highly labour intensive and also highly mechanised. Entire activity is mobile, seasonal, intermittant and, mostly inter connected. Completion period of projects ranges widely and calls for engagement and dis-engagement of labour from various trades, skills and professions. Duration of employment, quantum of work (work pressure), ardousness differs from one extreme to another. Construction labour is highly unskilled, more often than not migrant, with high turnover and frequantly seasonal drawn from agriculture. The workers are usually socially backward and uneducated with low bargaining power.

One of the major features of construction industry is that despite mechanisation, and may be due to mechanisation, it is highly prone to risks of accidents. Although it is difficult to obtain accurate statistics due to non-detection and non-reporting, the number of such accidents in most countries, especially the developed and the developing, frequently exceeds that in manufacturing industry. Factors contributing to this factor include :

- the high proportion of small firms and of self-employed workers;
- the variety and comparatively short-life of work in construction sites;

- the high turnover of workers;
- the large numbers of seasonal and migrant workers many of whom are unfamiliar with construction processes;
- exposure to the weather;
- the many different trades and occupations.

The Government of India have been progressively concerned about the welfare of these workers. The following enactments stood extended to the construction workers in various fields :

(i) Factories Act, 1948

(iii) The Contract Labour (Regulation & Abolition) Act, 1970

(iii) The Minimum Wages Act, 1948

(iv) The Payment of Wages Act, 1936

(v) The Payment of Gratuity Act, 1972

(vi) The Industrial Disputes Act, 1947

(vii) The Industrial Employments (Standing Orders) Act, 1946

(viii) The Trade Unions Act, 1926

(ix) The Workmen's Compensation Act, 1923 The Inter-State Migrant Workmen (Regulation of Employment and Conditions of Service) Act, 1979.

Still a need was being felt for a comprehensive Central legislation for this category of workers. Eventually the following two enactments have come on the Statute Book w.e.f. 20.8.96 initially brought in as Ordinances on 3.11.95:

1. The Building and Other Construction Workers (Regulation of Employment and Conditions of Service) Act, 1996; and
2. The Building and Other Construction Workers' Welfare Cess Act, 1996.

The legislation provides for regulating the employment and conditions of service, safety and health and welfare measures for the construction workers. In respect of the safety provisions the legislation conforms to ILO convention, No. 167 concerning safety and health in construction work. The Act also provides for creation of a Welfare Fund at the State level to be financed by contribution made by beneficiaries, levy of cess on all construction works at rates between 1 to 2% of the construction cost incurred by an employer and non-mandatory grants/loans by the State/Central Governments. The Fund is to be used for giving financial assistance to the families of beneficiaries in case of accident, old age pension, housing loans, payment of insurance premia, children's education, medical and maternity benefits etc. The Act also provides for certain other welfare amenities like temporary accommodation at or near work sites, creches, canteen, first-aid, washing facilities etc. The salient features of the Act are given in Table 2.

Table 2

(i) The Act is applicable to every establishment which employs or had employed on any day of the proceeding 12 months, 10 or more workers in any building or other construction work.

(ii) In the definition of establishment in the Act, individuals, who employ such workers in relation to their own residence the total cost of which is not more than Rs. 10 lakhs, are exempted.

(iii) Constitution of Central and State Advisory Committee to advise the appropriate Governments on matters arising out of Administration of the Law.

(iv) Registration of establishments employing construction workers and appointment of registering officers.

(v) Constitution of Welfare Boards by the State Governments

and registration of beneficiaries under the Fund and provision for their identity cards etc.

(vi) Provision for financing and augmenting resources of the Welfare Boards constituted by the State Government.

(vii) Provision for temporary living accommodation to all building workers within or near the work-site.

(viii) Fixing hours of normal working day, weekly paid rest day, wages for overtime, provision for basic welfare amenities like drinking water, latrines and urinals, creches, first-aid, canteens etc. for the building workers.

(ix) Making adequate provisions for safety and health for construction workers including appointment of safety and health officers for construction workers including appointment of safety committees and compulsory notification of certain accidents.

(x) Provision for appointment of Inspecting staff headed by Director General of Inspection at the Central level and Chief Inspector at the State level.

(xi) Special provision regarding fixing responsibilities on employers to ensure compliance of safety provisions and with regard to prevention of accidents, timely payments of wages etc.

(xii) Penal provisions for contravention, obstruction, violation of the Act.

(xiii) Application of the Workmen's Compensation Act, 1923 to building and other construction workers.

(iv) Empowering the Central Government to give direction to the States and to remove difficulties arising in giving effect to the provisions of the law.

The Rules containing detailed procedure for giving effect to various provisions of the Act with special emphasis on health & safety aspects of construction workers have since been notified on 19.11.190.

Those legislations are expected to improve the living conditions of workers engaged in the construction activities.

Home based workers

There is no autentic data regarding number of home workers in the country. However, as per the preliminary estimates available, the number varies from 30 million to 50 million home workers.

In India, home workers are mainly engaged in beedi rolling, garment making, agarbatti making, gem cutting, preparation of food items like papad making etc. Beedi rolling is one such activity which is largely carried out as home work and beedi workers who are mostly family based, number about 5 million out of which about 90 % are home workers (called Gharkhata workers). This constitutes less than 1 % of the total strength of home workers. Though there is no legislation which provide welfare measures to all home based workers, the Government have enacted the following legislations for the welfare of beedi workers:

(i) Beedi & Cigar Workers (Conditions of Employment) Act, 1966;

(ii) Beedi Workers Welfare Fund Act, 1976.

Constitution of Welfare Fund by levy of cess and utilising the proceeds for promoting welfare of workers both wage employed and self-employed, is an important plank of our policy. Under the Welfare Fund Acts, a number of schemes for the welfare of beedi workers are being implemented. These include health, maternity benefit, housing, education and recreation etc. In order to extent welfare facilities to beedi workers, it is necessary to identify these beedi workers and issue identity cards to them. So far, identity cards have been issued to about 32.93 lakh beedi workers. On the lines of Beedi Workers Welfare Fund, the Ministry of Labour propose to initiate the process of setting up Welfare Funds to extend similar welfare facilities to other categories of workers engaged in some of the following activities:

(i) Agarbatti Making;

(ii) Garment making including stitching & embroidery;

(iii) Preparation of food items like papad etc.

In order to process the setting up a Welfare Fund by enacting a law for the category of home workers mentioned above, a lot of spade work is required to be undertaken to identify the home workers, their working and living conditions, their genuine needs regarding housing, health, medical care, drinking water, sanitation and education of their children etc.

The Ministry of Labour has written to the State Governments to conduct a survey so that welfare schemes could be extended to them. The Government is also exploring the possibility of involving some NGOs of repute in this task.

Apart from other unorganised workers mentioned in this chapter there are many other categories of workers who are poor, illiterate, seasonally employed and scattered over remote corners of the country in both traditional and non-traditional sectors. They have not been able to take full advantage of socioeconomic facilities provided by the Government. The major categories of such workers are:

Beedi Workers	Brick-kiln workers
Cobblers	Fishermen
Hamal	Handicraft artisans
Handloom Weavers	Handloom & Khadi Weavers
Lady Tailors	Papad workers attached to SEWA
Physically Handicapped Self Employed persons	Primary Milk Producers
Rikshaw Puller/auto drivers	Safai Karamchari
Salt growers	Tendu leaf collectors
Urban Poor	Forest Workers

Sericulture Workers
Toddy Tappers
Carpenters
Leather & Tannery Workers
Powerloom Workers

LIC is operating a Social Security Group Insurance Scheme for the workers engaged in above mentioned occupations. Under this scheme insurance cover of Rs.5,000/- in case of natural death and Rs.25,000/- in case of accidental death is provided. Benefit of permanent disability due to accident has also been added. The Government are also implementing various welfare schemes for the welfare of unorganised workers such as Intergated Rural Development Programme (IRDP), Jawahar Rojgar Yojna (JRY), Employment Assurance Scheme (EAS), Indira Awas Yojna (IAY), National Social Assistance Programme (NSAP) etc. However, the plight of these workers is deplorable as they are deprieved of basic amenities at their work place. It is the endeavour of the Government to cover more and more categories of workers under welfare schemes such as are being operated by Ministry of Labour.

Bonded labour

Bonded Labour System has been abolished by law throughout the country with effect from 25th October, 1975. The responsibility for identification, release and rehabilitation of bonded labourers is that of the State Government who are responsible for implementation of the Bonded Labour System (Abolition) Act, 1976.

Reports received from 13 States where the incidence of bonded labour system has been reported namely Arunchal Pradesh, Andhra pradesh, Bihar, Gujarat, Haryana, Karnataka, Kerala, Madhya Pradesh, Maharashtra, Orissa, Rajasthan, Tamil Nadu and Uttar Pradesh indicate that the total number of bonded labour identified and released from bondage by the State Governments was 2,51,424 and almost all the bonded labourers identified so far have been rehabilitated. A meeting was held on 15,10,96 under the Chairmanship of then Union Labour Minister with the State Secretaries dealing with bonded labour in order to review the implementation of the Bonded Labour System (Abolition) Act, 1976 by the State Governments. The Labour Minister/ Secretary (Labour) called upon the State Government to complete the survey on bonded labour by 31.12.1996, The State Governments have reported that about 29,000 bonded labourers have been identified during the surey. The Government have advised the State Governments to rehabilitate these identified bonded labourers in least possible time.

The subject matter of bonded labour was also under consideration of the Surreme Court by way of WP (c) 3922/85. The matter came up for hearing again on 5.5.97 when Solicitor General of India placed before the court the further line of action suggested by Government of India for compliance by the State Governments. The Courts observed that the suggestions given by government of India are appropriate and directed the State Governments to comply with the suggestions and file their response the gist of the suggestions is that:

(i) Even though the Act, under Section 13 provides for constitution of vigilance Committees at the district as well as the subdivisional levels, it is obvious that these Committees are not function in effectively. These Vigilance Committees be activiated and should meet regularly with due seriousness and for ensuring that the State Governments may make periodic meetings of these Committees compulsory instead of leaving the option of convening the meetings with the local conveners. In any case the frequency of such meetings should not be less than once in two months. The District Magistrates and the Sub Divisional Magistrates should personally participate in these meetings and not be represented by other functionaries.

(ii) The non-official members of these Committees should be selected not for extending political patronage but on the basis of track record of social work taking into account their commitment and sensitivity to social issues in general and to the issue of bonded labour in particular. Under the overall supervision of these Committees an intensive door to door survey with the help of NGOs should be carried out to identify and enumerate the bonded labourers who may still be in bondage at least once in a year.

(iii) For the purpose of rehabilitation of bonded labourers, apart from assistance available under the centrally sponsored scheme, assistance from other welfare and poverty alleviation schemes should also be ensured through due converagence of all such schemes and programmes. Convergence in this sense would mean pooling resources from a veriety of sources and integrating the same imaginatively and skillfully to achieve the objective of qualitative rehabilitation.

(iv) A Committee headed by the Chief Secretary comprising of other concerned Secretaries who may directly or indirectly be concerned with this work., should be constituted to review the arrangements for conducting door to door surveys for identification and enumeration at bonded labour and to review the pace of implementation of rehabilitation efforts.

In the final hearing on 11.11.1997 the Supreme Court has transferred the case to National Human Rights Commission. The Commission has set up a Central Action Group to go into the various aspects of implementing the Hon'ble Court's orders.

A Centrally Sponsored Scheme was launched by the Ministry of Labour in 1978-79 under which the State Governments are provided financial assistance on matching (50:50) basis for the rehabilitation of bonded labourers. The scheme envisages provision of rehabilitation grant upto ceiling limit of Rs. 10,000/- per freed bonded labourer, half of which is given as central share. State Governments have been advised to suitably dovetail, the centrally sponsored schemes with other anti-poverty and employment generation programmes so as to pool the resources available under different schemes in order to ensure effective rehabilitation of released bonded labourers.

A proposal to modify the scheme so as to include the conponent of survey on bonded labour, awareness generation activities, seminars and financial assistance to NGO's is under consideration. A meeting with State Secretaries dealing with bonded labour was held on 2.12.98 to ascertain, inter-alia their views on proposed modification. All the State Govt. who participated in that meeting have agreed with the proposal to modify the Centrally Sponsored Scheme so as to make it more effective and purposeful in the process of rehabilitation of bonded labourers.

Contract labour system

Definition and scope

The system of employing contract labour is prevalent in most industries in different occupations including skilled and semi - skilled jobs. It is also prevalent in agricultural and allied operations and to some extent in the services sector.

Contracts can broadly be divided into two categories viz. job contracts and labour contracts. A job contract is one in which a person undertakes to produce a given result for the establishment through contract labour other than a mere supply of goods or articles of manufacture to such establishment. A labour contract is one in which a person supplies labour for any work of the establishment on payment of remuneration or commission.

The reasons usually advanced in justification of contract labour are :-

(i) Uncertainty about the Work in which such tabour is engaged;

(ii) The wide dispersal of areas in which work has to be performed; Difficulty of ensuring closer supervision by the employer or higher output by workers and

(iii) More cost effective:

The advantages which generally accrue to the employer through the employment of contract labour are the following:-

(i) Lower cost of production;

(ii) Employing labour without extending to them the fringe benefits;

(iii) Minimising the administrative set-up and reducing the over-head cost; and

(iv) Saving on additional investment for installation of plant and machinery by farming out the manufacture of components.

While the system operates across most sectors of economic activity, some of the identifiable areas in which it is most common include:

- loading and unloading of goods, raw materials, etc.,
- transportation,
- security services
- maintenance of buildings and plots
- packing and forwarding,
- job work in textiles,
- engaging of home based workers for the manufacture of detergent powders, garments beedies, etc,

Contract Labour, by and large, is neither born(on pay roll or muster roll nor is paid wages directly. The establishments which farm out work to contractors do not own any direct responsibility in regard to their labourers Generally, the wage rates to be paid and observance of working conditions are stipulate in agreements but in practice they are not strictly adhered to.

Inferior labour status, lack of job security and poor economic condition are three of the major characteristics of this category of workers.

The case against contract labour system

While considerable improvement has been achieved in the working and living conditions of dire labour in organised industries both due to state intervention through legislative and administrative measures and the activities of trade unions, the position is different in respect of contract labour even in organised industries. The benefits enjoyed by the direct labour under the labour laws such as Factories Act, 1948, the Mines Act 1952 the Shops and Commercials Establishments Acts enacted by different States, the Industrial Disputes Act, 1947, the Employees Provident Funds Act, 1952, the Minimum Wages Act, 1948, the Payment of Wages Act, 1936 etc. have not accrued to contract labour to any appreciable extent.

The conditions of contract labour in unorganised industries are still worse, because of the constraints such as (a) casual nature of employment, (b) ignorance & illiteracy, (c) small size of establishments with low capital investment per person employed, (d) scattered nature of establishments and (e) superior strength of the employer. If the minimum facilities are left to collective bargaining, standards are not likely to be uniform nor will the facility reach the less organised workers.

Thus while economic factors may justify the system

of contract labour, considerations of social justice call for its abolition or regulation.

The Contract Labour (R&A) Act, 1970

The conditions of labour in India were investigated from time to time by various commissions, and committees notable among them being the Royal Commission on Labour (1929-31), the Bombay Textile Labour Enquiry Committee (1937-39) the Bihar Labour Enquiry Committee (1938-40) and the Labour Investigation Committee (1943-46) which recommended abolition of contract labour system. Following the recommendations of the Planning Commission in second five-year Plan a number of studies were undertaken by the Labour Bureau. The Supreme Court in the case of Standard Vacuum Refinery Company of their workmen (1960-II-LLJ Page 233) made important observations and laid down certain criteria in respect of certain type of works on which contract labour should not be abolished. The Indian labour Conference at its 1 9th & 20th Sessions (1961-62) considered the reports of the Labour Bureau and recommended Legislative action for abolition of contract labour system in the type of work referred to in the Supreme judgement and measures for improving the working conditions of contract labour. A tentative draft bill the Contract Labour (Regulation) bill was considered by the 22nd and 23rd session of the Standing Labour Committee (1964-65) and on the basis of decision taken therein, the draft bill with suitable modification was introduced in the Lok Sabha on 13.7.67. The Contract Labour (Regulation and Abolition) Bill was passed by both the Houses of Parliament on 19.8.1970 and received the assent of th President on 5.9.1970.

Objects and purposes of the Act

The Contract Labour (Regulation and Abolition) Act, 1970 was brought on the Statute Book It regulate the employment of the Contract Labour i certain circumstances and for matters connected therewith.

Application

The Act and the Contract Labour (Regulation Abolition) Central Rules, 1971 have come into force with effect from the 10th February, 1971.

The Act extends to the whole of India. It applies to establishments and to contractors as define in Sec. 2 (1) (C) of the Act wherein twenty or mor workmen are employed or were employed on any day of the preceding twelve months as Contract Labour Establishments in which work only of an intermittent or casual nature is performed do not fall within th purview of the Act. An establishment wherein work i of intermittent or seasonal nature will be covered b the Act if it falls within the scope of the explanation below Sec. 1 (5) (b). As long as the nature of work performed in the establishment of the Principal Employe is not of an intermittent or casual nature, any Con tractor employing Contract Labour in relation to their establishment would be covered by the Act/Rules The contractor who undertakes a mere supply of goods or articles of manufacture to establishments such as wooden props to a Coal Mine, is not covered by the, Act. However, a Contractor engaged for th so called 'Job Contract' or 'Works Contract' who is required to produce a given result for the establishment other than mere supply of goods or articles manufacture is covered by the Act. Even the sub contractor who merely supplies contract labour for any work of the establishment is a Contractor within the meaning of the term in the Act.

The constitutional validity of the Act and th Central Rules were challenged before the Supreme Court, which examined and found that there is no unreasonableness in the measure (Gammon India Ltd. Vs. Union of India 1974-I>LLJ-480).

Appropriate Government

The jurisdiction of the Central and State Government has been laid down by the definition of th 'Appropriate Government' in Section 2(1) (a) of the Act. The definition has been laid down, through amendment by the Contract Labour (Regulation & Abolition) Ordinance, 1986, subsequently replaced by an amendment to the Act (14 of 1986) in the interest of healthy industrial relations and harmony in the implementation of the Act. With this amendment the Appropriate Government, would be the same in respect of an establishment under the Contract Labour (Regulation and Abolition) Act, 1970 as also the Industrial Disputes Act, 1947. However in the light of the judgement of the Supreme Court in Air India Statutory Corporation Vs United Labour Union and Others the Central Government have become the Appropriate Government in respect of all Central Public Sector Undertakings.

Prohibition of employment of contract labour

According to Section 10 of the Contract Labour (Regulation & Abolition) Act, 1970, the appropriate Government may, after consultation with the Central or, as the case may be, the State Advisory Board, prohibit by notification in the Official Gazette, employment of contract labour, in any process/ operation or other work in any establishment. Before issuing such a notification, the appropriate Government shall have regard to the conditions of work and benefits provided to the Contract Labour in that establishment and other relevant factors such as :-

(a) whether the process, operation or other work is incidental to, or necessary for the industry, trade, business, manufacture or occupation carried on in the establishment;

(b) whether it is of perennial nature, that is to say it is of sufficient duration having regard to the nature of industry, trade, business, manufacture or occupation carried on in that establishment;

(c) whether it is done ordinarily through regular workmen in that establishment or an establishment similar thereto;

(d) whether it is sufficient to employ considerable number of whole-time workmen.

Central and state advisory boards

Under Section 3 and 4 of the Act, there is provision for constitution of Central and State Advisory Contract Labour Boards to advise the Central/State Government on matters arising out of the administration of the Act. The Central Advisory Board -a tripartite Body was last re-constituted on 30th October, 1996. The term of non-official members of the Board is three years. Thirty-eight meetings of the Central Advisory Contract Labour Board (CACLB) have so far been held. The last meeting was held on 5th-6th January, 1999.

In matters relating to abolition of contract labour system, the Board normally constitutes a three member Tripartite Committee from amongst members of the Central Advisory Contract Labour Board representing the employers and workers and a Government official as Member- Convenor to study the issue in detail, The report submitted by the Committee is placed before the Central Advisory Contract Labour Board and keeping in view the recommendations of the Board, the Central Government takes a decision in the matter. At present, 12 such Committees are functioning either to study abolition of contract labour system or to consider the requests for exemption from prohibitory notification in various establishments.

It may be stated in this context that the advice of the Central Board or State Board is not binding on the Government. A single notification prohibiting employment of contract labour can be issued in respect of different establishments, if the operation and nature of work is similar in all these establishments. A decision taken by the appropriate Government after consultation with the Central Board or the State Board, as the case may be, and keeping in view the guidelines contained in Section 10 of the Act, is, however, subject to judicial review.

Code for reference and disposal of matter by the Central Advisory Contract Labour Board

In a landmark judgement dated 27.3.1996 in a group of Writ Petitions relating to contract labour in Air India, Indian Airlines and International Airport Authority of India, the Mumbai High Court had laid down what may be described as a code for reference and disposal of matters by the Central Advisory Contract Labour Board. The salient points of the judgement are given as under: -

(i) The appropriate Government takes a decision under Section 10 of the Act to prohibit or not to prohibit employment of contract labour in any process, operation or other work in any establishment under the delegated powers thereunder. It exercises discretion after complying with some fixed standards or upon the existence of some objective facts or conditions. It performs administrative and judicial functions or shortly 'quasi judicial' functions.

(ii) The appropriate Government can only take into consideration materials referred to in subsection (2) of Section 10 of the Act for taking the decision mentioned in sub-section (1) The appropriate Government cannot take into consideration any other material till it is placed before the Central Advisory Board.

(iii) The Central Advisory Board cannot refuse to perform its statutory obligation and cannot abdicate its functions to the appropriate Government.

(iv) The advice of the Central Advisory Board has to be respected except for just, strong and compelling reasons.

(v) The sub-Committee constituted by the Central Advisory Board under Section 5 of the Act has to aid and advise the Central Advisory Board and its opinion has to be given due weight.

(vi) It is impermissible for the appropriate Government to ask for comments on the report of the Central Advisory Board or of the Sub Committee from the concerned department/ authority in respect of the establishments of which the abolition of contract labour system is under consideration.

(vii) The decisions of the appropriate Government and of the Central Advisory Board are subject to judicial review.

The existing Central Advisory Contract Labour Board has so far held nine meetings and considered various issues relating to abolition of contract labour system in certain establishments including proposals for amendment to the Act and International Labour Organisation convention on contract labour.

The Central Government on the recommendations of the Central Advisory Contract Labour Board, have prohibited employment of contract labour in the establishment of National Thermal Power Corporation, New Delhi, Indian Oil Blending Ltd. Calcutta, Aeronautic Development Agency and Indian Oil Corporation, Mathura in various operations/ category of jobs during 1998-99, which are given in the Table 8.1 . The Bank of Baroda, New Delhi was granted exemption for a period of one year from the prohibitory Notification dated 09.12.1976 for engaging security personnel.

Registration of establishment and licensing of contractors

Section 6 provide for appointment of registering officers by the appropriate Government for the purposes of this Act. Section 7 provides for registration of principal employers with the appropriate authorities. Section 11 provides for appointment of licensing officers by the appropriate Government for the purposes of this Act. Section 12 provides that no contractor shall undertake or execute any work through contract labour except under and in accordance with a licence issued in that behalf by the licensing officer Section 12 further empowers the licensing officer to lay down in the licence such conditions including, in particular, conditions as to hours of work, fixation of wages and other essential amenities in respect of contract labour as the appropriate Government may deem fit to impose in accordance with the rules.

Welfare and health of contract labour

Section 16 to 19 of the Act lays down certain amenities to be provided to the contract labour viz canteens (Section 16), rest rooms (Section 17) sufficient supply of wholesome drinking water, latrines and urinals, washing facilities (Section 1 8) and first aid facilities (Section 19), and have been made obligatory.

Payment of wages

In order to guard against defaults in the matter of wage payment, Section 21 provides that a contractor shall be responsible for payment of wages to each worker employed by him as contract labour and such wages shall be paid before the expiry of such period as may be prescribed. The principal employer shall nominate a representative duly authorised by him to be present at the time of disbursement-of wages by the contractor.

Enforcement

In the Central Sphere, officers of the Central Industrial Relations Machinery (CIRM) have been appointed as Inspectors under the Act. It is their duty to ensure compliance with the provisions of the Act and the Rules framed thereunder and to launch prosecutions against defaulters. As regards the steps taken to stop employment of contract labour in all the prohibited categories of work, it is mentioned that regular inspections are being done by the Field Officers of the CIRM and prosecutions are launched against the management, whenever such violations are detected and adequate evidence is available to prove charges. From time to time, instructions/ directions have been issued to the field officers of CIRM and State Government for proper implementation of the Act.

The number of inspections carried out, prosecutions launched licences and registration certificates issued etc. under the Act in the Central Sphere by the Industrial Relations Machinery is given in Table 8.2. A number of representations/petitions have been received by the Chief Labour Commissioner (Central) under Rule 25(2)(V)(a)&(b) from the Contract worker of their unions claiming that the contract workers are performing the same or similar work as performed by the workmen employed by the principal employer. Out of 13 cases received till 1998-99 orders have been passed in one case by the Chief Labour Commissioner (Central) and 12 cases are under investigation. In order to facilitate speedy disposal of cases the Deputy Chief Labour Commissioner (C) as the authority to deal with these cases by amending this Rule has been notified.

At present there is no provision in the Act for absorption of contract labour in the event of prohibition of employment of contract labour in any category of work/ jobs under section 10 of the Act. There have been complaints that contract workers are being thrown out of employment in the jobs covered by the relevant notifications. In this contexts two landmark judgements have been passed by the Supreme Court in the cases of GSEB Vs Union of India and Air India Statutory Corporation Ltd. & Ors Vs United Labour Union & Others, on 9.5.95 and 6.12.1996 respectively.

In GSEB case, inter-alia , the Supreme Court recommended that :-

(a) all undertakings should on their own discontinue the contract labour who satisfy the factors mentioned in clauses(a) to (d) of Section 10(2) of the Act and abolish as many of the labour as is feasible as their direct employees.

(b) both the Central and State Governments should appoint a Committee to investigate the establishments in which the contract labour is engaged and where on the basis of the criteria laid down in clauses(a) to (d) of the Section 10(2) of the Act, the contract labour system can be abolished and direct employment can be given to the contract labour. The appropriate Government on its own should take initiative to abolish the labour contracts in the establishments concerned by following the procedure laid down under the Act.

(c) The Central Government should amend the Act by incorporating a suitable provision to refer to industrial adjudicator the question of the direct employment of the workers of the ex-contractor in the principal establishments when the appropriate Government abolishes the contract labour.

In Air India Statutory Corporation case, the Supreme Court have held that through there exist no express provision in the Act for absorption of employees in establishments where contract labour system is abolished by publication of the notification under section 10 (1) of the Act, the principal Employer is under statutory obligation to absorb the contract labour. The linkage between the contractor and employee stood snapped and direct relationships to restored between principal employer and contract labour as its employees. The award proceedings as suggested in Gujarat Electricity Board case being beset with incongruities and obstacles in the way of contract labour for immediate absorption, this part of the direction , the Supreme Court held is not correct in law.

The Governing Body of the ILO during its 261st Session in November 1994 undertook the preliminary examination of contract labour as an agenda item for the 1997 Session of the International Labour Conference. At its 262nd New Delhi - Session (April, 1995) the ILO Governing Body decided to include the contract labour in the agenda for the 85th Session of the ILC in 1997 under the Double Discussion procedure, i.e. for discussion in 1997 and 1998. The Government of India is one of the Governments who supported the discussion on Contract Labour.

While adopting the subject of Contract Labour "for its agenda in the ILC, ILO was moved by the in-creasing fragmentation and multiplication of employment patterns. A variety of non-standard and / or atypical forms of employing workers currently supplement traditional model of long-term employment relationship. A substantial increase in the use of the latter in the form of Contract Labour has been reported from many countries.

Contract Labour is the most common atypical form of work. The surveys conducted by the ILO has shown that the demand to regulate contract labour with a view to eliminating its possible negative consequences on the workers, have had limited success so far and seems increasingly difficult to pursue. Therefore, it was felt that any new International Labour instruments on the subject of contract labour should be sufficiently flexible and allow Member States to choose among different approaches to provide the needed protection. The ILO Off ice gave two options (i) adoption of a Recommendation which can provide important guidelines regarding protection to contract worker while leaving the Member States sufficiently flexible in choosing broad approaches and (ii) adoption of a Convention supplemented by Recommendation i.e. the Convention laying down the basic principles that should be applied to the protection of contract labour and the Recommendation which would provide for various approaches to implement these principles through national law and practices. The ILO Office obtained views of the Tripartite Constituents on the above through a questionnaire. The ILO Off ice had received replies from several Governments. 15 Governments were in favour of a Convention only, 37 Governments were in favour of a Recommendation only and 34 Governments were in favour of the adoption of a Convention supplemented by a Recommendation.

The subject matter of contract labour came up for discussion on 4.6.97 in a special Tripartite Committee constituted on the subject. The form of the instrument proposed was a Convention supplemented by a Recommendation and was adopted by the Conference at its 85th Session.

At its first sitting on 2.6.98, the 86th International Labour Conference constituted a Tripartite Committee for adoption of a Convention and Recommendation on contract labour under the double discussion procedure. Dr. L. Mishra, Secretary (Labour) was elected as the Chairperson of the Committee. Owing to the complex nature of the subject and the fact that the form and content of contract labour differs greatly between countries, the Committee could not propose the text of draft instruments to the conference for adoption. There remained serious conceptual, legal and terminological problems. The Committee adopted a resolution inviting the Governing Body of ILO to place these issues on the agenda of further session of the ILC with a view to the possible adoption of a Convention supplemented by a Recommendation pending completion of further examination of the issues within a period of next four years.

The Committee further recommended that meetings of the experts be held to examine issues especially identification of situations where workers require protection, appropriate ways of affording protection and the possibility of dealing separately with various situations, definition of such workers bearing in mind of different legal systems that exist and language differences and also to take other measures with a view to completing the work concerned by the Committee The Govt. of India is one of the Governments that whole heartedly supported the Convention supplemented by a Recommendation on contract labour. The outcome was disappointing in that many workers remaining unprotected would not have the benefit and support of an ILO instrument, which was needed urgently. The consensus reached was welcomed and a suggestion was made that the experts who would be assigned to study the issue should consider the particular situation of various regions such as South Asia, Latin America and the European Union as the national law and practice in each of these regions differed significantly. It was hoped that an agreement would be reached on the matter within the next four-year period.

Streamlining contract labour law

In the light of the experience gathered in the administration of the Act for more than two decades, and judgements of the courts, particularly , that of the Supreme Court in the matters of Gujarat State Electricity Board and Air India cases, a need has been felt to have a fresh look at the Act. While proposals have been received for amendment of the Act to make it more stringent and labour friendly, suggestions to exempt, certain categories of establishments from the purview of the Act or outsource certain activities in the context of ongoing programme of economic liberalisation have also been received from various Trade Unions, SCOPE and employers organisations like FICCI & CII . The Government, at the moment, has undertaken a thorough review of the Act with a view to bring about some amendments to the existing Act or introduce a new legislation. A committee of officials has also been constituted to examine the issues in details.

Table 3
Notifications issued under the contract labour (regulation and abolition) act, 1970 (1998-99)

Sl. No.	Notification No. & Date	Works/ Jobs prohibited
1.	U-23013/15/97-LW Dated 4.5.1998.	Employment of Contract Labour in the following works in the establishment of M/s. National Thermal Power Corporation Ltd., New Delhi. –Operator and instrumentation technician.
2.	U-23013/12/88-LW dated 13.7.1998.	Employment of Contract Labour in the following jobs/ works in the establishment of M/s. Indian Oil Blending Ltd., Calcutta. – Loading, unloading and carrying empty and filled drums and raw materials.
3.	U-23013/30/97-LW dated, 5.10.1998.	M/s. Aeronautical Development Agency, the National Aeronautical Laboratory Campus, Belur, Bangalore. (1) Helpers. (2) Messengers. (3) Attenders; and (4) Despatch Clerks.
4.	U-23013/15/97-LW dated 9.11.1998.	Employment of contract labour in the works in the various departments of Mathura Refinery and Marketing

Division of the Indian Oil Corporation Ltd. at Mathura.

Mathura Refinery

(1) Electrical jobs at different locations in the Refinery.

(2) Operations and maintenance of centralised air-conditioning plants and package units.

(3) Power supply for shutdown.

(4) Meter windings.

(5) Operation of centrifugal pumps and DG sets in Refineries.

(6) Chemical handling and solution preparation.

(7) Handling of jobs indifferent departments of the Refinery as attendants, helpers, operators in maintenance, instrumentation,

mechanical maintenance, fabrication and plant operation, including peons and clerks etc.

(8) Repair and maintenance of thermal insultation works.

(9) Operation and maintenance of electric jobs in the Refinery.

(10) Providing office services.

(11) Routine storekeeping and store handling other than occasional bulk handling of stores.

(12) Canteen services.

Marketing Division of Indian Oil Corporation Ltd. at Mathura

(13) Housekeeping work especially relating to sweepers.

(14) Liquified Petroleum Gas haulage work (loading and unloading of

Liquified Petroleum Gas cylinders).

(15) Liquified Petroleum Gas (Shifting, sealing, tagging of caps, 'O' ring fitting etc.)

Table 4

Enforccement of contract labour (R & A) act, 1970

S. No	Item	Year 1996	1997
1.	No. of Registration Certificates issued to principal Employers.	375	425
2.	No. of Licences issued to contractors	3613	4660
3.	No. of Inspections conducted	4653	3956
4.	No. of irregularities detected	72541	70709
5.	No. of prosecutions launched	3705	3330
6.	No. of convictions	2770	2240
7.	No. of contract labourers covered by licences.	4,89,776	5,88,67
8.	No. of licences revoked/cancelled	757	1371
9.	No. of registration certificates revoked	23	Nil

Inter-state migrant workers

Migration of labour is one of the accepted consequences of economic development. However, when this phenomenon occurs with increasing regularity in certain concentrations, particularly emanating from poor and backward regions, spread over vast distances to certain areas where these workers are compelled to work under exploitative conditions, it becomes necessary to look at the situation from the point of denial of human dignity & freedom and not merely from the point of employment. This phenomenon then is not merely one of voluntary labour movement, but of migration and transportation under duress, sometimes in situations akin to bondage which necessitates a stringent and unconventional approach.

Magnitude of migration

Migration has been a regular phenomenon in recent times involving people within a given geographical area or beyond the boundaries of a State or Nation As per 1981 Census figures there were 23.4 million Inter-state out-migrants. Of this, migration for employment accounted for 6.2 million representing 26% of the total. This includes intra-district, inter-district and inter-state migrants. About 5 lakh migrants were reported Seasonal' migrants migrating for less than one year. Two States Uttar Pradesh & Bihar alone account for 41.4% out migration. As large number of workers move between States without getting themselves registered it is difficult to have a absolutely correct data about the magnitude of such migration.

Reasons for migration

Freedom of movement in any part of the territory of India and freedom to pursue any avocation of one's choice is a fundamental right guaranteed by Article 19 of the Constitution. Migration being the movement of human beings in pursuit of certain cherished objectives like better employment and better wages there is apparently nothing wrong or objectionable to migration per se. Migration becomes objectionable only when it leads to exploitation culminating into human misery and deprivation of the irreducible minimum to which every worker as a human being and as a citizen is entitled It becomes objectionable when human greed, rapacity and acquisitive instincts overtake the finer aspects of human character and lead to denial of dignity, justice and inalienable human rights of certain underprivileged and downtrodden sections of human society.

Migration generally takes place on account of economic necessity. Uneven development, that is, inter-regional disparity in economic growth and disparity between different socio-economic classes has been identified by the National Commission on Rural Labour as the most important reason for causing migration. Development of capitalised agriculture in green revolution areas has increased the demand for labour. On the other hand stagnant agricultural development in dry areas has failed to provide employment to the poor in these areas. While better employment opportunities and higher wages in economically developed regions attract labour, non-availability of employment opportunities and consequent hardship in the under developed regions act as push factors in the migration process.

Wages and earnings of migrant labour

Wages for migrant labourers vary from sector to sector and region to region. Except in a few sectors and regions at a particular period in a year, migrant labourers by and large do not get minimum wages fixed under the Minimum Wages Act, 1948. In order to avoid payment of minimum wages and to get extra work in short time, payment by piece-rates is gaining ground. As a rule, hours of work are longer. Some studies also point out that migrant workers are prepared to work for lower wages than local labour. The perpetuation of this state of affairs is to some extent due to the fact that the migrant labour is unorganised.

The condition of women labourers is far more unsatisfactory. Wages to be paid to them are decided by the contractors. In spite of the provisions under the Equal Remuneration Act, which makes it obligatory for the contractor to pay equal wages to male and female labourers, more often than not the women labourers are paid lesser wages compared with the male workers. Sexual exploitation of the women migrant labourers especially the tribals is also a matter of deep concern. Studies of migrant female labourers in fish processing, construction work, quarrying etc. reveal the same pattern.

However, despite hardships and exploitation, the income of the migrant labour are higher than what they would have been able to earn without migration. As we have seen earlier the proportion of migrant labour is quite high for certain backward areas. As a result of the rise in their income from migration, their staying power has increased, the real wages have started rising in such areas during the eighties. The wage disparity between the developed and the less developed regions has started declining. The male-female disparity in wage rate is also coming down.

Problems faced by migrant labourers

Majority of inter-district and inter state migrants belong to the poorest sections of the society. Most of them are illiterate. They are lured by intermediaries who often exploit their helpnessless. By giving certain advance payments, the labour is forced into a kind of bondage. They are transported under unsatisfactory arrangements.

A majority of migrant labourers do not have a fixed place of work and keep shifting from one place to another. Generally they have to improvise an accommodation with no facilities at all. They are forced to work for lesser wages. This causes local pressures too and some times this leads to clashes between the migrants and locals. They have no bargaining power. They accept abject working conditions. In the event of disputes, they have little strength to withstand and to wait for dispute to be resolved by formal resolution machinery.

Applicability of labour laws to migrant workmen

Although labour legislations like the Minimum Wages Act, the Payment of Wages Act, the Workmen's Compensation Act and the Industrial Dispute Act etc. are applicable to all workers irrespective of their status as migrant or local subject to coverage of establishment in which they are employed but these laws have not been able to protect the interests of these workers. Therefore, Inter-State Migrant Workmen (Regulation of Employment and Conditions of Service) Act, 1979 (Act No. XXX of 1979) was enacted in 1979. The Rules under this Act were framed in 1980 and the provisions of the Act came into force from 2nd October, 1980. The Act intended to regulate the employment of Inter-state migrant workmen and to provide for their conditions of service and for matters connected thereto. The Act provides for the following :-

(a) Registration of principal employer/contractors (S.4) and licensing of all contractors (S.8) employing five or more migrant workmen;

(b) Issue of passbook to every inter-state migrant workmen with full details; (S. 12)

(c) Payment of equal wages for performing same or similar kind of work in an establishment alongwith local labourers which should not be less than the minimum wages fixed under the Minimum Wages Act; (S. 16)

(d) Payment of displacement allowance equivalent to 50 per cent of monthly wages or Rs. 75/- whichever is higher; (S.14)

(e) Payment of journey allowance including payment of wages during the period of journey; (S. 15)

(f) Provision of suitable residential accommodation, medical facilities and protective clothing as prescribed; (S.16) and

(g) Submission of report to the specified authorities of both the States and also relatives of the migrant workmen in case of a fatal accident cf serious bodily injuries to the workmen. (S. 16)

Important court judgement

The Supreme Court in their Judgment delivered on 16.7.90 in a writ petition filed by Dr. Damodar Panda vs. the State of Orissa and others directed "that every State/Union

Territory in India shall be obliged to permit officers of the originating State of migrant labour for holding proper enquiries within the limits of the recipient State for enforcement of the Act and no recipient State shall place any embargo or hindrance in such process". The directions of the Supreme Court in the above Judgment were conveyed to the all Labour Secretaries and Union territories on 1.10.90 for compliance. Since the State Governments and Union Territories are bound by the directions of the Supreme Court, there should be no difficulty now in appointing Inspectors by the originating State under section 20(3) of the Act for carrying out inspection in the State where the migrant workman is employed without any hinderance or objection, by the recipient State.

Recommendations of national commission on rural labour

The National Commission on Rural Labour (1987-91) had suggested certain amendments to the Act. Keeping in view the suggestions made by the Commission as also on the representation received from various interests group, the Government are considering certain amendment to the Act which include amendment of the definition covering the monetary limit for coverage on the lines of Industrial Disputes Act specifying the responsibility of employer and enhancing penalties for violation, providing for presence of workmen's representative at the time of disbursement of wages, transfer of claims to native places, permitting third parties to file complaints, summary trial of offences by Executive Magistrates, recovery procedure for amount due etc. The views of the State Governments have been invited on the proposed amendments.

Welfare schemes

The problem of migration is sought to be checked through a multi dimensional course of action through rural development, improved infrastructural facilities, employment generation, land reforms, increased literacy, financial assistance etc. Schemes like Integrated Rural Development Scheme (IRDP), Jawahar Rozgar Yojna (JRY), Employment Assurance Scheme (EAS), Self-Employment for Educated Unemployed Youth, Nehru Rozgar Yojna (NRY), Prime Ministers Rozgar Yojna (PMRY) and Targetted Public Distribution System are being implemented for the welfare of workers including Inter-state migrant workers.

During a workshop held at Chandigarh in September, 1997 by the Department of Sociology of the Punjab University in collaboration with the National Labour Institute, certain suggestions were made which are given below: —

(i) National Wage Policy: There should be a national wage policy so that bargaining power does not affect the migrant workmen adversely. There must be a scientific formula for fixation of rural and urban wages without consideration for poverty line but dignity of labour.

(ii) Migration process may be tailored to suit local labour demand and the surveys, studies and policy initiatives should be stream specific.

(iii) It should be borne in mind by the policy makers that migration is not a panacea for underemployment nor is the rural-urban wage parity, a panacea for migration. It is integrated rural development that holds the key to long term growth with equity and social justice.

(iv) Education Policy should not prepare the rural youth only for city jobs.

(v) It should be borne in mind that migration changes the financial conditions and hence the policy perception must change.

(vi) Tripartite vigilance committees may be created at places of concentration of migrant workmen.

(vii) Rehabilitation of workers on return. (viii) (ix)

(viii) Creation of a good data-base.

(ix) Gender sensitisation and better coordination between the voluntary organisations, National Human Rights Commission, National Commission for Women and Labour Department.

(x) Increased role of voluntary organisations like Sanjeevani, Anganwadis and Stri Sabhas.

(xi) For the purpose of data collection, village should be taken as a unit instead of a 'family' or an 'individual'.

Some of these targets can be achieved by creating community centres for the migratory population and setting up of Boards for registration and deregistration. Role of employment exchanges can be extended to meet seasonal demand and supply. The Government will take appropriate remedial action, if required, on these suggestions of the workshop while finalising the amendment proposals to the Act. The Government has also commissioned two studies in 1998 to examine the Went to which the provisions of the Inter-State Migrant Workmen Act are being implemented and identify the operational constraints of the Act and recommended strategies and policies for effective implementation of the Act.

9

Progress of Computerisation

Work profile of women

Women constitute a significant part of the work-force of India. A profile of women in the work-force of the country, bringing out the gander differential is presented in Table 9.1. As can be seen from the table, women lag significantly behind males in terms of work participation, employment, etc. However, there are some positive trends. While there has been marginal improvement in annual rate of growth of female employment, the annual rate of growth of employment of educated women is substantially higher.

Table 2 shows that work participation rate continues to be substantially less for females than for males. While there has been some improvement in the work participation rate of females since 1971, the improvement is not substantial especially in urban areas. Work participation rate for women which was 7.18 percent in urban areas in 1971 went up to only 9.74 in 1991. As against this, in the rural areas the female work participation rate has shown steady improvement since 1971. It has risen from 15.92 in 1971 to 27.20 in 1991. However, the female work participation rate continues to lag behind that of males. In 1991 it was a little over half of the male work participation rate.

Women's work participation rates differ widely from state to state. As brought out in Table 1, majority of women workers are employed in the rural areas. Amongst rural women workers, 87% are employed in agriculture as labourers and cultivators. Amongst women workers in urban areas, about 80% are employed in unorganised sectors like household industries, petty trades and services, building and construction, etc.

Table 1

Profile of women (relative to men) in the work-forc of India @

Category	Male	Female	Total
Total Population	439	407	846
Total Estimated Employment	243	89	332
Unemployment rate (1993-94)	2.60	2.44	2.56
Annual Growth of Employment in	3.57	3.64	3.59
Urban areas (1987-88 to 1993-94) Annual Growth of Employment in	2.25	0.87	1.84
Rural areas (1987-88 to 1993-94)			
Self-employment (1993-94) Urban-41.2	Rural-56.7 Urban-36.7	Rural-51.3 Urban-40.4	Rural-55.3
Work force participation rate (1993-94) Urban-51.3	Rural-63.8 Urban-12.1	Rural-23.4 Urban-32.7	Rural-39.1
Regular salaried employment (1993-94)	Rural-8.7 Urban-42.2	Rural-3.4 Urban-35.7	Rural-7.2 Urban-41.6
Casual wage employment (1993-94)	Rural-34.6 Urban-16.0	Rural-45.3 Urban-27.5	Rural-37.5 Urban-18.0
Unemployment rate of			

the Educated (Secondary & above) (1993-94)	Rural-8.9 Urban-6.9	Rural-24.3 Urban-20.7	– –

Table 2
Work participation rate in India, 1971-1991

Year	Total Urban	Persons Rural	Males	Females
1971	Total	34.17	52.75	14.22
Rural	36.33	53.78	15.92	
Urban	29.61	48.88	7.18	
1981	Total	36.70	52.62	19.67
Rural	38.79	53.77	23.06	
Urban	29.99	49.06	8.31	
1991	Total	37.68	61.56	22.73
Rural	40.24	52.50	27.20	
Urban	30.44	48.95	9.74	

Table 3
States/union territories according to levels of female work participation rates

10-20% (Female work participation)	20-30%	30-40%
Andaman & Nicobar	Daman & Diu	Andhra Pradesh
Bihar	Goa	Arunachal Pradesh
Chandigarh	Gujarat	Himachal Pradesh
Haryana	Karnataka	Madhya Pradesh
Kerala	Orissa	Maharashtra
Pondicherry	Rajasthan	Meghalaya
Tripura		Manipur
Uttar Pradesh		Nagaland
West Bengal		Tamil Nadu
Other States/ UTs:		
Less than 10%		

Employment of women in organised sector

The employment of women in the organised sector (both Public and Private Sectors) as on 31st March, 1996 was about 4426.4 thousand. This constitutes 15.8 % of the total organised sector employment in the country. The overall proportion of women's employment to total employment registered a gain of 0.4% when compared with the corresponding proportion of women's employment in 1995.

Employment of women was highest in the Southern Zone and lowest in the Central Zone. The increase in employment in terms of percentage was highest in the Southern Zone whereas the Eastern Zone recorded a negative growth of 4.24%.

The distribution of women employees in major industries reveals that community, social & personal services sector continued to absorb the majority of women employees being 2476.2 thousand. The lowest employment of women was noticed in electricity; gas and water Sectors.

In factory, mine and plantation establishments women workers constitute, 11 %, 7% and 36% of the total workers.

Table 4
Employment of women in the organised sector by states/UTs
(Employment as on 31st March, 1996) (in thousand)

Sl. No.	States/U.T	Public	Private	Total(3+4)
I	North Zone	430.9	128.5	559.4
1.	Haryana	59.9	22.4	82.3
2.	Punjab	92.3	277.2	119.5
3.	Himachal Pradesh	33.0	5.0	38.0
4.	Chandigarh (UT)	10.7	2.9	13.6
5.	Delhi	90.1	28.3	118.4
6.	Rajasthan	123.8	40.8	164.6

7.	Jammu & Kashmir	21.1	2.0	23.1
II.	Central Zone	325.5	77.1	402.6
8.	Madhya Pradesh	156.1	26.77	182.8
9.	Uttar Pradesh	169.4	50.4	219.8
III	North-East Zone	134.0	270.2	404.2
10.	Assam	71.4	257.6	329.0
11.	Manipur	12.3	3.1	15.4
12.	Meghalaya	15.2	0.6	15.8
13.	Mizoram	9.3	0.6	9.9
14.	Nagaland	10.8	1.0	11.8
15.	Tripura	14.9	77.3	22.2
IV	Eastern Zone	292.5	137.3	429.8
16.	Bihar	104.0	23.2	127.2
17.	Orissa	72.3	11.7	84.0
18.	West Bengal	116.2	102.4	218.6
V	Western Zone	504.3	291.7	7796.0
19.	Gujarat	147.2	75.9	223.1
20.	Maharashtra	342.2	207.8	550.0
21.	Goa	14.6	7.0	21.6
22.	Daman & Diu (UT)	0.3	1.0	1.3
VI	South Zone	944.0	8877.0	1831.0
23.	Andhra Pradesh	179.4	114.4	293.8
24.	Karnataka	199.0	273.8	472.8
25.	Kerala	159.9	255.77	415.6
26.	Tamil Nadu	397.8	241.4	639.2
27.	Pondicherry (UT)	7.8	1.6	9.4
28.	And. & Nicobar	3.3	0.1	3.4
	Total	22634.5	1791.9	4426.4

Table 5

Employment of women in the organised sector by major industry division (as on 31.03.1995)

(In thousands)

	Public Sector	Private Sector	Total
Agriculture and allied occupations	49.2	429.3	478.5
Mining and quarrying	65.0	16.4	81.4
Manufacturing	119.5	756.8	876.3
Electricity, gas and water	36.7	1.2	37.9
Construction	61.4	4.0	65.4
Wholesale, retail business and hotels and restaurents	15.4	25.1	40.5
Transport, storage and communications	157.6	4.5	162.1
Financial, Insurance, Real Estate and business services	169.1	39.0	208.1
Community, Personal and social services	1960.6	515.7	2476.2
Total	2634.5	1791.9	4426.4

Table 6

Employment of women in factories, mines and plantations ('000)

	1990	1991	1992	1993	1994	1995	1996	1997
Factories	499 (10)	507 (10)	524 (10)	530 (10)	591 (11)			
Mines	56 (7)	55 (7)	53 (7)	50 (6)	49 (7)	47 (6)	43 (6)	39 (6)
Plantations	558 (51)	572 (52)	556 (51)	568 (52)	629 (36)	633 (49)		

Table 7

Average daily employment of women in factories

Year (000's) (000's) Employment	Total Employment Employment total	Women's of women to	Percentage
1951	2,526.5	290.0	11.4
1956	2,882.3	301.4	10.5
1961	3,497.0	372.3	10.6
1966	4,068.9	364.7	9.0
1971	4,298.0	370.1	8.6
1974	4,633.2	440.1	9.5
1981	5,342.5	497.8	9.3
1985	5,207.0	493.5	9.5
1990	5,182.0	498.9	9.6
1991	5,211.8	507.1	9.7
1992	5,208.7	524.4	10.1
1993 (P)	5090.1	530.2	10.4
1994 (P)	5507.4	591.2	10.7

Table 8

Sex-wwise enrolment by stages/classes since 1951-school level

(in million)

Year	**Primary Primary**			**Middle/Upper**			**High/Hr.Sec**		
	Boys	**Girls**	**Total**	**Boys**	**Girls**	**Total**	**Boys**	**Girls**	**Total**
1950-51	13.8	5.4	19.2	2.6	0.5	3.1	1.3	0.2	1.5
1955-56	17.1	7.5	24.6	3.8	1.0	4.8	2.2	0.4	2.6
1960-61	23.6	11.4	35.0	5.1	1.6	6.7	2.7	0.7	3.4
1965-66	32.2	18.3	50.5	7.7	2.8	10.5	4.4	1.3	5.7
1970-71	35.7	21.3	57.0	9.4	3.9	13.3	5.7	1.9	7.6
1975-76	46.6	25.0	65.6	11.0	5.0	161.0	6.5	2.4	8.9

1980-81	45.3	28.5	73.8	13.9	6.8	20.7	7.6	3.4	11.0
1985-86	52.2	35.2	87.4	17.7	9.6	27.1	11.5	5.0	16.5
1990-91	51.0	40.4	97.4	21.6	12.5	34.0	12.8	6.3	19.1
1991-92	59.6	42.3	100.9	22.0	13.6	35.6	13.5	6.9	20.4
1992-93	60.5	44.9	105.4	23.7	15.0	38.7	15.0	7.7	22.7
1993-94	61.8	46.4	108.2	24.2	15.7	39.9	15.3	8.0	23.3
1994-95	61.7	46.3	108.0	24.0	15.3	39.3	15.7	8.4	24.1
1995-96	62.4	47.3	109.7	25.0	16.0	41.0	16.1	8.8	24.9
1996-97	62.6	47.9	110.4	24.7	16.3	41.0	17.2	9.8	27.0
1997-98	61.3	47.4	108.7	23.6	15.8	39.4	17.1	10.1	27.2

Table 9

Enrolment by stages (since 1951)

Year	Primary IV	Middle VI-VIII	Sec/Hr.Soc 10+2/Inter above)	Hr.Education (Degree &
1950-51	28.1	16.1	13.3	10.0
1955-56	30.5	20.8	15.4	14.6
1960-61	32.6	23.9	20.5	16.0
1966-66	36.2	26.7	22.0	20.4
1970-71	37.4	29.3	25.0	20.0
1975-76	38.1	31.3	26.9	23.2
1980-81	38.6	32.9	29.6	26.7
1985-86	40.3	35.6	30.3	33.0
1990-91	41.5	36.7	32.9	33.3
1991-92	41.9	38.2	33.8	32.3
1992-93	42.6	38.8	33.9	33.2
1993-94	42.9	39.3	34.3	33.5
1994-95	42.8	38.9	34.8	35.2

1995-96	43.1	39.0	35.3	37.1
1996-97	43.4	39.8	36.3	37.2
1997-98	43.6	40.1	37.4	36.4

Women's access to education and skills

Women's access to employment is to a significant extent, related to their access to education and skills. Women lag behind men in access to education as reflected by the sex-wise enrolment figures for different stages of education. The participation of girls at all stages of education has been increasing steadily over time as may be seen from Table 9.9. However, the percentages are still below fifty percent at all levels of education including higher education.

The Ministry of Human Resource Development (Department of Education) has brought under implementation several programmes for providing special access to education at all levels for women. Objectives of these programmes are universalisation of elementary education, vocationalisation of post secondary education and modernisation of polytechnic and higher technical education.

Vocational training for women

The National Vocational Training Institute (NVTI), Noida. (UP) and the 10 Regional Vocational Training Institutes (RVTIs) for women in different parts of India impart basic and advanced levels of vocational training to women in areas with high employment / self employment potential. Special attention has also been given for the modernisation and establishment of women's Industrial Training Institutes (ITIs) under the World Bank aided Vocational Training Project. A Women's Cell under the Directorate General of Employment and Training (DGE&T) coordinates with States in the matter of Vocational Training of women. The State Govt. and Union Territories also impart Vocational Training for women. At present there are 458 ITIs including ITI-

Wings for women having 36114 seats in 25 different States/ Union Territories. The programmes for imparting vocational training to women have been dealt in greater detail in Chapter 9 Para 11 part II of this Report. Training of women in Indian Institute of Worker's Education (IIWE)

The Indian Institute of Workers Education, Mumbai has established a separate cell on "Women and Child Labour" and evolved advanced training programmes for the women activists of Central Trade Union Organisations/ Federations and Women's Organisations who are involved in the upliftment and welfare of women and child labour in the country. Modular syllabus for the advanced training programmes on the theme of women and child labour has been prepared by the cell. From 1992-93 to September, 1998, 224 women activists were trained in the various training programmes conducted by the Women and Child Labour Cell of the Institute.

Table 10

Employment of women-protective legal provisions

S.	Name of Enactment	Protective Provision No.
1.	The Beedi & Cigar (Conditions of Employment) Act, 1966	–Provision of creches for the benefit of women workers. When 50 or more Workers women are employed in employments covered by the 1st and 2nd laws. When 20 or more women are employed in employments covered by the 3rd and 4th laws. When 30 or more women are employed in employments covered by the 5th law.
2.	The Plantation Labour Act, 1951	Women workers to be provided time off for feeding children.
3.	The Contract Labour	–Not to be required to work beyond

	(Regulation & Abolition) Act, 1970	9 hours between 6 AM and 7 PM - with the exception of mid-wives and nurses in plantations
4.	The Inter State Migrant Workers (Regulation of Employment & Condition of Service) Act, 1979	–Separate toilets and washing facilities to be provided in employments covered by the 3rd and 6th laws.
5.	The Factories Act, 1948.	–in factories, women are not engaged in cleaning, lubricating or adjusting any part of prime or transmission machinery; maternity leave upto 12 weeks with wages to be provided.
6.	The Mines Act, 1952	–Employment in mines below ground prohibited.
7.	Maternity Benefit Act, 1961	–Maternity benefits to be provided on-completion of 80 days working. –Not required to work during six weeks immediately following the day of delivery or miscarriage. –No work of arduous nature, long hours of standing likely to interfere with pregnancy/normal development of foetus; or which may cause miscarriage or is likely to affect health to be given for a period of one month immediately preceding the period of six weeks before delivery. –On medical certificate, advance maternity benefit to be allowed. –Rs. 250.00 as medical bonus to be given when no prenatal confinement and post natal care is provided free of -charge.
8.	Equal Remuneration	–Payment of equal remuneration to

	Act, 1976	men and women workers for same or similar nature of work provided under the Act and also under the provisions at Sl. No. 4. –No discrimination permissible in recruitment and service conditions except where employment of women is prohibited or restricted by or under any law.
9.	Employees' State, Insurance (General) Regulation, 1950	–Claim for maternity benefit becomes due on the date medical certificate is issued for miscarriage, sickness arising out of pregnancy, confinement or premature birth of child. –Claim for maternity benefit becomes due on the date medical certificate is issued for miscarriage, sickness arising out of pregnancy confinement or premature birth of child.
10.	Beedi Workers Welfare Fund Act, 1976.	–Appointment of women member in the Advisory and Central Advisory Committee is mandatory under the Acts at Sl. Nos. 10 to 13.
11.	Iron Ore Mines, Manganese Ore Mines and Chrome Ore Mines Labour Welfare Fund Act, 1976.	–do–
12.	Lima Stone and Dolomite Mines Labour Welfare Fund Act, 1972.	–do–
13.	Mica Mines Labour Welfare Fund Act, 1946.	–do–
14.	The Building and	Representation of a woman member

Other Construction Workers (Regulation of Employment and Conditions of Services) Acct, 1996	on Building and Other Construction Worker' Welfare Boards. Provision for maternity benefit to female beneficiaries of the Welfare Fund. Provision for creches where more than 50 female construction workers are ordinarily employed.

Assistance to women job seekers

The Employment Exchanges took special care to cater to the job needs of women registered with therin. During January-September, 1997 they placed 460,11 women in various employments.

Special cell for women labour

The Ministry of Labour has set up a Women Labour Cell in 1975. The intention was to focus attention on the lot of working women with a view to improving it. The Cell has the following functions :

(i) Formulation and coordination of policies and programmes for the female tabour force within the frame work of national manpower and econonmic policies.

(ii) Maintaining liaison with other Government agencies to secure effective implementation of the programme in respect of women workers.

(iii) Monitoring the implementation of the Equal Remuneration Act, 1976 for promotion of employment of women.

(iv) Setting up of an Advisory Committee under the Equal Remuneration Act, 1976 for promotion of employment of women.

(v) Giving grants-in-aid to Non-Governmental Organisations/ Voluntary Organisations to formulate and execute action-oriented projects for women tabour.

Equal remuneration

Most of the States and Union Territories have appointed competent authorities under the Equal Remuneration Act, 1976 and have also set up Advisory Committees under the Act. Annual returns are called for by the special cell from the State Governments in order to monitor implementation of the Act. In most cases the response from the State Governments has not been encouraging. However the available data as reported by them has been compiled along with the data on enforcement of the Act in the Central sphere (Box 9.2).

The following social welfare organisations have been recognised under the Equal Remuneration Act, 1976 for the purpose of filing complaints in courts against employers for violation of the provisions of the Act:

— The Centre for Women's Development Studies, New Delhi.

— The Self Employed Women's Association, Ahmedabad.

— The Working Women's Forum (India), Madras.

— The Institute of Social Studies Trust, New Delhi.

An important activity of the Cell is to convene the meeting of the Central Advisory Committee which has been constituted under the Equal Remuneration Act, 1976 and follow up the recommendations made by the Committee. Another important activity of the Women Cell is to examine and process project proposals to carry out studies on matters affecting women workers and also to fund programmes aimed at improving their economic well being. Several projects aimed at improving the working conditions of women and raising their economic level were processed by the Women Cell of the Ministry of Labour during 1997-98.

The Cell has also processed and sanctioned other studies and action-oriented projects of far reaching significance. The study on health hazards faced by women construction workers under implementation in the King George Medical College, Lucknow is one such project. A list of studies and action oriented projects sanctioned by the Ministry of Labour and currently under implementation is as under:

— Mahila Arthik Sanskritik Evam Shekshik Vikas Sansthan, Varanasi, Uttar Pradesh for handicraft training to women labour.

— Magadh Social Development Society, Patna, Bihar for training women workers in masonry trade.

— Mahatma Gandhi Khadi and Gramodyog, Orissa for training women workers in masonry trade.

— King George Medical College, Lucknow for conducting study on the incidence of cervical disc diseases among women labour.

— Sudha Mahila Samaj Kalyan Parishad, Nalanda Bihar for training women labour in masonry trade.

— Research Integrated Social Development Action, Andhra Pradesh for training women in carpentry trade.

— Development Education and Welfare Institute, Tamil Nadu for training women labour in leather goods trade.

— Resource Centre for Human Affairs, Dt. Nellai Kattabomman, Tamil Nadu for training women labour in fibre knitting.

— Institute for Plantation Agricultural and Rural Workers, West Bengal for organising women labour.

— Atma Seva Sansthan, Vaishali, Bihar for training women labour in construction trade.

— Council of Youths for Development and Cooperation, Imphal, Manipur for training women in masonry trade.

— Jana Vikas Society, Andhra Pradesh for organising women labour.

Position of implementation of the equal remuneration act, 1976

(in nos.)

Inspections Detec- ted		Viola- tions Recti- fied	Viola- tions Launc- hed	Prose- cutions	Convic- tions	Acqui- tals
State/UTs						
1996	12534	376	65	a	6	.1
1997	15381	1878	178	48	34	10
Central						
1996	4809	4692	5241	1050	801	39
1997	4195	4722	4223	1144	537	27
1998	2350	6360	2429	548	208	'13

Child Care Centres

Statutory provisions have been made in certain labour laws for organising child care centres for the benefit of women workers. The Beedi & Cigar Workers (Conditions of Employment) Act, 1966 and the Building and Other Construction Workers (Regulation of Employment and Conditions of Service) Act, 1996 provide for establishment of creches for the benefit of women workers. The Plantation Labour Act, 1951 provides that the women workers be provided time-off for feeding children.

Future strategy

In the context of economic liberalisation, the quality of women's employment will depend tip several factors.

Chief amongst these are access education and skill development training. In be these areas women continue to lag behind men. The solution lies in creating conditions and opportunities which are conducive for women to work in increasingly productive and remunerative sectors of the economy with freedom. The issues requiring priority attention in the coming years are:

(a) Creating and strengthening an accurate e authentic data-base on women workers in sectors of employment , covering both organised and unorganised sectors. This could used as a tool of planning for both legislative as well as administrative intervention by the Government to protect and safeguard the interests of women workers in different fields of work and under different conditions of employment.

(b) Technological changes tend to displace women more than men primarily on account of lack of education, orientation, training and skill development programmes. Such programmes for women workers, therefore, need to be given high priority with a view to enabling women workers to improve their productivity and access to quality employment and also to enable them to take up new jobs involving technological changes.

(c) Carrying out research studies on problems of women workers, their employability and the extent of their displacement on account of technological and various other changes.

During the Ninth Five Year Plan, Women Cell has two major schemes in the area of Women Labour, details of which are as follows:

(i) Strengthening of Women Labour Cell: The Government has enacted the Equal Remuneration

Act, 1976. The Women Cell has been created in the Ministry to monitor implementation of the above Act. A Central Advisory Committee has been set up to advise the Government on providing increasing employment opportunities for women. Similarly, the State Govts/Union Territories have also constituted Advisory Committee in the States/ Union Territories to monitor implementation of the Act in the State Sphere.

(ii) Grants-in-aid to voluntary organisations: This scheme was introduced with the intention of furthering Government policy of helping women workers to become aware of their rights and opportunities and also become economically independent. The benefits expected to accrue through this scheme are yet to reach any substantial number of women workers in the unorganised sector. Therefore, the scheme has been retained during the Ninth Five Year Plan.

10

Economic Emigration

Migration of workers from India to other countries is not a new phenomenon. Factors which have influenced such migration of workers to other countries, inter alia, include the gap between the demand and local labour supply, the wage differential between the country of origin and country of arrival, the possibility of finding a suitable job in the country of arrival, distance (whether physical, cultural of religious), the extent to which the national group is present in the country of arrival and the migration policies as a measure of acceptance of foreign employers. In the recent years, additional factors which have affected migration include internationalisation of production, trade and finance, globalisation of economic network, liberalisation in movement of capital and technology, change in the life style of the returning migrants etc. Some persons temporarily emigrate in search of opportunity to upgrade their skills. India has a vast reservoir of well trained technical manpower (Table 11.1). In recent years, a large number of Indians have been able to find lucrative jobs abroad and thus participate in the economic and industrial development of the country of employment.

Immediately after Independence, labour outflows from India were made up almost entirely of permanent migration in so far as the proportion of migrants who returned to India, after a particular period was negligible. A large proportion of these migrants were persons with professional expertise, technical qualification or other skills perceived to be scarce or needed in labour importing countries. For an overwhelming proportion of these migrants, the destinations were the United States of America, Canada and the United Kingdom. Emigration of Indian labour towards the Middle East, especially to the oil exporting countries, is a recent phenomenon which began in the mid 1970s. The hike in the oil prices during 1973-74 and afterwards led to a considerable increase in the revenue of oil producing and exporting countries in the Gulf region. As a result, development programmes which included creation of amenities like schools, hospitals, houses, improvement of transport and communication etc. were taken up. This resulted in a spurt in demand for not only highly skilled technical experts but also semi-skilled and unskilled workers. Therefore, the main outflow of emigrant workers over the last few years has been to the Gulf countries where a few million - Workers are estimated to have been employed. The maximum number of Indian workers are in Saudi Arabia(1.3 million). Other major employers of Indian workers are UAE (1.2 million), Oman, Kuwait and Bahrain. The number of workers who were given emigration clearance for contractual employment abroad in the past few years and data on distribution of labour outflows are presented in tables.

Table

Emigration for employment over the years

Year	*No. of workers (in lakhs)*
1985	1.63
1986	1.14
1987	1.25
1988	1.70

1989	1.26
1990	1.44
1991	2.02
1992	4.17
1993	4.38
1994	4.25
1995	4.15
1996	4.14
1997	4.16
1998	3.55

Two important characteristics of migration to the oil exporting countries of the Middle East are that the migrant workers to these countries are generally persons who are at the lower end of the spectrum Of skills, as also of incomes and that an overwhelmingly large proportion are temporary migrants who return to India after a short period of contractual employment.

It is seen that during 1998, there has been a steep decline in the number of persons emigrating for work to other countries. This is primarily because of reduction in the number of persons going to Saudi Arabia. It is reported that there is a general slump in the employment market in Saudi Arabia because of the following reasons:

(i) Increasingly determined efforts to enforce Saudisation resulting in replacement of ex-Remittance patriate labour by Saudi Nationals in as many areas as possible;

(ii) more rigorous scrutiny by Saudi Authorities before visas for recruitment from India are cleared; and

(iii) general economic constraints as a result of fall in oil prices.

The employment of Indian workers abroad helps to earn foreign exchange and thereby adds to the foreign exchange reserves of India. The private transfer of foreign exchange from the year 1980-81 is given in Table 11.5. As may be seen from the table there has been increase in the remittance of foreign exchange during the year 1995-96 and 1996-97 over the previous years resulting in increase in the foreign exchange reserves.

Statewise figures of workers granted emigration clearances/ENCR endorsements during the years 1994, 1995, 1996 1997 and 1998.

State	*1994*	*1995*	*1996*	*1997*	*1998*
Andhra Pradesh	34,508	30,284	29,995	38,278	30,599
Assam	616	537	514	776	513
Bihar	6,785	5,867	5,816	6,369	14,569
Gujarat	12,802	12,182	11,991	1'2,792	8,528
Goa	1,571	969	962	1,024	945
Haryana	745	794	892	929	1;,.692
Himachal Prades	312	251	277	61	207
Jammu & Kashmir	632	567	611	228	709
Karnataka	32,266	33,196	33,761	40.396	11,535
Kerala	1,54,407	65,529	1,67,325	1,56,102	91,720
Madhya Prades	5,815	4,248	4,141	3,397	6,429
Maharashtra	32,178	26,312	25,214	25,146	24,657
Manipur	2	5	7	07	
Meghalaya	6	2	3	04	
Orissa	3,612	3 685	3,441	3,511	2,079
Punjab	12,445	11.852	11,751	12,414	26,876

Rajasthan	27,418	28,374	19,221	2,8,242	19,824
Tamil Nadu	70,525	65,737	64,991	63,,672	69,793
Tripura	2	-	-	-	1
Uttar Pradesh	22,815	T8,932	18,962	17,754	33,728
West Bengal	2,020	2,278	2,377	2,254	3,765
Delhi	3,816	3,281	2,892	2,494	5,535
Pondicherry	87	52	7t	74	285
Sikkim	-	-	-	-	1
Chandigarh	-	-	-	-	78
Others	-	-	-	-	1,236
TOTAL	4,25,385	4,115,334	4,14,214	4,16,424	3,55,164

Table

Private Transfer (Receipts)

Year	*Remittances in*	
	US $ min.	*Rs.Crore*
1980-81	2707	2136.7
1981-82	2333	2082.8
1982-83	2525	2431.0
1983-84	2568	2648.3
1984-85	2509	2981.9
1985-86	2219	2715.5
1986-87	2339	2990.6
1987-88	2724	3532.7
1988-89	2670	3865.4
1989-90	2295	3823.9
1990-91	2069PR	3711.0PR
1991-92	3587	9418.9

1992-93	2651	8124.0
1993-94	5265	16513.0
1994-95	6200	25416.0
1995-96	3506PR	28660.2PR
1996-97	12367PR	43968.1 PR
1997-98	11830	43764.4

The legal frame work

Emigration check on Indian passports has been in vogue since 1922. Prior to 1981 when the work pertaining to overseas employment was transferred by the Ministry of External Affairs to the Ministry of Labour, the Emigration Act was administered by Ministry of External Affairs (MEA). With the increase in the quantum of emigration in mid 1970s due to oil-boom in the Gulf countries and various shortcomings noticed, the Emigration Act 1922 was repealed and the Emigration Act, 1983 was enacted which came into force w.e.f. 30th December, 1983. The Emigration Act, 1983 deals with the emigration of Indian workers for overseas employment on contractual basis and seeks to safeguard their interests and ensure their welfare.

Under the Emigration Act, 1983, only the Recruiting Agents registered with the Ministry of Labour can conduct the business of recruitment for overseas employment after obtaining a Registration Certificate (RC) from the Protector General of Emigrants. The Certificate is granted after taking into account Recruiting Agent's financial soundness, trustworthiness, adequacy of premises, experience in the field of handling manpower export etc., and after obtaining security ranging from Rs.3 lakh to Rs. 10 lakh in the form of Bank Guarantee depending on the number of workers to be deployed. The scale of security is as follows:i)

(i) upto 300 workers - 3 lakh

(ii) 301 to 1000 workers - 5 lakh

(iii) 1001 workers and above - 10 lakh

The security is intended to secure due performance of the terms and conditions of the Registration Certificate and to meet the cost of repatriation of any recruited worker in the event of his being stranded abroad. Under Section 16 of the Emigration Act, 1983 an employer can recruit any citizen of India for employment in any country or place outside India either through a Recruiting Agent competent under the Act to make such recruitment or directly in accordance with valid permit issued by the Central Government under Section 15 of the Emigration Act. Indian workers are also deployed by the Indian Project Exporters on the projects undertaken by them overseas and emigration clearance to such workers is given by the Protectors of Emigrants (POEs) after the Project Exporters have obtained appropriate clearance from the Ministry of Commerce/Reserve Bank of India. The recruiting agents are authorised to charge as service charges from each worker at the following rates:-

Category	*Maximum service charges*
Unskilled workers	Rs. 2,000/
Semi-skilled workers	Rs. 3,000/
Skilled Workers	Rs. 5,000/
Other than the above	Rs. 10,000/-

A new Office of Protector of Emigrants (POE) has been set up w.e.f. 4.1.1996 at Hyderabad to cater to the needs of intending emigrants. The other off ices of POEs are at Mumbai, Calcutta, Chandigarh, Cochin, Delhi, Chennai and Thiruvanathapurarn. The offices at Delhi and Mumbai account for more than 75% of the total emigration from India in a year. Emigration Check

Required (ECR) Category.

Categories of persons whose passports have been endorsed as 'Emigration Check Required I (ECR), if intending to travel abroad for non-employment purposes, are required to obtain 'suspension' from the requirement of obtaining emigration clearance. The persons seeking ,suspension' are required to submit an application in the prescribed form, produce return ticket and passport with non-employment visa. Earlier, they were also required to furnish proof of drawal of foreign exchange to finance their visit abroad or a sponsorship declaration. The requirement of proof of drawal of foreign exchange has been dispensed with from April, 1991.

The 'suspensions' are granted by the eight off ices of Protector of Emigrants and sixteen authorised Regional Passport Offices. The Immigration authorities at the International Airports grant 'suspension' in emergency cases. Basically, those travelling abroad as tourists and whose passports carry ECR endorsement obtain these suspensions. The total number of 'suspensions' granted by the Protectors of Emigrants during the last few years is given in Table.

Table

Suspension of emigration clearance

Year	*No. of suspensions granted (in lakhs)*
1987	4.68
1988	3.52
1989	2.76
1990	2.51
1991	2.37
1992	1.95

1993	1.53
1994	1.48
1995	1.51
1996	1.54
1997	1.56
1998	2.81

Emigration check not required category

Section 22 of the Emigration Act, 1983 provides that no citizen of India shall migrate unless he obtains emigration clearance from Protector of Emigrants. However, with a view to facilitating the movement of the workers, seventeen categories of persons have been exempted from this requirement and have been placed under 'Emigration Check Not Required' (ECNR) category. (Box 11.1). As such they are entitled to get the endorsement of "ECNR" on their passports from the Passport Offices showing proof of their eligibility. They are not required to obtain any clearance from the Offices of POEs before seeking employment aborad.

In addition to above, a worker belonging to any of the following six çategories and having valid employment Visa endorsed on his/her passport can either approach the concerned POEs or the Passport authority through a registered Recruiting Agent for ECNR endorsement on his/her passpost:

(i) Supervisors (all professions);

(ii) Skilled workers (all professions)

(iii) Semi-skilled workers (all professions);

(iv) Light/Mediurn/Heavy Vehicle Drivers;

(v) Clerical workers of all categories including Stenographers, Store-keepers, Time-keepers, Typists etc.;

(vi) Cooks excluding those who seek employment in household duties (as cooks)

Persons going to Pakistan, Bangladesh and to the countries in North America and Europe (excluding CIS countries) are exempt from emigration check formalities. The pilgrims going for Haj and Umrah in Saudi Arabia and those pilgrims travelling with the declared purpose of performing Ziarat to Saudi Arabia, Syria, Iran, Iraq Jordan and Egypt were exempted from the requirement of obtaining suspension from 'Emigration Check Requirement' from POEs/Passport Offices w.e.f. 12.5.1992, 8-1-93 & 22.10.1993 respectively. Sana (Yemen) was added to the list of countries exempted from the requirement of obtaining emigration suspension for performing Ziarat w.e.f. May,1997. From 14th July, 1998 Japan, New Zealand and Australia have also been added to the list of countries for which emigration check is not required.

Recruiting agents

The registration of recruiting agents under the Emigration Act, 1983 commenced from January, 1984. From January,1984 till 31.12 98 Registration certificates were issued by Office of the Protector General of Emigrants to 3077 recruiting agents. This figure includes nine State Manpower Export Corporations established in the states of Uttar Pradesh. Andhra Pradesh, Kerala, Punjab, Tamil Nadu, Karnataka, Himachal Pradesh, Haryana and the Union Territory of Delhi. Major concentration of recruiting agents is in Mumbai, Delhi, Chennai and Thiruvanathapuram.

Manpower exports for projects

Apart from recruitment Agents, Indian emigrants are also deployed abroad by Indian Project Exporters on the projects undertaken c by them overseas. The Project Exporter has to obtain appropriate clearance from the Ministry of Commerce/Reserve Bank of India before he is permitted to deploy R workers abroad. For projects valued at less than Rs. 2 is crores, the Reserve Bank of India is empowered to grant clearance. For projects valued at over Rs. 2 crores the approval of Ministry of Commerce is required to be taken before emigration clearance is granted. Where the a, Project Exporters send the workers in a group they are required to furnish Bank Guarantee ranging from Rs.20,000/- to Rs. 5 lakhs depending upon the number 1, of workers to be deployed. The workers going abroad on an individual basis (either through Recruiting Agents or Project Exporters) or directly through a foreign ernployer are required to deposit security for one-way-air-fare from the place of employment to the place of' origin.

Redressal of grievances

While as a result of liberalisation of the policy, the number of persons going abroad has increased, the emigrant workers are facing serious difficulties bordering on exploitation in foreign countries as would be evident from the following type of complaints which are received by the PGE/POEs.

- The contract of the workers signed by them in India is unilaterally changed to the disadvantage of the workers by the foreign employers,
- Sometimes the workers are put to jobs different from the one for which they were recruited in India.
- Sometimes the worker is not given any employment at all by the sponsor. Instead he/she is required to look for a job himself/herself and in return he/she is forced to pay a part (30%) of his/her salary to the sponsor.
- Even the registered recruiting agents charge much higher fees than prescribed by the Government for the emigrant workers. The fee actually charged in many cases is alleged to be as high as 15-20 times of the prescribed service charges.

- Many employers do not pay wages in time and terminate the employment contract prematurely.
- In some cases, workers have complained of unsatisfactory living and working conditions, harassment, delayed payment of death and disability compensations etc.

Complaints against Recruiting Agents are enquired into with the help of police authorities and the concerned Indian Missions abroad and action is taken, as appropriate in each case in accordance with the provisions of the Emigration Act, 1983 and Rules framed thereunder. Complaints against un-registered recruiting agents are referred to the concerned police authorities for investigation. Complaints against foreign employers are taken up with the Indian Missions abroad. In addition, departmental action is taken against erring agents by way of suspension and cancellation of Registration Certificate. Registration Certificates of 19 agents were suspended during 1997. The following two complaints received during the last four years require special mention:

(i) Fourteen female para - medical staff in Yemen got stranded due to non-availability of jobs with the sponsor. The Protector General of Emigrants took up the matter with the Embassy of India, Sana'a, Republic of Yemen and alternative employment was arranged for thirteen of them. One of them who showed reluctance to work there returned to India. The Registration Certificate of the Recruiting Agent who had sent them to Yemen was suspended.

(ii) 137 Indian workers got stranded in Abu Dhabi as the Italian Company, Fochi International, for whom they were recruited, became in solvent before the arrival of the Indian workers there. On receipt of the complaint, the Protector General of Emigrants took up the matter with the Embassy of India in

Abu Dhabi and after considerable efforts alternative employment was provided to 91 workers. Out of the remaining 46 workers who opted to be repatriated, 37 worker's were repatriated by the Embassy at the cost of the Government to be later reimbursed by the concerned Recruiting Agents, who had recruited them. The entire expenditure except an amount of Rs.1.65 lakh, 'incurred on their repatriation has since been recovered from the Recruiting Agents. The remaining 9 workers returned after making their own arrangements. Action has been taken against the erring Recruiting Agents by suspending their Registration Certificates.

The Protector General of Emigrants and other senior officers of the Ministry of Labour hold public hearings twice a week on Tuesday and Fridays from 11.30 AM to 12.30 PM at Shram Shakti Bhavan, New Delhi. Public Hearing System has been extended w.e.f. August, 1993 to the off ices of the POEs located in Mumbai, Calcutta, Chandigarh, Cochin, Chennai and Thiruvanathapuram where intending emigrants, recruiting agents, project exporters etc. can meet the senior most POE for redressal of his/their grievance, for obtaining any information on various aspects of emigration, lodging their complaints etc. on every Tuesday and Friday from 11.30 AM to 12.30 PM without any prior appointment. During the period January to December, 1998, 1418 petitions were handled at these public hearings.

Strict vigilance is also enforced to secure proper conduct of the officials handling emigration matters.

11

Employment Scenario

Rural development implies both the economic betterment of the people as well as greater social transformation. Increased participation of people in the rural development process, decentralization of planning, better enforcement of land reforms and greater access to credit and inputs go a long way in providing the rural people with better prospects for economic development. Improvements in health, education, drinking water, energy supply, sanitation and housing coupled with attitudinal changes also facilitate their social development.

Rural development is, in fact, the pivot of administration at the Central, State and district levels in India. Various steps for the betterment of villages have been taken from time to time. Rural development has remained one of the constant and increasingly conscious goals of our Five Year Plans from their inception. As such, in the Ninth Five Year Plan also, high priority has been given to rural development and employment.

Rural poverty is inextricably linked with low rural productivity and unemployment including underemployment. Hence, it becomes necessary to improve productivity and increase employment in rural areas. Moreover, more employment needs to be generated at higher output. It is true that over the last two decades there has been a considerable decline in the incidence of rural poverty. However, a large number of persons continue to live below the poverty line. Hence, there is a need for continued direct State intervention for poverty alleviation. While the programmes for self-employment and supplementary wage employment would continue in the Ninth Five Year Plan, these would be redesigned in order to make them more effective as instruments of poverty alleviation. Apart from this, they would be integrated with the various doctoral programmes as well as the area development programmes within the umbrella of the Panchayati Raj institutions.

The decline in rural poverty is attributable both to the growth factor and to the special employment programmes launched by the government in order to generate more incomes in the rural areas. Hence, in its more limited interpretation, rural development has been confined to a direct attack on poverty through special employment programmes, area development programmes and land reforms. Some of these programmes are discussed below.

The Integrated Rural Development Programme (IRDP) is a self-employment programme aimed at enabling poor families to cross the poverty line, via access to income-generating assets and training. During the Eighth Plan, a system of concurrent evaluation of the IRDP was introduced. Various rounds of the concurrent evaluation revealed that while it had been successful in providing incremental income to the poor, in most cases this was not enough to enable them to cross the poverty line. Thus to make self-employment programmes more effective in the Ninth Five Year Plan, there will be a shift in strategy under IRDP. Several modifications have been made in order to improve the efficacy of the programme via higher levels of investment, better infrastructural support and strengthening of linkages, as also by a shift towards a group/cluster approach.

Training of Rural Youth for Self-Employment (TRYSEM) aims to enable the rural youth to take up self-employment ventures in different spheres across sectors by giving them assistance under IRDP. During the Ninth Plan, TRYSEM will be revamped in its design, curriculum and method of training in order to improve the employment opportunities of the poor. It will focus on activities in which the rural youth are already engaged and where there exists a potential for skill up gradation or else on activities which would enhance production under the group-cluster approach.

The success of several women's groups under Development of Women and Children in Rural Areas (DWCRA), which is based on a group approach, suggests that group dynamics work if people are organized into homogenous self-help groups for taking up income generating activities. A mechanism for replicating the successful DWCRA groups would be evolved. Besides, a greater integration of DWCRA with IRDP and TRYSEM will be attempted to provide women's groups with greater access to financial resources and training.

In the Ninth Plan, a new initiative for social mobilization will be taken up, for creation self-managed institutions of the poor. A mechanism for training of social animators to assist the poor to from their own organizations and articulate their felt needs and aspirations would be taken up.

The Jawahar Rozgar Yojana (JRY) was the only wage employment programme at the beginning of the Eighth Plan. The primary objective of the programme is generation of supplementary employment and creation of rural infrastructure required for more sustained employment. However, funds under this scheme went into every single village, though the amounts varied as States were allocated resources on the basis of the incidence of poverty. Apart from JRY, there is another wage employment programme known as the Employment Assurance Scheme (EAS). Both these schemes provide employment for a short duration in the form of casual manual work, during the lean agricultural season. So far, the EAS is being implemented in 3,206 blocks but will be universalized by 1997-98. In the Ninth Plan, this scheme would also be implemented through the PRIs.

In order to provide a greater thrust to shelter and irrigation facilities for the weaker sections, the Indira Awaas Yojana (IAY) for rural housing and the Million Wells Scheme (mws) for provision of open wells/family water harvesting structure were made separate independent schemes since January 1996. In the Ninth Plan, IAY will receive a greater thrust as it is one of the identified basic services for complete coverage in a time-bound manner. The scope of MWS will now be expanded to include borewells/tubewells and lifting devices.

The area development programes confined to drought-prone and desert areas were reviewed and redesigned in an attempt to restore the ecological balance through soil and moisture conservation. Preparation of watershed plans for a unit of 500 hectares with involvement of all members residing in the watershed was made mandatory. Training of functionaries in area planning and watershed management will be expanded.

Access to land remains a key element of the anti-poverty strategy in rural areas because rural poverty is largely among the landless and marginal farmers. In the Ninth Plan, emphasis has also been given to land reforms. The programme of action for land reforms would include the following: (i) detection as well as redistribution of ceiling surplus land; (ii) updating of land records on a regular basis; (iii) tenancy reforms providing for recording the rights of tenants and share-croppers; (iv) consolidation of holdings; (v) preventing alienation of tribal lands; (vi) providing access on a group basis to the poor on wastelands and common property resources; (vii) leasing-in and leasing-out of land will be permitted within the ceiling limits; (viii) preference to women in the distribution of ceiling surplus land and legal provisions for protecting their rights on land.

Given enough resources with the government, there is no reason why rural development and through it the eradication of rural poverty cannot be achieved during the five year period of the Plan with hundred per cent success. There is need for continued direct State intervention for poverty alleviation. While the programmes for self-employment and supplementary wage employment would continue in the Ninth Plan, these would be redesingned in order to make them more effective as instruments of poverty alleviation. It is necessary that these programmes are integrated with the various sectoral programmes as well as the area development programmes within the umbrella of the Panchayati Raj institutions.

An important change envisaged in the Ninth Plan is to make self-employment programmes more effective through a shift in strategy under Integrated Rural Developnment Programme (IRDP), from an individual benefiviary approach to a group and/or cluster approach would include development of skills of the rural poor through an inbuilt training component, upgradation of technology, establishment of forward and backward linkages, availability of appropriate infrastructure and markekt tie-ups. It is good that the scheme of Training of

Rural Youth for Self-Employment (TRYSEM) is now going to be revamped thoroughly in order to improve the employment opportunities of the poor. It is common knowledge that the artisans in rural areas, despite their rich heritage and skills, belong to the poverty group. Therefore, to improve their skills and production capabilities, they would be provided with modern tool kits as well.

A significant aspect of rural growth would be the improvement in the status of rural women. In this context, already the Development of Women and Children in Rural Areas (DWCRA) has been quite a siccess story in empowering women and in improving their economic status, though only in selected States so far. A mechanism for replicating the successful DWCRA groups would be evolved during the NInth Plan, while it would be integrated with IRDP and TRYSEM to provide womens' groups with greater access to financial resources and training. A country wide Employment Assurance Scheme is also intended to be launched during the Ninth Plan so that during the lean agricultural season, some manual work of casual naure may be given.

Rural poverty is largely among the landless and marginal farmers. Therefore, access to land remains a key element of the anti-poverty strategy in rural areas. Ninth Plan has laid down th e following programme of action for land reforms during the plan period:

- Detection as well as redistribution of ceiling surputs land;
- Upgradation of land records on a regular basis;
- Tenancy reforms providing for recording the rights of tenants and share-croppers;
- Consolidation of holding;
- Preventing alienation of tribal lands;

- Providing access on a group basis to the poor on wastelands and common property resources;
- Leasing-in and leasing-out of land will be permitted within the ceiling limits; and
- Perfernce to women in the distribution of ceiling surplus land and legal provisions for protecting their rights on land.

Social sector

Seven basic services have been identified for priority attention with an all-out effort for their complete coverage in a time-bound manner. These are safe drinking water, availability of primary health service facilities, universalisation of primary education, provision of public housing assistance to all shelterless poor families, nuturitional spport to children, and such other aspects as already mentiones before. The Panchayati Raj institutions will function as effective institutions for olcal self-government and social justice and implement schemes in social services.

The village and small industries sector (VSI) has rightly been chosen as the focal point for triggering off the growth process. Industries of this sector will be provided sufficient incentives and support to facilitate their growth and employment potential. Quite importantly, foreing investment will not be allowed to displace these industries. Investment limit for such industries has now already been raised by the government in order to enabele them to achieve economies of scale. It is hoped that the items reserved for production in them will continue to remain so. The VSI sector is to meke a dent in the regional disparities in terms of industrial and overall growth all over the country.

With all the sectoral financial and physical targets laid down, any plan cannot be successful unless the strategy to achieve its various targets is quite sound, practical and does not go awry. The approach paper contents that while it is feasible to achieve a seven per cent growth rate on the basis of the existing behavioural paramenters for private savings and investment, regular and significant revision of the pervasive underpricing of irrigation services, electricity, railway passenger fares, postal and telecommunication rates, perroleum and other mineral prices is required so that both the value-added and savings of these sectors improve substantially and are not eroded.

It is important to realize that for the target growth rate of seven per cent, investment would need to be of the order of 28.6 per ment of GDP. And this would have to be achieved despite a drop in the incremental capital-output ratio (ICOR, its decline shows improvement in efficiency) from 4.34 per cent.This, therfore, brings us to the aspect of allocation and optimal use of funds for doing so. It is expected that this cecline in ICOR would be achieved due to economic reforms, elimination of outdated technologies, higher energy and material efficiency in the industrial sector.

It is also imperative to maintain a balance between thg capital-intensive industry and labour-intensive industry to achieve the plan targets.Ancillary industries should take over manufacture of the componets of the industry set-up through the foreign direct investment route. All said and done, there fully aware of the dimension of resource mobilization. Therefore, it is necessary that both the Centre and the States work out programmes in concrete terms to meet the financing requirements of both infrastructure development and poverty alleviation schemes.

The Nehru Rozgar Yojana has been designed to provide employment to the urban unemployed and under-employed poor. The employment contemplated is of two types: one relates to the setting up of self-employment ventures and the other type relates to provision of wage employment through the creation of socially and economically useful assets and shelter upgradation programmes in urban areas. The programme has three schemes: (i) scheme for setting up micro entreprises and providing training and infrastructure support for urban poor beneficiaries. This scheme is operative in all urban settlements; (Ii) scheme of wage employment for creation of socially and economically useful public assets in the jurisdiction of urban local bodies. This scheme is applicable in : (a) towns with less than 20,000 population; and (b) towns with population from 20,000 to one lakh: and (iii) scheme of employment through housing and shelter upgradation in low income neighbourhoods mainly for the urban poor and economically weaker sections and training and infrastructure support for promotion of construction skills among beneficiaries. This scheme is applicable in settlements with population below 20 lakh.

While the target group of the Yojana is urban poor, women beneficiaries and beneficiaries belonging to scheduled castes and scheduled tribes will constitute special target groups. The main achievements of the scheme for the period ending December 1994 are; (i) Scheme of Urban Micro Enterprises (SUME); subsidy to the tune of Rs. 127 crore and institutional finance (in the form of bank loans) to the tune of Rs. 381 crore (approximately) i.e. three times of the subsidy have been sanctioned to 6.21 lakh beneficiaries since the inception of Yojana in 1989. Under the Training and Infrastructure Support component, 1.50 lakh beneficiaries have been trained/are undergoing training for skill upgradation; (ii) Scheme of Urban Wage Employment (SUWE): under this scheme, the states/union territories have reported expenditure of Rs. 213 crore till 31 December 1994 on creation of public assets in low income neighbourhoods and 380 lakh manadays of wage employment have been generated for the urban poor: (iii) Scheme of Housing and Shelter Upgradation (SHASU : HUDCO has sanctioned schemes from various states/union territories worth Rs. 292 crore (subsidy of Rs. 55 crore and loans upto Rs. 237 crore) involving upgradation of more than 7.27 lakh dwelling units till 31 December 1994.

The Scheme of Integrated Development of Small and Medium Towns (IDSMT) was launched in the year 1979-80 with the following objectives: (a) achieve more balanced urban development in the country; (b) provide infrastructural facilities to support employment generating activities; (c) evolve resource generating schemes for local bodies for the purpose of proper operation and maintenance of the infrastructural facilities so created; (d) develop growth poles for the betterment of rural hinterlands adopting a regional approach; and (e) arrest migration from areas to large/metropolitan cities.

The budget allocation for IDSMT Scheme has been raised from Rs. 80 crore in the Seventh Plan to Rs. 155 crore in the Eighth Plan. It is expected that 300 towns will be covered uner the scheme during the Eighth Plan period. Upto 31 March 1995, 232 towns have been covered under the revised scheme of IDSMT and Central assistance of Rs. 57.5 crore released. This amount includes Rs. 45.84 crore for 232 new towns and Rs. 8.15 crore for on-going schemes in 57 towns. It also includes Rs. 3.52 crore approximately on account of grant-in-aid released to 20 state governments and one union territory administration for defraying the expenses incurred on preparation of project reports of 190 towns covered under the revised scheme of IDSMT.

Large metropolitan cities like Calcutta, Bombay,

Madras, Hyderabad and Bangalore make significant contributions to the national economy. Therefore, their prosperity and efficient functioning are of national concern. Many problems in these cities are due to massive migration from rural areas and smaller towns all over the country on which the city authorities have little or no control. The state governments are not in a position to make adequate investments in infrastructure in such cities on account of their limited resources and their priority to sectors lie agrculture irrigation education health, etc. Keeping in view of the persistent demands from the state governments and based on the recommendations of the National Commission on Urbanisation, a Centrally-sponsored scheme for infrastructure development in mega cities having population of four million and above as per 1991 Census has been introduced from the year 1993-94. The scheme is called the Mega City Scheme. The main features of the scheme are: (i) the scheme would be applicable to Bombay, Calcutta, Madras, Bangalore and Hyderabad; (ii) the scheme would be administered through the Ministry of Urban Developmnt and funds would be channelised though a special institution at the state level; (iii) the funds from Central Government are to be used as equity support/seed capital for the institition The sharing between Central Government and state government would be 25:25 per cent and the balance 50 per cent is to be met from institutional finance, through public financing institutions or capital market; (iv) the institution would provide project related finance for urban infrastructure including water supply, sewerage, soild waste management, etc; and (v) finance will not be provided for health, education, electricity MRTS/LTRS, etc., under this scheme. The projects to be included under the scheme would be under three categories: (a) Projects for basic services where minimum returns are not expected–for these laons could be at 8.5 per cent; (b) Projects in which user charges could be levied–for these loans could be at 12 per cent and (c) Projects which are remunerative and for which loans would be given on market rate of interest.

To ensure viability of the institution described at (iii), the above three categories of projects would be financed in the ratio of 30:3:40 as a rough indication. The intention is that the overall package (rather than each project) should be viable in the sense of creating a sizeable corpus for future investment.

The scheme would be implemented during the Eighth and Ninth Five Year Plans. The following Plans allocations from the Central Government are proposed for the five cities.

The project for each mega city should consist of a judicious mix of remunerative and non-remunerative schemes so that the total basket is economically viable. The project outline envisages a mix of projects with different gestation periods; as far as possible, projects with long gestation periods are to be avoided. Projects of regional singificance are to be given priority. The priorities would be decided by the state governments. However, the criteria for prioritisation of projects could be: (a) compatibility with the perspective structure plan for the metropolitan region; (b) selectivity in terms of significant impact in particular and desirable sectors or complementarity to an existing or completed large project for speedy accrual of benefits; and (c) shorter gestation period so as to ensure completion of a significant proportion of the project during the Eighth Plan period.

The state goverments are required to designate one institution as the coordinating and monitoring agency for the entire range of mega city project activities. The following agencies are since chosen to be the designated agencies: Bombay Metropolitan Region Development Authority (BMRDA); Calcutta Metropolitan Development Authority (CMDA); Madras Metropolitan Development Authority (MMDA); Hyderabad Development * and Finance Corporation (KUIDFC). The designated agencies will monitor the implementation of various schemes as well as resource mobilisation for the revolving fund. A state level project sanctioning committee will approve the projects during 1995-96. A budget allocation of Rs. 84 crore has been made as Central assistance for the scheme.

Entrepreneurship

Entrepreneurship is the character, practice and skill that combines innovativeness, readyness to take risk, sensing opportunities, heightened initiative, perceiving and mobilising potential resources, concern for standard of excellence, persistence in achieving the goal, positive orientation to problem solving and constant strive for growth and excellence. When all these attributes are developed in one person, the person becomes entrepreneur. Such entrepreneurs can be found in any field-may it be industry, business, education, public or professional bodies, but wherever they go they create a land mark, turn the direction and attain hights.

in economic field "entrepreneurship refers to identifying/innovating ideas, product and services; mobilising resources, organising production/services and finally marketing them covering the risk with constant strive for growth and excellence". There are enough historical evidences to suggest that whenever the number of such person has grown in a society or country that society and country has attained greater prosperity at that point of time. Every country, therefore, needs a large number of entrepreneurs who can set up industries, business and services of various types for attaining national prosperity.

Experiences have shown that two major factors have played significant role in developing entrepreneurship. One of them is the development of human factors-the entrepreneur himself. Another major factor is the development of environment where entrepreneurial activities can flourish and grow.

The human factor refers to the attitude, desire and motivation of an individual, his capability to perceive the environment changes and opportunities as well as his ability to solve the problems which he is likely to face. The training is effective in developing allthese aspects of human factors provided it is planned well with balanced emphasis on all the aspects. Training has played crucial role for all such strategies.

Emergence of Two Models: Experimentations in Assam and other States in India jointly by SIETI, respective state governments and SIDO led to the emergence of the SIET Integrated Model for entrepreneurship Development.

The model advocated for local agency is to conduct selection tests to identify potential entrepreneurs; followed by training that include achievement motivation; economic insight for selection of project and project formulation and skills in production marketing and financial management. After training the local agencies organise support for obtaining infrastructural facilities including institutional financing. The Classical Model was tried in several parts of India and yielded good results in States like Jammu & Kashmir, Assam, Karnataka and Andhra Pradesh.

Almost simultaneously, another entrepreneurship model popularly known as 'Gujarat Model' emerged out of the rich experiences gathered by Centre for Entrepreneurship Development (CED) in Gujarat. During

1971 CED was jointly sponsored by Gujarat Industrial Development Corporation (GIDC) Gujarat State Financial Corporation (GSFC), Gujarat Industrial Investment Corporation (GIIC) and Gujarat State Industrial Corporation (GSIC). The 'Scientific selection of potential entrepreneurs through psychological tests and exercises and follow-up after training through a local project leader were the major innovations in the programme. The content of training included motivation laboratory, management & organisational skills, and other incentives. The project leader assisted the trainees in preparing the project and kept on counselling till their enterprises were set up. The close interlinkage between the various development agencies ensured getting finance sanctioned, machinery ordered and raw-materials supplied at appropriate time and place.

The above two models provided basis for several experimentation and schemes by central and state government as well as by NGOs. Among those which were initiated during 1970s and contributed significant experiences from both their success and failure are Andhra Pradesh Crash Programme 1971; * Scheme for Training of Young Engineers (TYE) 1972; XISS Entrepreneurship Development Programme for Tribals (1972); J & K Self-Employment Programme 1974; Maharashtra MSSIDCP Programme 1974; Scheme for Entrepreneurship Development Programme 1978; and Training for Rural Youth for Self-Employment (TRYSEM) 1979 (the important experiences from such efforts have been recorded in the Status Analysis Report by NIESBUD).

The experiences gathered through these efforts provided adequate evidences that imputs such as finance, technical know how, machinery & equipment, or infrastructural facilities like land, sheds etc. are critical but not enough for developing entrepreneurship.

The supply of all of them (not one of them must be accompanied with adequate information), appropriate selection of potential entrepreneurs, training and strong follow-up. In the absence of one, others were found infructuous.

Significant efforts made in India reviewed in the following pages offer rich experiences needed for formulating few strategies for developing entrepreneurship for various target groups.

In 1962, the Small Industry Extension Training Institute, popularly known as SIET, was established at Hyderabad. In collaboration with SIET, Prof. David CMc Clelland formulated and conducted the famous experiment at Kakinada and Rajahmundri in East Godavari District of A.P., to test the impact of Achievement Motivation Training on developing entrepreneurship. The experiment which continued upto 1965 raised hopes of developing entrepreneurs through Achievement Motivation Training. It further broke the myth that "entrepreneurs are born and not made". The experience was published in book form entitled 'Motivating Economic Achievement' in which the authors summarized the impact:

"Achievement Motivation training is especially likely to change men who are incharge of their business probably because they take the scope and independence to carry out new ideas and plans, further, if a man already is somewhat dissatisfied with himself, but sees himself as someone who can intitiate specific action to solve specific action to solve specific problems, he is likely to respond to training with specific and visible activity".

The earlier attempts for developing entrepreneurship were made in the 1960s under the programme 'Intensive Campaign'. The Agencies created during the 1950s to supply input and technical information were involved in organising such campaigns. The techniques used to collect funds during the early '60s were adopted to develop entrepreneurship. The campaigns were launched with two objectives:

- Motivating entrepreneurship;
- Dispersal of small industries.

The campaign procedure, however involved 11 steps such as meeting in localities to discuss various kinds of incentives, assistance, and facilities provided; demonstration with the assistane of a mobile van; exhibition of films; personal discussion about the prospects of projects; visits to local industrial units; matching the product with entrepreneurial investment capacity; distribution of printed publicity materials; filling up forms for hire purchase; verification for registration; utilisation of idle capacity and discussion on possibilities for development and improvement of existing industries, etc. It was expected that prospective entrepreneurs would decide about an entrepreneurial career. During the campaign, persons were shown ready-made indusrial project schemes and/or were assisted to develop schemes which they could start.

On the spot announcements about sanctioning the schemes were made. However the results were far from satisfactory. The final sanction of the scheme from Headquarters took a long time. By then, many of the prospective entrepreneurs had decided not to go further. Some who proceeded found that they had gone into business without studying its prospects and of their competence as successful businessmen. Many District Collectors cautioned against such a campaign, as it was finally they who had to answer for its failure and meet the frustration of the community. The main shortcoming of the campaign, regarded as the first organised step to develop entrepreneurship in India on a large scale, was that it failed to consider that business development is not an instant action. It is rather a process that stretches over a period of years, and requires continuous involvement and follow-up. Besides, once the campaigns were concluded, there were no local agencies left to support them in obtaining resources, both to set up and run their enterprise.

In order to fight the problem of unemployment among educated persons, the Ministry of Industry formulated the following two schemes:

In 1971-72 the scheme intended to provide package assistance to prospective entreprenuers, which included in-plant training and creation of a separate cell at the State level to look after the programme. The programme included training/setting up an Industrial Estate in each state and providing initial finance for purchase of machinery.

The scheme aimed at developing entrepreneurship among engineers and technical diploma holders. In all 29 institutions were identified to impart 3 months training. This programme began in 1972 along with some changes. In the context of rising unemployment among engineers, the Ministry of Industry in 1970 devised a special scheme for training of unemployed engineers, in Industrial Entrepreneurship, with a view to orienting them towards small scale industries, and motivating them to take up self-employment by setting up SSI units of their own. This training was imparted largely through 13 SISIs and 11 designated institutions. The course include topics such as achievement motivation, entrepreneurship and small industries, planning for small industry, procedural formalities for starting SSI, market survey, preparation of bankable project reports, knowledge of institutional set up for promotion of SSI (including details of facilities assistance/incentives offered by such institutions), introduction of management of small industry including book-keeping. Besides task, lectures, discussions, case studies and film shows, participants were taken on field visits to industrial untis. After training, assistance in implementing the various procedural formalities right upto the permanent registration stage was also offered. The duration of training was 3 months and trainees were given a stipend of Rs. 250/- p.m.

Altogether 335 courses were conducted, training 9003 engineer entrepreneurs, of whom 1642 were reported to have set up their own units. This meant an overall success rate of 18.24% during the period 1970-71 to 1980-81. Of the 6757 profound trained by SISIs, 1323 (19.58%) had set up their own industrial units. The designated institutions trained 2246 persons, of which 319 (14.20%) were reported to have set up their own industries. Three designated institutions of MNREC, Allahabad, IIT, Delhi and IIT Kanpur, did not maintain data. If data relating to these is corrected, the success ratio improves to 20.37%.

In 1971, the Andhra Pradesh Government launched a crash programme for Entrepreneurial Development. To begin with, the programme was confined to the two cities of Hyderabad and 14 backward districts of the State. The entire staff of the Department of Industry was mobilised, and teams of technical officers were drawn from the Department of Industries, SIDC, SISI and the Regional Research Laboratory, to scrutinise each scheme submitted by a large number of entrepreneurs in response to the advertisement. After scrutinising and selecting the schemes, the Technical Committees worked to give a viable shape to the sophisticated schemes. Nationalised banks and the State Financial Corporation approved finance for the schemes. After obtaining the financial sanction, implementation committees consisting of atleast two officers, were formed to deal with the problems encountered in the formative stage of the industries. Similarly, to procure the necessary machinery, an advisory committee consisting of technical experts in different disciplines, representatives of banks, with the joint director of industries as convenor, was formed.

This committee helped entrepreneurs to procure quality machinery at competitive rates. In plant training at industrial establishments and training in modern management techniques was arranged by the State Government at SISI and SIET. In less than 9 months before March 1973, 483 units started production, due to effective backing up of the prospective entrepreneurs with credit facilities, training, and above all the ready accessibility and supply of inputs. The success was an excellent example of the impact of responsible administrative action, and later on the Andhra Pradesh Government created a task force to carry out such activities.

The three decades of continues growth have brought maturity to the movement of entrepreneurship development in India. Till the beginning of the 1960s, entrepreneurship remained a topic of academic and philosophical discussion by economist, sociologist and psychologist. The attempt was to accurately define and describe entrepreneurship, its nature and functions. Such description were markedly influenced by respective academic disciplines. Although most of these descriptions were partly true, yet none of them had the quality of describing entrepreneurship as a whole. Towards the end of the 60s, two very significant contributions were made in the field of entrepreneurship. These were:

— Establishment of positive linkages between entrepreneurship and economic prosperity. 1 and

— Emergence of strong hypothese that entrepreneurship can be developed through planned efforts.

The former helped acceptance of entrepreneurship development for achieving economic prosperity and the later facilitated experimentation with various strategies for developing entrepreneurship.

In 70's varieties of strategies and models of developing entrepreneurship were developed, repeated and replicated. As a result entrepreneurship was identified as important vehicle of industrial development which is evident by the emergence of about 1.7 million SSI enterprises creating jobs for more than 10 million workers in the sector.

During 80's the structure and functions needed for promoting entrepreneurship become more or less clear and entrepreneurship attained the status of a movement. At national level during 1982-83 National Science & Entrepreneurship Development Board (NSEDB) and National Entrepreneurship Development Board (NEDB) were created under the Chairmanship of the Prime Minister and Union Minister for Industry respectively. Two national resource institutions, i.e., National Institute for Entrepreneurship & Small Business Development (NIESBUD) at New Delhi and Entrepreneurship development Institute of India (EDII) at Ahmedabad were established during the same period. Presently more than 700 organisations including 7 state level entrepreneurship development institutes, 27 SISIs under SIDO, 17 TCOs, 20 Engineering and Technical Institution, 7 STEOs and a host of non-governmental organisations are engaged in developing entrepreneurship. SIDO alone has trained more than 50.000 potential entrepreneurs during 78-88 and one Centre for Entrepreneurship Development of Gujarat trained more than 10,000 potential entrepreneurs since its inception. In this way thousand of people get opportunities to be developed as entrepreneurs. But the coverage is still far less as compared to the potential available in the country. We may have to took into the infrastructural facility, availability and accessibility to information and technology and develop enormously large cader of trainers and poromoters to reach both urban and rural population. To illustrate, during the 8th Five Year Plan, as per the modest calculations, the country needs about 13,000 trainers, promoters for training potential entrepreneurs as against few hundred which are available today.

The mid 70s witnessed the crystallisation of an integrated model for Entrepreneurship Decelopment (EDP), consisting of stimulatory, support and sustaining activities. This was replicated and very widely with minor variations. The present decade is shaping up to be "age of entrepreneurial explosion". It is visiable as a significant programme in national development plan. During 80s, the structure and function needed for promoting entrepreneurship have become more or less clear. With growing emphasis by the Government and the matching enthusiasm by NGOs, entrepreneurship has now attained the status of a movement.

The movement of entrepreneurship development in India, however, started as part of the total strategy of small industry development. The dynamic SSI policy has strongly supported the cause of entrepreneurship development and both have mutually supplemented each other.

Presently, Small Scale Industries in India are defined by investment limit of Rs. 6 million (Rs. 7.5 million for ancillary units). Besides manufacturing, services, maintenance and processing enterprises are also included in SSI. The tiny sector which has been given the distinctive position is defined as consisting of those units having investment less than Rs. 0.5 million.

The response to such dynamic policy has been very rewarding. The growth of SSI Sector has been one of the most impressive. Between 1973-74 and 1986-87 the number of SSI increased by over 3 folds from 0.416 million to nearly 1.457 million. Presently (1990) their number is estimated as 1.7 million. Employment in this sector has risen more than double from nearly 3.47 million to 10.14 million. The value of Production in terms of current prices increased ten times (Rs. 72,000 million to Rs. 722,500 million). In the field of export, SSI conribution was recorded as approximately 30 per cent of the country's total exports.

More impressive than these statistics is the number crossing 5,000 products which are manufactured in the small scale sector. Beginning with the production of simple consumer goods, the small scale today manufacturs several sophisticated, precision items using latest technology. Some of the sophisticated items precision items using latest technology. Some of the sophisticated items produced in SSI sector include T.V., electronic disk calculator, micro-wave components, electro-medical equipment, miniature bulbs, optical lens, digital measuring equipments, air-conditioning equipments, electric motors, machine tools, authomobile and scooter parts.

Small enterprises in India were also found more economical than large enterprises in terms of capital investment and development generation. Further, small enterprises are providing learning ground for imparting, managerial, entrepreneurial and technical skills. They also provide an outlet for creative urge among individuals to persue excellence in product design and innovations resulting into competitive culture and problem solving orientation which usually lack at the initial stage of development but are basic to socio-economic prosperity.

The most significant aspect of small industry development is that this sector has stimulated vigorously the economic activity of a far reaching magnitude and created a sense of confidence among very large number of small entrepreneurs about their strength and vitality.

Consultancy

The Indian consultancy scenario is a rich blend of both "self-developed" technology on one hand and "acquired" know-how on the other. When the country emerged into freedom in 1947 the Indian Economy was at a low ebb with impoverished resources, processes and infrastructure designed to meet vested requirements and an environment wherein the wherewithal for nurturing and training technical and managerial talent was hardly there. The country soon took stock of the situation. National priorities were identified and a well conceived policy of "planned development" was adopted. Economic re-generation & growth forced an important segment in these planning programmes with socio-economic factors, like medicare, education, technical training, employment etc. appropriately dovetailed. It was recognised that for all these programmes or activities it was essential to nurture, encourage and develop an effective cadre of professionals, both technical and managerial. The concept of consultancy was thus ushered in and gathered strength gradually.

In the course of these four score and more years-in an environment of growth and development-the Indian consultant has been sufficiently exposed not only to the technological development and consultancy practices in other countries but also is a part of the indigenous consultancy culture that has evolved as an achievement towards the national objective of self-reliance. India's commitment to self-reliance in engineering skills has ensured a fairly good growth of the consultancy sector.

As a part of the overall strategy for industrial development, the utilisation of indigenous design and engineering inputs is one of the key factors. The sixties and seventies witnessed the emergence of several consultancy organisations, with specialisation in various sectors of industry. Some of these were set up in collaboration with foreign organisations while many others were set up totally with local expertise.

According to a survey recently conducted by the Consultancy Development Centre (CDC) and the Federation of Indian Export Organisations (FIEO), Both non-profit institutions set up by the Government of India to service Indian Consultancy-there are more then 1400 consultancy organisations and individual consultants (both management and technical) rendering services in various aspects of industrial and non-industrial sectors of the economy.

The trend of growth of consultancy during the periods 1940-1988 is shown in the Table below:

Growth trend of Indian consultancy

Period	Annual growth %
1940 - 60	5
1961 - 80	43
1981 - 88	52

During the course of the last 5 years the number of consultancy firms in the country has country has increased from 700 to 1400; the consultancy turnover from Rs. 500 to Rs. 1000 crores; employment in the consultancy profession from 40,000 to 80,000 and exports of consultancy services from Rs. 50 to Rs. 120 crores.

In spite of this growth, and keeping in mind that the consultancy culture has assumed some dimensions in

India's national economic infrastructure only recently, Indian consultancy, in spite of its achievements, is yet in its nascent stage.

Techno-economic studies and feasibility surveys

Project Identification, pre-investment appraisals, final location, engineerings surveys, market surveys.

Energy

Power generation, transmission and systems analysis, hydro and thermal power generation, nuclear and atomic energy, oil and gas installations, energy conservation, geothermal energy and non-conventional energy sources, pipelines and offshore engineering, power distribution, hydro-electric power projects.

Water resources

Dam engineering; irrigation; river hydraulics; drainage, flood forecasting and control, water resources development and management; investigation for water resources; water treatment and distribution; waste water treatment and diposal systems; barrages; navigation locks; water conductor systems; canal structures and anti sea-erosion measures etc.

Geosciences, minerals and mining

Soil and geotechnical investigations, testing, ground strengthening exploration and project installation etc. for ferrous, non-ferroud and metallurgical industries.

Construction

Design-basic and detailed engineering for buildings and dams, ports, harbours, tunnels, towers, etc. Installation and commissioning, site management and supervision of construction, rehabilitation and expansion of existing units, post commissioning assistance, operation and maintenance services.

Transport

Travel demand studies, identification of transport options, system choice, selection of route alignment, financial and social cost benefit analysis.

- Roads and Highways: Techno-economic feasibility studies, detailed engineering and design for express ways, state national highways and feeder roads, fuel economy studies and construction supervision.
- Railways Electrification, Signaling and Telecommunication System: Route survey, system design, electric power supply, HT-LT substations and controls. Route relay interlocking, centralised traffic control, automatic block signalling, automatic train control systems including train supervision, passenger information systems, microwave systems, VHF and UHF systems and mobile train radio communications.
- Inland Water Transport: Pre-investment appraisals, hydro-graphic-surveys, techno-economic feasibility cum traffic studies, develpoment of infrastructural and terminal facilities, river engineering, prevention of silting, design and construction management.
- Airports: Feasibility studies, surveys and traffic forecasting, airport master planning, design and engineering of pavements, building, terminals, maintenance bases and hangars, construction supervision, airport management and maintenance system, aircraft hangers.

Ports & harbours

Development, improvement and modernisation of ports including dry ports and fishing harbours, regulation of port operations, assessment of infrastructural facilities, hydrographics and land survey of coastline and project management.

Management

Management consultancy, including economic studies, market research, financial evaluation, system design including computer software and telecommunications etc.

Telecommunication

Local telephone system, transmission system, computer and communication, industrial consultancy for all items used in telecommunication, architectural design for telecommunication buildings, communication management, training and manpower development.

Manpower training and development

Assessment of training needs, planning and setting up training infrastructure, management of training institutions, designing courses and curriculum planning, development of tailor-made training programmes with classroom in structions and on the job training.

Electronic data processing

Hardware selection and software development for management information systems, computer aided designs, financial accounting, inventory control and production control.

Inspection

Quality assurance programmes, installation and improvement of quality control and documentation, quality audit, qualilty certification thorough stage and final inspection, vendor rating, S.Q.C. valuation and capacity assessment.

Marine engineering

Naval Architecture, Freighters, Dredging, Ship Design.

Urban engineering

Urban planning, urban development, drinking water treatment and supply.

Another DSIR initiative has been the setting up of the Cosultancy Development Centre with the active co-operation of the of the National Association of Consulting Engineering (NACE), Association of Consulting Engineers (ACE) and the Federation of Indian Export Organisations (FIEO) in the Ministry of Commerce. CDC is the brains-trust of the Indian consultancy profession, fully equipped with the necessary equipment and professionals to:

- service the information needs of the Indian Consultant and day-to-day requirements.
- provide a computerised data base with CAD/CAM facilities.
- organise short and long-term training programmes for young engineers.
- institute schemes for recognition of outstanding consultancy performances.
- facilitate transfer of technology.
- conduct studies/surveys on topics of interest to the profession.
- publish periodicals, journals and publicity literature.
- organise visits of outgoing and incoming experts and delegations related to the profession.
- embark on any other activity or programme designated to ensure that the consultancy culture premeates at all concerned levels in the country.

The Department of Scientific and Industrial Research (DSIR) has thus taken effective and innovative steps that have ensured, for Indian Consultancy, growth and development inputs so as to merit both national and international attention. Some of the objectives achieved by DSIR have been:

- Promotion of a consultancy culture in all economic sectors, more particularly industry.
- Encouraging consultancy linkages between laboratories and end-users.
- Encouraging increased use of indigenous know-how and technology, with consequent reduction in imports.
- Stimulating the export growth of consultancy services.
- Establishing better linkages between research, academic institutions and consultants.
- Ensuring a more effective and rational utilisation of investment, whether in industry, in agriculture or in infrastructure.
- Making available opportunities for training and moulding young engineers in the context of national priorities.
- Creating a data base for collection and dissemination of information related to consultants, consultancy and technology.
- Providing financial assistance to consultancy promotion organisations or consultants as a 'catalytic' input to generate in them greater interest to participate in important fora for interaction with more knowlegeable or experienced counterparts, both at the national and international levels.
- Encouraging consultants to design and publish effective literature and documents for projection to potential endusers of consultancy.
- Initiating schemes of awards to recognise and encourage talent.
- Setting up suitable infrastructure for servicing the subject and the profession.

The following are the main indicators which serve as tangible factors for ascertaining the impact of these promotional schemes for the growth and development of consultancy services in the Seventh Five Year Plan Period which has just ended:

– Number of consultancy firms	:	Increase from 770 as of five years ago to 1700 as of now
– Consultancy turnover	:	Rs. 500 to Rs. 1000 crores
– Employment in consultancy Profession	:	40,000 to 80,000
– Exports	:	Rs. 50 to Rs. 125 crores

The Indian Economy is all set to achieve a much higher growth than hitherto, with significant institutional changes. From a little over 3% growth in the sixties and seventies, the eighties have witnessed 4 to 5% growth, thus raising hopes of a better performance in the nineties. Though the impact of the population growth still remains a matter of serious concern, with a planned growth of 6% or more, built-up by an inherent strength of its agricultural economy, rapid and sustained development of the industrial sector matched by giant strides in infrastructural and other areas of development, India can look forward to the future with optimism and confidence.

Industry, which was highly protected in the past, is today opening-up with a deliberate policy of liberalisation. The planners with their vast experience of the past four decades with regard to the changing structure of economy and its increasing sophistication, feel that it should be possible only if it is backed up by technical upgradation and a growth strategy based on self-reliance, in which independent consultancy would naturally have an important role to play.

The country has just crossed the threshold of its Eighth Five Year Plan, the main components envisaged as growth factors during the NIneties are energy & power; telecommunications; electronics; informatics with focus on computers; industry particulalry steel, textiles, cement, fertilisers, petro-chemicals, crude oil, sugar and plastics; agriculture and food packaging; urbanisation with emphasis on overcoming housing shortages and small scale and rural industries.

All these and the other provision incorporated in the Plan will obviously need more trained personnel and professionals, which presupposes an enlarged and more important role for Indian Consultants.

The Technology Policy Statement (TPS) of the Government of India, 1983, has recognised perhaps for the first time, the need to promote and develop new skills in consultancy. The Policy includes technology transfer as one of the important objectives and lays emphasis on difusion, international competitiveness in technology exports and also building up technical cooperation steps in this direction that could substantially contribute to enhancement of indigenous consultancy capability and improvement of potential for exports of technologies and services.

The Department of Scientific and Industrial Research (DSIR), under the Ministry of Science and Technology, has already initiated effective follow-up on the recommendations and observations embodied in the Technology Policy Statement. The Plan of DSIR on "Promotion and Support to Consultancy Services" has essentially been directed to strengthening and developing the technological and management capabilities of Indian consultants, so that their service are utilised more effectively and on a wider scale, by a larger number of users with reduced dependence on foreign sources. The enhancing of indigenous consultancy capabilities is also aimed towards building up larger exports of projects, technologies and services as well increased commercialisation of indigenous technologies.

The DSIR programme of action on the TPS is, by and large, centered on the following provisions of the TPS viz:

Encouraging Engineering consultancy to ensure speedy technology and industrial development with appropriate utilisation of indigenous materials, plant and machinery. Engineering Consultancy is projected as an essential link between R & D institutions and the industry for promoting effective transfer of technology. Where foreign technical collaboration or consultancy is considered important, indigenous engineering consultancy in both private and public sectors is sought to be involved and promoted on a sound professional basis in the context of the overall national perspective of. * "

The Department and its agencies seek to promote capabilities in design engineering, for the transformation of know-how to commercial production. This is considered particularly important in areas relating to agricultural production, agro-industries, metallurgical, chemical and petrochemical proccesses: machine tools, industrial machinery, and capital goods as well as construction and erection of entire plants. Building up of these capabilities is considered to have a beneficial catalytic impact on the utilisation of indigenous efforts that have resulted in products and process know-how. Existing design engineering capabilities are sought to be strengthened and upgraded and interaction encouraged between design engineering organisations, academic and research institutions and industry.

Recognising the necessity to maintain international competitiveness of products, services and technologies that have export potential, special strategies have been formulated to create conducive conforming to optimum international standards. It is acknowledged that in the international scenario, the need for building-up domestic in the services sector is assuming greater significance and in the context of protective and restrictive trends in trade, including technology transfer. It is realised with the services sector is accounting for larger opportunities in developed economies compared to the manufacturing sector and has hence to prepare itself to meet the future challenges as per the changing technological and economic environment at the global level.

A major initiative by DSIR is the launching of the scheme entitled "Promotion and Support to Consultancy Services". Under this scheme financial support is provided to organisations/institutions for promotion of design engineering and consulting services through measures such as:

- extending incentives to Consulting Engineering firms to document their experiences in major projects, particularly abroad.
- encouraging R & D efforts of consultancy organisations.
- Empanelling eminent engineering professionals on a retainer basis for assistance to consultancy organisations and entrepreneurs.
- providing fellowiships to promising engineers as apprentices with reputed consultancy organisations and arranging their training and exposure to the consultancy ethos.
- organising seminars, workshops etc. and preparing publicity material such as video films, directories,

brochures and catalogues particularly for projection abroad.

- assisting consultants in pilot studies and in building up infrastructural facilities in relation to commercialisation of indigenous know-how.
- enhancing the capabilities and supporting activities related to accelerated technology transfer, particularly in the context of TCDC.
- building up linkages with various institutions/ organisations.
- encouraging the availability of consultancy services to the small scale sector, on preferential terms.

In a country of such vast dimension like India-with its varied geographical, climate, cultural and economic scenarios, as also the differing priorities of the different states and regions, along with the differences in the natural endowment of each region, the Indian consultant has had different back-drops in the course of his development. Apart from the projects and programmes launched in different parts of the country, by different authorties and in respect of varying subjects, the authorities in India have taken special care to set up specialised academic and training institutes to help in the creation of an effective technological and professional cadre. The sources of Indian consultancy are several. The include:

- Public Sector Consultancy Organisations.
- Consultancy Wings of Public Sector Undertakings.
- Independent Consultancy Organisations in the Private Sector.
- Consultancy Organisations as part of the Private Sector Undertakings.
- State level consultancy Organisations.

- R & D Laboratories under the CSIR and other Cooperative Research Institutes.
- IITs, Engineering Colleges, Universities and other Academic Institutions.
- Management Institutions.
- Societies.
- Non-resident Indians who have come back to India.
- Individual consultants based on their long and rich professional experiences.

Though it has not been possible to assess exactly the number of professionals employed in the total consultancy profession, according to a tentative estimate made by the CDC and FIEO, in the light of a survey for their Directory, there are about 80,000 professionals now providing consultancy either individually or through institutions or organisations. The distribution based on number of professionals employed in consultancies is given below:

There are large organisations set up by the Government in the seventies. Initially they were formed either for export of consultancy, or for specific sectors such as power, fertilisers, roads, railways etc.

There are consultancy organisations set up around the same time as in-house consultancy. The captive consultants are part of large industrial, financial or contracting commercial enterprises.

These are medium and small size organisations set up and owned by independent practising consultants;

This is a relatively new type of consultancy which is of recent origin. A large number of senior officials both from Government and Industry on retirement from responsible positions provide consultancy in a variety of fields of their specialization-sometimes individually and at times, as a group.

Indian Consultancy covers a wide range of disciplines such as:

Agro based Industries	–	Housing
Airports	–	Hydrogeology
Architecture	–	Hdroelectric Power
Auditoria	–	Hy drological Surveys
Bricks & Tiles	–	Industrial Estate
Bridges	–	Industrial Process Engineering
Bus Transport	–	Hospitals
Ceramics	–	Hotel Development
Cement and Cement Machinery	–	Irrigation/Flood Control
Cold Storage	–	Land Reclamation
Coal & Coal based industries	–	Material Handling
Computer Services & Software	–	Man made fibres
Chemicals including fine and heavy		
Chemicals	–	Mineralogy
Drugs & Pharmaceuticals	–	Mineral Exploration
Dams	–	Non-ferrous Metal Processing
Drainage	–	Waste Utilisation
Effluent Treatment	–	Pharmaceuticals
Electricals	–	Pipelines
Electronics	–	Ports & Harbour
Engineering Industry	–	Pulp & Paper
Energy Conservation	–	Petroleum
Environmental Studies	–	Petrochemicals

Fertilisers	–	Pesticides & Insecticides
Food Processing	–	River/Sea Transport
Farm Mechanisation	–	Rubber
Ferrous & Non Ferrous Metallurgy	–	Soil Engineering
Geological Surveys	–	Structural Design
Geophysical Surveys	–	Subways
Geo. Tech. Engineering	–	Telecommunications
Heating/Ventilation/AC	–	Textiles
Hides & Leather	–	Thermal Power
Highways/Roads	–	Traffic Studies
Townships	–	Urban Planning

The spectrum of services covered by the Indian consultancy profession includes, among others, the following:

- Project Identification
- Preparation of Project Profiles
- Market Information & Detailed Market Surveys
- Pre-investment Profiles
- Techno-Economic Feasibility Reports
- Technology Evaluation/Procurement
- Materials Management
- Operation & Maintenance
- Design of Plant & Machinery
- Manpower Training
- Trouble Shooting and Debottlenecking
- Setting up R & D facilities
- Turn Key Projects
- Personnel Recruitment
- Production Planning

- Products Mix & Inventory Management
- Packaging Guidance & Support
- Technical Guidance & Support
- Personnel Management
- Financial Management
- Market Survey & Marketing Strategy
- Supervision of Construction & Commissioning
- Project Management
- Study of Sick Units
- Expansion and Diversification of Existing Units
- Preparation of Loan Applications for Financial Institutions.

The decade of the Eighties has witnessed a significant rise in export of Consultancy Services from India. The India Consultant is becoming increasingly popular in several world markets, because of his inovative and professional inputs, competence and competitive fees. In the last 10 years the export performance of Indian consultancy registered in increase from a modest Rs. 20.6 million in 1977-78 to over Rs. 1250 million in 1988-89.

The major areas in which Indian consultants have secured assignments are:

- Infrastructure consisting of Power generation & transmission, Ports, Telecommunication, Railways, Roads, Airports etc
- Agro-based Industries.
- Engineering Industries.
- Process Industries.
- Management Consultancy including Software.

The nature of services rendered includes preparation of feasibility reports, detailed project reports, engineering supervision, project implementation, civil structural and architectural designs, management, operation and maintenance of plants and services, design of equipment and plants, studies on rehabilitation of sick units, export of specialised software and application packages and to some extent computer aided design engineering. Some Indian consultants have also executed projects on turn-key basis.

Nearly 50% of the export earnings in the Management Consultancy section has been accounted for by the export of Computer Softwares. More than 80 Consultancy Organisations have exported software during the year 1987-88.

The markets for Indian Consultancy have included Austraila, Algeria, Bangladesh, Baharin, Belgium, Colombia, Cyprus, Denmark, Ethiopia, Jamaica, Japan, Jordan, Kenya, Kuwait, Libya, Laos, Malaysia, Mauritius, Mexico, Mozambique, Nigeria, Netherlands, Nepal, New Zealand, Oman, Philippines, Pakistan, Qatar, Switzerland, Singapore, Seychelles, Saudi Arabia, Sudan, Syria, Spain, Sweden, Thailand, Tanzania, Turkey, UK, USA, Ugada, UAE, USSR, Venezuela, YAR, Zambia, Zimbabwe, etc.

A summary of export earnings for the period 1978-79 to 1987-88.

Listed below are some of the major consultancy assignments abroad which have been won by Indian firms:

- Cement Plants at Saudi Arabia, Jedah, Iraq, Libya and South Yemen.
- Petrochemical Plant in Iran.
- Integrated Steel Plant in Nigeria.

- Rural Development Projects in Oman, Indonesia and Commonwealth of Dominica.
- Airports in Libya and Algeria.
- Public buildings in Southern Arabia, Tanzania, Oman.
- Irrigation and hydro projects in Burma.
- Power station in Malaysia.
- Solftware to U.K., West Germany, Austraila and USA.
- Gas Pipeline project in Nigeria.
- Management of Railways in Nigeria.
- Setting up of one million tonne direct reduction electric furnance steel plant in Nigeria.
- Thirty five telecom projects in 10 countries of Asia, Middle East, Africa and Kuwait.
- Transportation Plan for Sohar and Salalah, Sultanate of Oman.
- Municipal Roads in Abu Dhabi, UAE.
- Integrated Development of North Eastern Part of Sana'a, Yemen Arab Republic.
- Structure Plant for Salalah Coastal Plains, Oman.
- Comprehensive Area Development at Jibroo, Oman.
- Muscat Development Plan at Oman.
- Integrated Urban Development Plan for Sohar Town at Oman.
- Development of Muttrah Saq at Oman.
- Capital Complex at Muscat, Oman.

- Salalah Town Improvement at Oman.
- Bank Housing projects, Sana'a, Ymen Arab Republic.
- Labour Township Development at Sana'a, Ymen Arab Republic.
- Social Housing Complex at Bausher, Oman.
- Housing and Area Development at Dubai, UAE.
- Bustain Hotel Water Supply Scheme, Muscat, Oman.
- Water Supply for Taqa and Sudh Towns at Oman.
- Water Supply for Azaiba, Ghala and Bausher, Oman.
- Sewerage System for the Information City of Qurum, Iran
- Sewerage and Drainage for Bandar Abbas, Iran

There are three major associations of Consultants in India. They are:

(a) National Association of Consultancy Engineers (NACE)–Members are from corporate organisations--public and private. Their office is at:

Confederation of Engineering Industry
23-26 Industrial Area
Lodhi Road
New Delhi - 110003.

(b) Association of Consulting Engineers (ACE)—Members of ACE are mainly the independent consultants. Their office is at:

Association of Consulting Engineers
E-12 Defence Colony
New Delhi - 110024.

(c) Management Consultant Association of India (MCAI)—Members of MCAI are the management consultants both corporate (private and public) and also individuals. The office of the MCAI is at Bombay. They also have regional chapters at Delhi, Calcutta, Madras. Pune. Bangalore.

Recently another association called the "Association of Consulting Civil Engineers" (ACCE) has been formed. They also have regional chapters at Delhi, Calcutta, Bombay, Hyderabad, Madras, Bangalore etc.

It should be noted that the members of NACE and ACE are essentially tecnical consultants.

All these associations registered under the Indian Societies Act.

At present there are no exclusive institutes or agencies for imparting training in consultancy. Most of the Consultancy Organisations provide training to their new recruits and executives themselves. However since the Consultancy Development Centre came into being, it has set for itself a major task of organising training programmes to consultants and users of Consultants. CDC courses are open not only to Indians but Nationals of other countries as well. The short term and long term courses conducted by the CDC are:

	Topic		*Period*
(i)	Training for Graduate Engineers	:	1 year
(ii)	"How to select & use consultancy"	:	5 days
(iii)	"Effective use of consultancy"	:	3 days
(iv)	"Data management & correlation"	:	3 days
(v)	Programme for Advancement of Consultant Effectiveness (PACE)	:	3 days
(vi)	"How to do Consultancy" (for professionals & academicians)	:	2 days

(vii) CAD/CAM : Every Saturday with overall 75 lectures and 35 sessions.

The Management Consultancy Association of India (Bombay) is running a two year distance learning programme on Management Consultancy.

The Management Development Insitute, Gurgaon also conducts short-term courses on topics like Consultancy marketing etc.

The National Productivity Council of India conducts courses on specific areas like energy conservation, productivity improvement, Quality Control or other topics of interest to consultants.

In the colourful and fascinating "Texture" of a successful economy, infrastructure represents the 'weft and webs' of such an economic texture. Infrastructure is defined as 'the underlying capital of a society embodied in roads and other transportation and power and other public services. Sometimes it is referred to as social overhead capital. In a broad sense, infrastructure can also include the health, skills, education and other qualities and endowments of a population. Long range investment in infrastructure is often referred to as 'autonomous investment' which also includes long-range investment aimed at introducing major innovations. The capability of Indian Consultancy Organisations in the area of infrastructure includes Energy, Railways, Roads, Air ways, Ports and Harbours, Water Construction and Communication etc. as outlined briefly below:

Consultancy experience and capability in the energy field in India is impressive. India's ambitious energy programmes cover both conventional and non-conventional sources. On the one hand are the well-established hydro, thermal and nuclear power stations and on the other hand are the relatively new energy ventures with bio-gas, solar and tidal power.

The magnitude of development of this sector can be appreciated by the rate of growth since 1947, the year when India got freedom. The then installed power generating capacity was only 1360 MW which has multiplied 40 times during the last 40 years to the current level of 55000 MW (of installed capacity) with a target of 104000 MW by the year 1990-95. Sixty six per cent of the power generation is from thermal plants, thirty one per cent from hydro electric projects and the rest through nuclear and non conventional energy sources.

Indian consultancy organisations, both in the public and private sectors, are now capable of offering total turn-key packages for both conventional and non-conventional sources of power generation. A noteworthy feature of this development is that concurrent with the design and engineering capabilities, the fabrication capability for power equipment such as high pressure boilers, turbo generators up to 500 MW capacity, various auxiliary equipment, switching stations, circuit breakers, computerised process control system, transmission equipment, etc. have aslo been developed. Indian consultants and machinery manufactures are now in the world market bidding competitively for design, fabrication, supply and installation of power projects on a turn-key basis.

Indian expertise in power generation and transmission has also been exported to various developing countries. Among the major foreign assignments successfully executed by Indian firms are (i) thermal power station in Thambous (Iran) (ii) 1000 MW thermal power station in Saudi Arabia (iii) hydro electric project in Bhutan (iv) Homs power station at Libya (v)

Power transmission system in the Sultanate of Oman (vi) hydro-power generation in the Sultanate of Oman (vii) hydro-power generation in Iraq.

The Indian coastline about 5700 Kms. long has ten major operational ports and the 11th is under construction. In addition there are 19 intermediate and about 230 minor ports. While the operation and administration of these ports are carried out by statutory autonomous port trusts which have acquired considerable experience and expertise in port management, the technology for port construction is available with a number of private consultancy organisations. These organisations have not only built major ports in India but have also undertaken and completed similar projects in other parts of the world such as (i) rehabilitation of ports at various in Burma (ii) development of the Surabaya and Belawar ports in Indonesia.

The largest carriers of both men and material in India are the 'Indian Railways'-with a 62,000 Kms. long rail route and a network density of 1.9 kms/100sq. kms an average daily passenger load of about 3.5 million and an average annual freight carriage of about 320 million tonnes. This is considered the fourth largers railway network in the world and perhaps the largest in Asia. The Indian Railway, which is 135 year old, is today a totally self-reliant system in most aspects of operations including construction, traffic, maintenance and management. The study of transport planning systems with special reference to railways in Cuba, preparation of a feasibility study in Ethiopia, the rehabilitation of workshop and rolling stocks in Sudan and the operation and maintenance of the railway networks in Turkey, Libya, Zimbabwe, Ghana, Jordan, Nigeria, Iran etc. are typical examples of the successful projects executed abroad by Indian Railway Consultancy Organisations.

The Indian road network is one of the largest in the worked. The total road length, including the natioal highways, the state highways and other roads, exceeds half a million Kms. Considerable experience in roads construction and management has been gathered by consultancy organisations both in public and private sectors who are in a position to provide consultancy in every aspect of road construction and maintenance. Latest examples of the Indian consultancy capability in the area of roads & bridges, is the bridge across the Yamuma river in Delhi now under construction and considered the widest in Asia and the cable-stayed-bridge on the river Brahmaputra in the north eastern region.

A number of road construction projects in Libya, roads and road bridges in Iraq and similar projects in the Yemen Arab Republic have been completed by the Public Sector. India private consultants in this area have not lagged behind. Some of the major road projects constructed by private consultancy organisations abroad are the Flyover at Qatar; Bridge over Meherabad Airport, Ruseifa Interchange at Jordan; Trishuli Bridge & Devighat Bridge at nepal and railway bridges in Algeria and bridges in Iraq and Iran. The Indian consultant has also developed considerable capability in building roads in hilly tracks and inaccessible areas and maintaining them.

The International Airports Authority of India, a Government of India organisation, is a pioneer in airport design and constructrion. The 95 airports constructed, maintained and operated by the IAAI, handle anually about 80 million passengers, over 200 million tons of cargo and approximately 34,000 tons of mail. About 45 international carriers operate through major Indian airports. The IAAI has expertise in diverse fields ranging from airport pavement design construction of terminal buildings to airport lighting, communication and navigation, cargo terminals, computer aided designs and operating systems, airport management etc. A noteworthy feature which has gained international recognition of their air field pavement design is the concept based on layered system which is tailor-made to the requirement of site conditions.

The IAAI has rendered a variety of consultancy services including turnkey projects, in various countries such as Libya, Maldives, South Yemen, People's Democratic Republic of Yemen, Algeria, Nauru, Mauritius, etc.

India has numerous achievements in telecommunications. Cities, towns and villages having telephones have gone up from 659 to over 35,000 and the number of telephones has gone up twenty seven times from 1,68,000 to 45,00,000. Telex facilities have been provided to 220 cities and towns. Over 170 countries are connected with International Subscriber Trunk Dialing (ISTD) facility besides 500 towns and cities which are already in the national STD hook-up. Commercial production based on these designs is expected to commence soon. Worldwide computer to computer communictation has just commenced. Electro-mechanical exchange are replacing manual exchanges leading to programme controlled analogue and digital electronic exchanges. The thrust towards modernisation is a continues process. With the strenth of such accumulated and well-developed knowledge in telecomunications, India now holds a commanding position in telecommunication consultancy.

Telecommunication Consultants India Limited (TCIL) is the only organisation of its kind in India that has developed and designed several integrated telecommunication systems covering long distance radio links, dedicated land lines, underground mine communication and mobile links. TCIL has executed a number of major telecommunication projects in other parts of the world such as the installation and maintenance of different types of the electronic PABX in Kuwait, installantion, commissioning and testing of 600 kms. micro wave system in Turkey, management of telecommunication centre in Nigeria, operation of cable network in Jordan, operation and maintenance of the micro wave network in Saudi Arabia, besides a number of similar jobs in other countries like Sri Lanka, Bhutan, Maldives, Abu Dhabi and Iraq

Perhaps the major area of strength in Indian consultancy in construction. This includes industrial building, housing-both urban and rural, bridges, flyovers, multi-story buildings, hotels, stadia, etc. This is almost a domain of private consultancy organisations who have developed enormous design and construction capability. There are also some public sector organisations engaged in construction activities. Numerous Indian architects, reputed contractors and a number of R & D institutions have all contributed to the competent construction consultancy base in India.

Water resources development for multiple benefits and generation of power through hydel schemes to meet the energy needs of the country, have been occupying a key position in all the developmental plans in India during the last 40 years. The major areas developed include river systems, irrigation, flood control, water conservation and ground water development.

With an experience of several decades in all aspects of water resources development, the Central Water Commission has the expertise and know-how of the latest technique and designs of river valley projects, dams barrages, navigation locks, water conductor systems, canal structures, power houses, dam safety devices, storm water drainage system, anti-sea erosion measures, collection and collation of hydro-meteorological data, flood forecasting etc. The Central Water Commission and the Water & Power Consultancy (India) Limited, a public sector organisation, have executed a number of projects abroad. Some of these are the Sedewayi Project (Burma), Salma Dam (Afghanistan), Khanabad Barrage Project (Afghanistan) etc.

The National Buildings Construction Corporation Limited (NBCC), a Central public sector company, under the administrative control of the Ministry of Urban Affairs and Employment, continued to fulfil its commitments to the development of infrastructure in the country and development of projects both within India and abroad. The Corporation from a mere beginning of simple building construction activities in the early 1960s has now established itself in high-tech construction, real estate sector, etc. It is proud to be ranked as a number one company in the country for construction of high rise chimneys, TV towers, silos, etc. It has become a MOU signing company from 1992-93. Based on evaluation of its performance on MOU parameters, its performance has been rated as 'Good' by the Department of Public Enterprises.

In view of the liberalisation and de-regulation of the economy, the Corporation has entered into an agreement with M/s. Balke Durr Cooling Tower Limited, a world leading German company in the field of designing, planning and construction of cooling towers and thermal power plants to take up the cooling tower projects in India and abroad.

Hindustan Prefab Limited (earlier known as Hindustan Housing Factory), New Delhi has been in existence since partition of the country and became a fully-owned Government company in 1955. It was the first company in India which specialised in manufacturing of Prefab Housing using light weight autoclaved concrete. Presently it is engaged in the construction of pre-stressed concrete bridges, railway sleepers and electric poles. The company also does a large amount of construction work at site including prestigious World Bank projects.

The company has earned a name for itself in Northern and Western Railways' guage conversion works. It has completed all the bridges in Delhi-Rewari Section, Jodhpur-Merta Road-Phulera Section, Rewari-Hissar, Sirsa-Bhatinda Section, Jodhpur-Jaisalmer Section and the Sabi river bridge on the Rewari-Jaipur Section. The last named bridge has been a landmark for the company. Within a period of one year, 89 spans were completed along with sub-structure. It also manufactures various other precast concrete components for the PWDs and the New Delhi Municipal Council. The company has also done a Real Estate Project in South Delhi and quality housing at HUDCO Place, New Delhi. It has acquired an all India stature with projects in Delhi, Haryana, Bihar, West Bengal, MP, Maharashtra and Gujarat.

The National Capital Resgion Planning Board (NCRPB) has been set up with statutory powers under the NCR Planning Board Act, 1985, to plan and promote a balanced and harmonised development of the region which covers an area of 30,242 sq km comprising the whole of Delhi (1,483 sq km) and part of the three adjoining states of Haryana (13,413 sq km), Rajasthan (4,493 sq km) and Uttar Pradesh (10,833 sq km). The NCR is envisaged to be developed in accordance with the policies and programmes enunciated under the Regional Plan-2001 for NCR which is in force since January 1989. The development steategy evolved by the NCR Planning Board include, *inter-alia,* the integrated development of new townships alongside the existing priority towns selected for accelerated development, by providing commensurate infrastructure support both at regional and local levels to create economic momentum in their growth and expansion, which, in turn will generate abundant employment opportunities and higher income for its people. In accordance with this strategy, the Regional Plan envisages to deflect about two million people by the year 2001 of the following priority towns: (i) Meerut; (ii) Bulandshahr; (iii) Khurja; (iv) Hapur; (v) Panipat; (vi) Rohtak; (vii) Palwal; (viii) Rewari; (ix) Dharuhera; (x) Bhiwadi; and (xi) Alwar.

Besides the above, the Regional Plan also envisages to develop 34 subregional centres within the NCR and five counter-magnet areas outside the NCR located in Punjab, Madhya Pradesh, Rajashtan, Haryana and Uttar Pradesh. This development can be made practically functional only if it is backed and supported by regional physical infrastructure and economic linkages. With this in view, the Regional Plan also emphasises the development of proper transport (expressways and highways and railways), tele-communications, power and other regional infrastructure along with providing for a package of fiscal measures to help decongest the Capital.

For the overall development of the Region in accordance with the Regional Plan-2001, the Board has estimated an overall investment of Rs. 45,000 crore by 2001, out of which, about Rs. 17,000 crore is required for infrastructure development by the public sector (Centre, NCRPB, states and their implementing agencies), and Rs. 28,000 crore by the private sector for creating economic infrastructure as well as housing and other facilities. For the Regional development projects both by Central ministries and the NCRPB jointly with state governments, the Board has approved an investment programme of Rs. 3,813 crore for the Eighth Plan (1992-97) of which Rs. 1,868 crore is for stae sector projects, and Rs. 1,967 for Central sector projects.

The Central sector schemes relate to the augmentation of rail network, construction of expressways, laying of telecommunication network, etc. while those under the state sector involve the development of new townships, costruction and maintenance of regional roads and providing transmission and distribution network for power supply

The genesis of Central Public Works Department (CPWD) can be traced to 19th century when Ajmer Provincial Division was created in 1863. The department acquired a size and stature from the year 1911 when it had to play a key role in creation of infrastructure for shifting of National Capital from Calcutta to Delhi. During this period, the Department constructed the Rashtrapati Bhawan, North Block, South Block, Parliament House, etc. The Department was formally constituted as CPWD in 1930. Presently, the CPWD with its headquarters located at New Delhi, headed by Director General (Works), is having its offices all over the country. It has zonal chief engineers at Delhi, Bombay, Calcutta, Madras, Siliguri, and Shillong. The CPWD provides integrated construction management services from project concept to completion stage. The scope of its activities extends to construction of residential, non-residential institutional and educational buildings, sports complexes, hospitals, runways, airports, computer centres, embassies, *samadhis* and landscaping works. The CPWD has even gone to the borders of the country at the remote and difficult areas and has executed fencing roads and flood lighting.

The *Vigyan Bhawan* at Delhi which was extensively damaged by fire in April 1990 has been renovated and refurnished to the international standards recently by CPWD. It has constructed a highly challenging and time bound project at Hall of Special Displays at Pragati Maidan, Delhi costing nearly Rs. 20 crore within six months time to meet the deadline for India International Trade Fair 1994. The Hall was inaugurated and dedicated to the nation by Hon'ble Prime Minister of India on 19 November 1994. The CPWD constructed fencing in Punjab, Rajasthan sectors in over 780 km length. Another about 700 km of road in Indo-Bangladesh border in West Bengal sector has also been completed and fencing in 185 km has been completed. The Indo-Pak borders have been provided with flood lighting in over 800 km length. The works of re-development of *Vijay Ghat* and *Kisan Ghat Samadhis* are nearing completion and *Vir Bhumi,* the *Samadhi* of former Prime Minister late Shri Rajiv Gandhi, is in progress. The other important buildings in progress in Delhi are Parliament Library Building, Intelligence Bureau building and Indira Gandhi National Open University and extension of Supreme Court, National Security Guard Project at Gurgaon and *Bhasha Bhawan* (Ministry of Culture) at Calcutta. Infrastructural support for National Festivals such as 15 August at Red Fort and 26 January at *Rajpath* in Delhi are being managed by CPWD.

The CPWD has taken a lead in environment friendly construction. The landmark decision ha been taken to ban the use of solid wood in its construction starting from April 1993. It has introduced various possible wood substitutes available such as medium density fibre boards, waste wood particle boards, pressed steel, cement based particle boards and PVC. Further, some more wood substitutes lie red mud, polymer glass, reinforced gypsum board and rice husk are bing developed with the assistance of research laboratories. Usage of plantation timer like rubber wood, eucalyptus and bamboo is also being promoted. This will help protect the environment both by stoppage of cutting of forests and usage of waste which otherwise litter up the usable land The flyash bricks, which are ecofriendly are being used on some works as a substitute for traditional bricks. The energy efficient housing project consisting of 135 quarters adopting solar passive architecture at Delhi has been completed. The efforts are also in progress for developing appropriate housing cluster and design of individual dwelling units with thermal comfort and day lighting.

The CPWD also provides consultancy services for various public sector organisations and autonomous bodies for their planning and designs of major buildings, projects, complex structures, air conditioning and electrical installations, etc. It has all in-house facilities for planning, designing construction management and human resource development and undertakes deposit works of various nature from different autonomous agencies. CPWD has a mindset for quality assurance and has taken a quantum jump in this field by establishing the first ready mix concrete plant facility for all consumers in the city of Delhi. It has also risen to the need of the present day project management system, considering the modern client-contractor relationship, and has modified its contract forms which are used by almost all Government/semi-government bodies in India.

Other careers

Youth from rural areas migrate to cities in search of jobs and vocational pursuits. They are generally ignorant that wider opportunities are lying at their door steps which they are not able to recognize for lack of proper knowledge, training and sills. They are educated at schools and colleges where apart from book knowledge there is no in—flow for recent developments in the economic activities opening new avenues for self—

employment in their own villages or neighbourhoods. Merchant Banking and Financial Services are such areas in where no knowledge of this concept of practical know—how is provided to the youth at college level because their teachers themselves are ignorant about new developments.

This focuses on two main aspects:

— Which are the areas in rural surroundings where merchant banking and financial services of different types could offer employment or self—employed opportunities for the educated youth in rural and semi—urban areas?

— How the youth could be prepared for doing these activities in rural areas?

The first question requires a probe into those few activities out of well–defined list of merchant banking and financial services activities which are useful to rural economy and can be taken up to serve the rural folks engaged in farming, animal husbandary and allied agricultural activities besides normal commercial outfits engaged in supplying the consumers goods of day to day household needs.

There are several non—fund based and fund based activities from the point of view of rural economic conditions. One must understand the scope and coverage of a few of such activities and select out of them the appropriate ones suiting rural background for gainfully engaging the rural youth.

Generally, the non—fund based activities include selling corporate securities offered under capital issue management and private placement of securities, credit/ fund syndication, corporate counselling, NRI counselling, trustee management, portfolio management, managing mergers and amalgamation or takeovers, management of buy—ins and buy—outs, financial engineering and capital restructuring, corporate reorganisation, inter-corporate investments of funds, lease booking, etc.

Whereas fund based activities are underwriting of equity/preference share, bonds and debentures to new capital issues, dealing in money market instruments particularly arranging for certificate of deposits, commercial paper and treasury bills, inter–corporate deposits, undertaking equipment—leasing, venture capital financing, working capital financing, mutual fund activities, and dealing in secondary market, after obtaining membership of stock exchanges, inter corporate placement of fund, etc.

For doing some of the above activities, the service provider has to be registered with Securities Exchange Board of India (SEBI) under SEBI Act, 1992 and the specific regulations and rules provided therefore. The services which require prior authorisation from SEBI are both primary as well as secondary capital market activities. Amongst primary capital market activities, requiring SEBI authorisation, are merchant banking activity relting to capital issues management, underwriting of capital issues and rendering capital issues related advisory services. The activities of Registrar to the Issues and bankers to the issues do fall within the ambit of SEBI and required registrations. For the secondary market activities the important role is played by stock broker and subbroker. Both of these intermediaries require registration with SEBI. Portfolio management is another service to cater to the needs of investors in both the markets that require SEBI approval. Other activities requiring SEBI approval are credit rating, factoring and mutual funds.

Out of the above merchant banking and financial services, there are several activities which can be carried on very well by the rural based educated youth on commission basis as agents. These activities are selling public issues as sub—brokers, selling units of mutual funds as agents of mutual funds, selling insurance products of insurance companies, mobilising as agents the savings of rural folk for banks or company's fixed deposits, postal saving schemes, acting as agents of portfolio managers, running chit fund schemes, etc. against commission basis.

The rural based youth will be in a better position to render these services to rural community for several reasons, for example:

— The know the savers, investors personally and they can repose confidence in them to buy investment products.

— They will be serving the rural folk at their door steps which will save time and money, i.e. the expenses to be incurred in going to cities for the same purpose.

— The big merchant bankers and other business runners need not spend money on marketing efforts as the rural based youth will be acting for them as agents, local representative at nominal charges.

— The rural economy will develop as a result of spread effect and linkages being established through these financial services activities.

Apart from the above activities, there is a very big scope for carrying in rural areas the fund based activities which suits the rural community. These activities could be as under:

— Leasing of agricultural equipment to rural folk for carrying on farming, allied agricultural activities by supply of equipments like tractor, trollies, etc.

— Providing consumer finance for purchasing durable consumer goods for household needs to rural people like, vehicles, TVs, refrigerators etc.

The history of economic development of industrially developed nations of Europe and America shows that the pace of economic development is accelerated through merchant banking and financial services and if these activities are started in rural areas it will help in revitalising our economy.

The next question is how to start these services in rural areas. Given the presumption of ignorance and lack of knowledge amongst rural educated youth non—government voluntary organisations should be encouraged through government to create awareness in the semi–urban and rural areas involving the district planning and block development machinery and Zila Parishads and Panchayats while holding seminar, symposium etc. In north, Indian Institute of Merchant Banking, a non—government voluntary organisation, promoted by some dedicated academics and professional merchant bankers based at New Delhi has been imparting training through professional development courses by correspondence in merchant banking, financial services, stock market operations, investment counsellling and agent's operations.

Resettlement and re-employment

In order to maintain a youthful profile of the Armed Forces, over 55,000 service personnel are retired/released every year at a comparatively young age. Majority of service personnel at the time of retirement are at an age where they have numerous unfinished responsibilities which necessitate their taking up of a second career. The Government is seized of this problem of rehabilitating them through provision of employment in organised sector or through self-employment. The welfare of ex-servicemen has been accepted as a national responsibility.

The Directorate General of Resettlement (DGR) under the Ministry of Defence (MOD) has been set up to look after all matters connected with resettlement and welfare of ex-servicemen and their dependents. A Kendriya Sainik Board under the Chairmanship of *Raksha Mantri* has been established for laying down general policy for the welfare of ex-servicemen and their dependents, for the administration of welfare funds, and also for coordinating the work of the Sainik Boards in the country. At the state level, the Rajya Sainik Boards, and at the district level the Zila Sainik Boards, have been established. The Government of India bears 50 per cent of the expenditure incurred on the organisations of Rajya and Zila Sainik Boards, the remaining expenditure is borne by the respective state governments.

Resettlement activities for the retired/retiring service personnel consist of the following: (a) training programmes to reorient retiring Defence personnel towards civil emploment; (b) providing re-employment opportunities in government/semi-government/public sector organisations and (c) schemes for self-employment.

In order to equip retiring service personnel for employment, suitable training programmes have been devised. They equip them for employment in civil organisations and for self-employment. For retiring service officers, the following training programmes were introduced during 1994-95: (a) Diploma in Industrial Security and Labour Laws; (b) Coaching for Air Line Transport Pilot Licence/Senior Commercial Pilot Licence/Commercial Helicopter Pilot Licence; (c) Consultant in ISO-9000; (d) Quality Assurance Manager ISO-9000 and (e) Deputy Quality Assurance Manager ISO-9000. Up to March 1995, 882 officers were trained. The vocational training, ITI training and on the job training are presently being conducted for retiring Service personnel other than officers.

Re-employment constitutes a major means of rehabilitation of ex-servicemen. To achieve this goal both the Central and state governments have provided various concessions/facilities. These include reservation of posts, relaxations in age/educational standards, priority in employment etc. The Central Government has reserved 10 per cent of Group 'C' and 20 per cent of Group 'D' posts for ex-servicemen in Central ministries/ departments. The percentage of reservation in public sector undertakings and nationalised banks in these are 14½ and 24½ per cent respectively. Besides, there is 10 per cent reservation for the post of Assistant Commandants in para-military Forces. Reservation under the state governments varies from two per cent to 20 per cent. There is no reservation for ex-servicemen in Bihar, Kerala and Megahalaya.

DGR has been nominating ex-servicemen security agencies to various PSUs and private sector organisations. These security agencies provide employment opportunities for officers and other ranks. There are over 173 ex-servicemen security agencies which are registered with DGR, of which 130 have been sponsored for work. This alone has generated employment opportunities for over 6,419 ex-servicemen and over 250 officers.

There is considerable scope for absorption of ex-servicemen in para-military forces like CRPF, BSF, ITBP, CISF, etc. However, the response of ex-servicemen for joining these forces has been generally poor. With a view to achieve fuller utilisation of reserved vacancies, special recruitment rallies were organised in selected states. During 1993, special recruitment drives were conducted by CISF.

The concept of Ecological Task Force was mooted in 1992 for the purpose of restoring the forest cover in regions where significant deforestation had taken place. These units were initially raised in three states *viz.*, Uttar Prasdesh, Rajasthan and J&K. The task forces are manned by ex-servicemen who are paid salaries as per TA scales. Every individual, irrespective of his rank prior to retirement, is re-employed as a sepoy. Ministry of Defence provides officers to command these units.

Self-Employment

Important schemes for self employment for ex-servicemen are SEMFEX-I, SEMFEX-II and SEMFEX-III. These schemes have been launched in collaboration with the Small Industries Development Bank of India, NABARD and the Khadi and Village Industries Commission for providing extensive self-employment opportunities for ex-servicemen and their dependents.

The SEMFEX-I Scheme was launched in April, 1987. Under this Scheme, financial assistance is provided to ex-servicemen to set up small industrial projects for self-employment. Loans under this Scheme are provided by the respective State Financial Corporation. As on 31 December 1994 there were 6,686 beneficiaries and the amount sanctioned is to the tune of Rs. 179.27 crore since inception.

The SEMFEX-II Scheme was launched in January 1988 by the DGR in collaboration with the National Bank for Agricultural and Rural Development (NABARD) to provide assistance for agricultural and allied activities. Under the Scheme, financial assistance up to Rs. 7.5 lakh for setting up of industrial units/service establishments is given. The ceiling of Rs. 7.5 lakh is, however, not applicable for setting up of units relating to agro-industries. Since inception and up to December 1994 loans amounting to Rs. 12.30 crore have been sanctioned to 2,352 beneficiaries.

The SEMFEX-III Scheme was launched in October 1991 in collaboration with the Khadi and Village Industries Commission (KVIC). It provides self employment opportunities for setting up village industries under the purview of KVIC. Under this Scheme, ex-servicemen and their widows are eligible to take up self-employment ventures. Financial assistance for such ventures is provided under a liberalised pattern of assistance by the KVIC. The loans granted to village industries under this Scheme carry a rate of interest of four per cent and there is no interest on loan for *Khadi* units. The Scheme is picking up. Up to December 1994, a loan of Rs. 1.42 crore was sanctioned in 188 cases.

Schemes have also been launched in collaboration with Bombay Mercantile Cooperative Bank and Oriental Bank of Commerce to provide financial assistance to ex-servicemen and their widows on easy terms. In addition to the above schemes for financial assistance, certain other measures have also been taken to assist ex-servicemen in their self employment ventures. These are: (a) Allotment of sheds/plots; (b) Price subsidy to ex-servicemen units; (c) Allotment of surplus class V-B vehicles; (d) Allotment of repairable typewriters and duplicators; (e) Transportation of bulk LPG; (f) Allotment of Mother Dairy milk booths, fruit and vegetable outlets; (g) Transportation of coal and (h) Allotment of petroleum product agencies.

Welfare

Before April, 1993 there were four separate funds *viz.*, amalgamated Special Fund for War Bereaved, War Disabled and other ex-Servicemen/serving personnel; (i) Flag Day Fund; (ii) ST Dunstan's (India) and KSB Fund and (iv) Indian Gorkha Ex-Servicemen's Welfare Fund These separate funds have been merged into an 'Armed Forces Flag Day Fund'.

The Kendriya Sainik Board (KSB) administers 'Armed Forces Flag Day Fund' for the welfare and rehabilitation of ex-servicemen, war widows, disabled service personnel and their dependents. The total corpus of the fund, as on 31 March 1995 was Rs. 45.60 crore. The corpus of the fund is invested with Banks/PSUs. The income accruing from interest is utilised for the various welfare activities. In the year 1994-95, Rs. 2.20 crore were spent on the major welfare activities. Financial assistance is also provided to institutions such as Paraplegic Homes at Kirkee and Mohali, Cheshire Homes, Military Hospitals, St. Dunstan After Care Organisations and Homes for taking care or old and physically handicapped ex-servicemen and their dependents. Financial assistance is also provided to individual ex-servicemen suffering from serious diseases for treatment in civil hospitals in case they cannot be treated in Military Hospitals and have not availed similar assistance from any other source. During 1994-95, a sum of Rs. 20,59,719.60 was sanctioned for the treatment of serious diseases.

To collect reliable data about ex-servicemen/widows population and update it on a regular basis a census of ex-servicemen is being carried out by DGR through Zila Sainik Boards (ZSBs) with effect from 15 May 1992. The Scheme envisages registration of retired defence service personnel with their ZSBs and issue of I-cards to the eligible ex-servicemen/widows. As per the feedback received, a total of 12.01 lakh ex-servicemen and 2.06 lakh widows have been registered and were reported to be surviving as on 31 December 1994.

The Government has been granting various concessions to ex-servicemen from time to time. The major concessions granted to different categories of personnel or their dependents cover assistance in the field of education, reservation for wards in professional institutions, reservations in Sainik Schools and Military

Schools, medical treatment, assistance for construction/repair of houses, financial assistance for the marriage of daughters, canteen facilities, rail and air travel concessions. Besides, financial assistance from the Raksha Mantri's Discretionary Fund (RMDF) is given to old and infirm exservicemen and to their widows in indegent circumstances.

The revised rates of financial assistance are: (a) Assistance to old infirm ex-servicemen/widows of ex-servicemen Rs. 250 per month for two years; (b) Marriage of daughters of ex-servicemen/widows in penury Rs. 4000; (c) Repair of house for ex-servicemen/widows in penury Rs. 5,000; (d) Medical treatment-depending upon the nature and gravity of ailment subject to a maximum of Rs. 8,000; (e) Education of children of ex-servicemen/widows in penury Rs. 35 per month per child for up to three children up to class X and (f) Other cases in respect of ex-servicemen/widows in penury (like natural calamities, accidental death or where RM/RRM feel that the case deserves sysmpathetic consideration–no single transaction to exceed Rs. 8,000.

Inter-ministerial committee

In pursuance of the recommendation of the high level empowered committee headed by the *Raksha Mantri* on improvement in the retirement pensions of Defence Personnel, the Ministry of Defence constituted an Inter-Ministerial Committee to deal with the problems of ex-servicemen other than those relating to pensionary matters. Accordingly, a committe under the chairmanship of an Additional Secretary in the Ministry of Defence was set up. This committee included representatives from the Ministry of Finance, Ministry of Law, Department of Pension and Pension and Pensioners' Welfare and other relevant organisations. The Committee considered 53 demands of ex-servcemen. It has recommended/partly recommended 33 demands, noted that five demands were not found justified. The demands which have already been accepted by Government are: (i) Permission for commercial employment after retirement; (ii) Provision of Soft Seed Capital Assistance under SEMFEX-II Scheme; (iii) Non-allotment of oil production agencies to ex-servicemen/widows; (iv) Reservation in purchase from ex-servicemen entrepreneurs; and (v) Issue of Last Pay Certificate along with discharge certificate.

Employment programmes

In working out the size of the wage employment programmes, we have to ensure that at least one member of every family below the poverty line gets employment for a minimum of 100 days in a year to cover the seasonal unemployment. The 38th round of NSSO has estimated about 44 million families below the poverty line in rural areas (in 1983—84) and providing employment to one member each of such families for 100 days would requre employment generation of 4,400 million mandays.

If we take the poverty estimates of the 43rd round of NSSO and average size of family as 4.5, there are about 30 million families who are below the poverty line. To provide 100 days of employment to one member of each family, 3,000 million mandays will be required. At present, abut 24 million persons have got themselves registered under EAS and this figure would go up as EAS will be implemented throughout the country (till October 1996, EAS was limited to 3,206 blocks only).

The poor people seeking employment could roughly go up tc 35 million or so, when EAS would be extended to the entire country in 1997—98. During the normal years, we, therefore, have to generate about 3,000—3,500 million mandays in a year to meet the assurance of 100 employment to all those rural poor who need and seek employment. At present, the weighted average minimum wage is about Rs. 30 per manday and taking into account the wage material ratio of 60 40, thecost of generation of one manday would be Rs. 50. For generation of 3,000—3,500 million mandays,l we would reqquire Rs. 15,000—16,500 crore every year.

Given the resources, it may, however, not be possible for the Indian economy to support such a massive programme. But then, the implementation of the Maharashtra EGS show that all the poor may not turn up for the kind of work provided under wage employment programmes. The actual requirement of funds would be somewhat less than the projections above. The provision of Rs. 60,000 crore in the Ninth Plan for rural employment, the major portion of which would go to the wage employment programmes, should, therefore, be sufficient to take care of the lowest rung of poverty.

The wage employment programmes in India started from the experimentation/pilot phases, in the 1960s and the 70s and then consolidated in the 80s and are now moving towards a scenario which guarantees employment, although it is beyond the economic capacity of the Centre for the present. We are in the assurance kind of scenario, where the implementation of EAS would certainly mitigate the hardships of the poorest of the poor in the rural areas by providing employment and food security in terms of increased purchasing power and distribution of food grains.

The point that the present wage employment programmes in India are based on the vast experiences of the implementation, would strengthen our optimism in the Ninth Plan in which we would be moving towards a full employment situation. It is also heartening to note that during the Ninth Plan, EAS along with JRY would become perhaps the largest wage employment programme of its kind anywhere in the world.

We are on the threshold of the Ninth Five Year Plan, where available indications are that Rs. 60,000 crore will be provided for rural employment and a major portion of this allocation will be going for the wage employment schemes like the Jawahar Rizgar Yojana (JRY) and the Employment Assurance Scheme (EAS). India lives in villages, where agriculture provides employment to about teo—thirds of the population.

Agriculture, being seasonal in nature, cannot provide employment year round. The continuous increase in population worsened the unemployment problem in rural areas and the Indian economy has, therefore, always been in less than full employment situation, which itself experience seasonal agricultural peaks and troughs. There has always been a fap betweenf full employment situation and the actual availability of employment.

This gap becomes worse in lean agricultural season and alarming during droughts and famine—like conditions. To bridge this gap, various wage employment programmes were launched by the Centre from time to time, like the Food for Work Programme (FWP) in 1977, the National Rural Employment Programme (NREP) in 1980, the Rural Landless Employment Gurantee Programme (RLEGP) in 1983, the Jawahar Rozgar Yojana (JRY) in 1989 and the Employment Assurance Scheme (EAS) in 1993.

Wage employment programmes

FWP: The culmination of earlier experiences of the implementation of wage employment programmes was the Food for Work Programme (FWP) which was started as a non—plan scheme to augment the funds of State governments for maintenance of public works on which large investment had been made in the past by utilizing available stocks of food grains. There were, however, lot of expectations from the programme but is did not make much headway in the beginning due to certain constraints inherent in the scheme itself. On review of this programme and the difficulties experienced by the States, the scheme was liberalized to include all ongoing plan non—plan works and new items of public and community works. The basic objectives of FWP were to generate additional gainful employment for unemployed and underemployed persons in the rural areas and to improve the incomes and nutritional levels (as wages were to be paid in food grains). While generating employment, durable community assets were to be created which would strengthen the rural infrastructure and result in higher production and better living standard in rural areas. The idea was also to utilize thesurplus food grains for development of human resources and employment creation.

A total of 979.32 million mandays' employment was generated during the period from 1977—78 to 1979–80 (September). This scheme became very popular in the rural areas and came to be recognized as a major instrument of rural employment. A number of deficiencies were also noticed in the implementation of the Food for Work Programme including erratic disbursement of food grains as wages, delay in measurement ofearth work, non—durability of the assets created under the programme, inadequate technical supervision of works and the lack of proper supervision which led to dilution of technical requirement of the projects.

NREP: The FWP was restructured and renamed as National Rural Employment Programme (NREP) in

October, 1980 as a culmination of previous experiences in this field. The programme became part of the VI Five Year Plan from April, 1981 andwas implemented as a Centrally—sponsored scheme on a 50:50 sharing basis between the Centre and States with the three—fold objectives of generation of additional gainful employment, creation of durable comunity assets and raising of the nutritional standards of the rural poor. The programme envisaged an outlay of Rs. 1,620 crore including the States' matching share during the VI Plan period to generate additonal employment opportunities to the extent of 300 to 400 million mandays per year, simultaneously creating durable community assets.

Sixth Plan & RLEGP: During the VI Plan, the total expenditure on implementation of NREP was Rs. 1,873 crore as against the outlay of Rs. 1,620 crore including the States'share. The target of employment generation as envisaged under the Plan was also achieved. The total employment generation during the period was 1,775.18 million mandays.

The midterm appraisal of the VI Plan, however, pointed out that the hard core of rural poverty pertaining to employment opportunities particularly for the landless during the lean agriculture periods, (when work in agriculture is scarce) had to be tackled in a much more direct and special manner. It was, therefore, though that at least one member from each landless household should be provided employment up to 100 days in a year. With this end in view, the Rural Landless Employment Guarantee Programme (RLEGP) was launched in August, 1983, as a fully funded programme by the Central government and was implemented in additon to the National Rural Employment Programme covering the entire country.

During the VII Plan, an expenditure of Rs. 7,809.93 crore was made and 3,496.30 million mandays' employment was generated under NREP and RLEGP. While these two programmes have been able to exceed the financial and physical targets, it has not been possible to provide 100 days of employment to at least one member of each landless household in a year as envisaged under RLEGP.

For want of good opportunities in India, talented young men and women are now seeking employment with American software firms. We seem to have an edge in the field of software, which is internationally recognized. The Ninth Plan should provide a framework to utilise the talent within the country. There is no use in simply appealing to the young people in the name of national interests without giving them an opportunity and a fair deal to utilize their talent.

It is comforting that the Ninth Plan approach has spoken of the need to nuture and support fully scientific talent with exceptional capabilities. The approach paper says that facilities comparable to international standards will be offered to them so as to enable them to carry out outstanding research within the country. More Centres of Excellence will be created and they will be encouraged to function in close co–ordination with institutions of higher learning to supply future manpower needs for thenational S & T programme.

The preoccupation with the demands of the rising middle class has led to an obsession with consumer goods in the production pattern of the country. While there is nothing basically wrong in catering to this market, the needs of the majority of the people below the poverty line have been given less importance. This is a pity because many of the CSIR laboratories have done excellent work that is relevant to the poor in the villages but is should be applied on a large scale.

The late Dr. Y. Nayudamma pleaded for a social bias in scientific applications. He pointed out that it is fashiionable (and paying) to do research in frontier areas. But not all frontier areas are relevent or urgent to the needs of our country. While no one denies the right of a talented person to contribute to the world's pool of knowledge whithout any national inhibitions, it is essential that the major emphasis should be to make life a bit easier for the underprivileged among us. This calls for a change in the value system. At present, none would rate a researcher n say, cowdung utilization high. AddressingWestern–oriented priorities gives better recognition!

When Dr Nayudamma assumed charge of the CSIR, he drastically reduced hundreds of needless procedures that had only delayed matters. He proved to be an excellent administrator.

However, red tape has great attraction for scientists, who want to become administrators. Even Fellows of the Royal Society have succembed to the lure of power, though, thanks to our ministers, powers to such technocrats have been effectively reduced.

Frustration: This brings out a deeper problem. The lure of easy money in banking and management has drained S & T areas of young talent. This has led to a lot of frustration among scientists. It is a pity that only a handful of science talent marit scholars end up with science degrees or as scientists. To be a scientist is no longer socially, financially or intellectually attractive. Our scientific establishment, with a few exceptions, lack in good public relations. Most scientists cannot communicate their work and ideas in a user—friendly manner. They generally (with some exceptions) look down upon those who try to popularize their work. Their sights are set elsewhere. Humility, which is the halmark of a true scientist has become a rare quality! Their dialogue is addressed to ever—narrowing circles of a few highbrows! In sum, the main issues in S & T involve several hard choices.

First, the lion's share now going to Space and Atomic Energy calls for a review. People are disillusioned why Space should continue to get so much money. However many big rockets are needed, for instance, to launch our INSATs which in any case last for more than seven years now—a days? If there is no scope for exports of rocket subsystems, where is the rationale for the huge outlay on big rockets? A credible answer is called for to justify the status quo. While remote sensing satellites and rockets for launching them may be justified, it is difficult to convince the common people about the need for large boosters, when such rockets are commercially available elsewhere at reasonable prices (which are only occasional expenses). In Atomic Energy also, there has been no convincing answer to the problem of safety. If it is a rocket or a plen, the damage from failure is limited. In the case of nuclear waste contamm nation,l the consequences affect generations and are simply too tragic for words. With all the massive investments, nuclear power accounts for an insignificant portion of the power supply. The position may change but as of now, people do not have high hopes about it.

Second, agriculture needs a new deal in terms ofinfusing environmentally—friendly technologies particularly in reducing the use of chemical fertilizers.

Third, let the industry pay for R & D useful to it. There is no justification to protect obsolete industries. This is a false patriotism. The government can then concentrate on socially significant research where profit—driven industries hesitate to go in. Foreign technology for consumer items should be limited to upgrading items of mass consumption. The Western culture of creating non–essential wants (through advertising) need not be encouraged.

Above all, there should be a wider debate (not confined to scientists only) on the S & T issue. The worst scenario would be public indifference, making it easy for a few scientists (with their own selfish agenda) to call the shots.

Critical issues

Faith in & Use of Selection Procedure : The massive publicity and tremendous thrust given by the Government coupled with the increasing unemployment among educated youth caused in influx of seminal enthusiastic individuals to take up entrepreneurial career. Enthusiasm creates a complex problem for the support agencies in the matter of choice of individuals to given necessary support for enterprise launching and management. There is always a danger by supporting those who are not genuinely interest but have been attracted to the support programme for many other reasons. The resources used for developing such persons by way of investment on training etc. often go waste. Besides being wastage of scarce resources, the wrong selection may also contribute to the volume of entrepreneurs facing closure and sickness. Therefore, there is a need for choosing right type of people to be given support facilities. A three-tier system commonly used for selection purpose includes "the analysis of application blanks"; psychological tests and group planning exercises"; and "personal interview". Presently each of the above areas are given different weightage by different organisation. Also there is variation in selection of psychological tests, games and exercises for selection purposes. The standardising of such selection procedures requisites longitudinal studies spread overt long period of investigations. The administrators generally do not support such longitudinal studies. Since empirical evidences are lacking many organisations avoid conducting selection tests or apply a non-standard procedure as per their convenience (some time which). This erode the quality of EDP and may endanger even its credibility in the long run.

Industry specific information play vital role in selecting, designing and deciding the size of units, and market strategy. The inadequate information prevents entry into an Entrepreneurial venture. The lack of information also contribute considerably to the wrong decision resulting into sickness. Often the healthy units also have been reported stagnating format of appropriate information. Problems are acute and the national organisation set up for collection, storage and dissemination of such informationm may require heavy reinforcement or even decentralisation at lower level. The existing network of industrial information is proving the major hurdle in accelerating the process of entrepreneurship develoment.

Technology is fast changing. What is new technology today is likely to be obsolete in next five years. It is more true in case of the technology adopted by small entrepreneurs in general. With a change in technology, the unit loses its capabilities of competitiveness. Subsequently, entrepreneurs are continuously worried about the product development in given period of time but their access to latest technology is very poor. Many of them do not have internal R&D and trade totally dependent on the technology/processes developed elsewhere. The urgency, however, is often not appreciated by research staff of technical institutes/ centres of excellence. This is one of the major hurdles in promoting Hi-Tech small industry. Mere physical proximity between researchers and industrialists may not necessarily eliminate the barriers which inhibit the meaning full interaction resulting into development and flow to technology. This issue requires continues attention an innovations in formulating strategy for the development quick flow and transfer of appropriate technology to the small entrepreneurs.

The human factor refers to the attitude, desire and motivation of individual, his capability to perceive the environment change and opportunities as well as his ability to solve the problem which an entrepreneurs is likely to fact. The training is effective in developing all these aspects of human factor provided it is planned well with balanced emphasis on all aspects. An analysis of the development process that helps emergence of people opting for entrepreneurial career in the society and succeeding in setting and running self-employment activites, reveals that it follow a sequence of development in individual personality, capability and ability.

The first generation of entrepreneur requires to develop:

- Entrepreneurial quality/motivation;
- Capability for enterprise launching/motivation;
- Ability for enterprise management; and
- Sense of responsibility to the society that promote/support them.

These aspects related to individual behaviour, abilities and capabilities follow the logical sequence of development which ultimately drive prospective entrepreneurs to actual entrepreneurial career.

The training has been the common component of most of entrepreneurial development programmes conducted by various organisations. Of course training conducted by these organisations vary in terms of their duration, content and methodology. Probably depending on the availability of faculty and orientation of the organising agencies, the emphasis shift towards one or the other. Training varies in methodology as well.

Of late, the efforts have been made to standardise such training by evolving 'Model Syllabi' for entrepreneurship development training at national level. But the issue related to standardisation of training in order to achieve the desired result is still alive to ensure the minimum standard.

The growth in number of small business is very rapid all over the world. But the percentage of small business unit facing closure or sickness are growing significantly. One of the every 12 units started in US is facing closure every year. In India, according to the data available with the RBI, the number or sick units during 1982 was as high as 50,549 out of 10,44,405 units claiming 5.6% SSI units becoming sick. The Reserve Bank of India defines a unit as sick if "it has incurred cash loss for one year and in the judgment of the bank is likely to continue to incur such losses for the current year as well as the following year and which has imbalance in its financial structure such as, current ratio of less than 1:1 and worsening debt equity ratio (total outside liabilities to the net worth)". According to the diagnostic study of a sample conducted by the Development Commissioner (SSI) India, the major causes of sickness are:

- 30% due to shortage of working capital/inadequacy and untimely assistance from the banks.
- 22% due to scarcity of raw-material.
- 13% due to lack of demand.
- 10% due to management deficiencies.

No account has been given for the remaining 25% except for the first case which explains for 30% sickness, the remaining factors can be broadly attributed to the management functions. Even if certain percentage is assigned to environmental factors, beyond the control of the owner/manager of small business, considerable percentage of sickness appears to emerge from management inadequacies. Moreover, against the great potential of further growth and graduating small business to medium & large industry, the majority of small business units beyond large are found stagnating with same level of operation. The dominant factors may be the lack of management insight & competency. The great growth potential demand greater emphasis to devise content and methodology for management education, training and consultancy.

Most of the modern management techniques have been developed for the use of large business establishments. Theoretically and in principle these hold good also to small business management. But their scale of operation and the need of specialist for their application appear to be the major bottleneck in the use of such management techniques in small business management. This suggests testing and adaptation of such management practices.

The small entrepreneurs is up against considerable odds, when he goes out looking for funds either fixed or variable capital financing. This is not because the finances are not available or schemes have not formulated for meeting varieties of need for capital financing. India is probably one of those countries which have multiple schemes launched by various financial institutions under the leadership of IDBI. Although various schemes have been instituted, they are all functioning at a sub-optimal level. The kind of venture capital support that is needed to nurture and sustain small technologically innovative and dynamic business is perhaps not present in most of the developing countries. The another hurdle in raising capital financing by small entrepreneurs more often arise out of the comparison with medium and large industries. In a comparison to medium and large industries small entrepreneurs are often very helpess in providing assets and security which on paper, not required but in practices never ignored. Again for the purpose of industrial growth and rehabilitation of sick units the necessary funds should flow fast.

For sustaining entrepreneurship, the capital financing requires that the officials belonging to both industrial extension system and financial institutionms develop comprehensive understanding of health of industrial untis, posses diagnostic skill to assess the health and acquire counselling skill to influence needy SMI to implement remedial growth measures and above all develop favourably attitudes towards extension approach which is basically opposite to the concept of a donor.

Entrepreneurship Development has been found a forceful movement to fight the acute problem of growing unemployment. When it has been attempted sincerely and systematically, it has yielded very rewarding results. In the past, many mistakes have been committed as a part of 'hit and miss' trial methods. The success is bound to be there provided we formulate strategy by understading the concept, process and techniques of developing entrepreneurship. One area of caution is also necessary to understand the similarity and distinction between entrepreneurship and self-employment. All entrepreneurs are self-employed but all self-employed are not necessarily entrepreneurs The tendency to ignore such differences may make the strategy weaker. A diluted strategy for developing entrepreneurship may result in failure and consequently the task of piece-rate-workers. Both may be necessary and useful at different stages but should be attempted with clear-cut distinctions and omitting the confusion by titling the programme differently.

Middle-class families (middle-income group) seem to be the direct benefitciaries of EDPs. This group is important in terms of both number and influencing public opinions. In the course of developing entrepreneurship, the supply of inputs (including finance) plays a crucial role. Instead of treating such inputs as development requirements, there may be a tendency to use them as a means to earn favour. There may be temptation to politicize the whole movement.

The entrepreneurship movement which started in India, in mid sixties have proved its potential. Now the dynamics and methodology are clear, strategies are more or less standardised. The scope and coverage, however, is so vast and widespread that the movement requires active involvement and enthusiasm of all the government voluntary organisations and social reformer. Through entrepreneurship, it is possible to build new economic order with progressive socio-psychological make-up.

Assurance

The experience of implementation of NREP/RLEGP over the years showed that whereas the Government of India's objective in starting these programmes was to tackle the problems unemployment of unskilled rural labourers, the distribution of funds by the States in different regions and districtis did not follow this logic. The funds did not invariably go to the areas of concentration of unemployed landless and rural labour. It was found in the evaluation of NREP that about 53 per cent of villages did not take up even a single work under NREP for nine years or so its implementation. The wage—employment resources were being used b the States as a substitute for their plan/non—plan schemes. The assets being created were not economically productive. The system of approval of the projects/schemes was such that it left much to be desired. In spite of the clear guidelines

thatthe felt needs of the vijllage people should be reflected in the works programme, there was not nmuch involvement of the people at the grass roots level in identifying the works and implementation of these programmes.

It is against this background that the financial year 1989—90 became an important landmark in the history of the wage employment programmes in India when a massive programme of Jawahar Rozgar Yojana (JRY) was launched by merging NREP and RLEGP. The expenditure under the programme is shared between the centre and the States on a 80:20 basis. Apart from the commitment of the government to empower the village level institutions, one ofthe reasons for the launching of JRY was to take the wage employment programmes to each and every village in the country (see Chauhan, 1997a). Another landmark was the year 1993—94, when the element of assurance was added in the wage employment programmes by launching the Employment Assurance Scheme (EAS) in 1,746 blocks (see Chauhan, 1994a). During the year, JRY was also strengthened and deepened, particularly, in the backward districts by launching the intensive JRY. The last year of the VIII Plan (ie 1996—97) has been another landmark when the purely asset—oriented programmes were delinked from JRY and EAS is broadened and extended to include the entire country under its ambit. Now we are witnessing a phase of assurance of employment although it falls short of the right to work. The question is: can we provide the right to work to all or not? For the present, it is beyond the economic capacity of many of the less income countries like India to guarantee right to work. The right to work has also its legal connotations.

The concept of right to work which has been considered by the Supreme Court in some of its judgments as an Implied Right enshrined under Article

21 of the Constitution of India, guaranteeing, 'protecton of life and personal liberty' and hence right to life. The concept of right to work has two different implications. In the first place, right to work can be interpreted to mean right of every citizen to get employment according to one's qualifications, training, aptitude, etc. The other simpler version of right to work is to ensure that at least unskilled work will be available for all willing workers at a minimum prescribed wage. The first concept is difficult to implement in a liberalized kind of economy where a major part of the employment generation is in the private sector. Again, where the government does not have direct control over the direction of investment in the economy, it would be difficult for it to ensure that all citizens are provided employment according to their qualifications and training. What is feasible in a free economy like ours, is to bring about a match etween the skill, aptitude, etc, of citizens and the availability of employment through a process of planning.

The planning could relate to both supply and demand side, viz provision of trained manpower through appropriate control over manpower training and absorption of skilled labour in various labour intensive industries etc. This sort of matching skills with available employment has to be planned over a period and can be achieved only in stages. Guaranteeing work to every citizen according to his or her skills is, no doubt, a country hardly leaves any choice with the Indian planners.

Article 41 of the Constitution under the Chapter 'Directive Principles of State Policy' has directed the State, within the limits of its economic capacity and to make effective provision for securing right to work among the other socially desirable provisions. The economic capacity of the Indian economy even cannot afford guarantee of employment or minimum wage for the present. Hence the assurance of 100 days of work in the form of casual manual work.

Is there a need for basic changes? Some people, educationists included, consider that basic changes are not necessary. They are satisfied with the existing system and their argument is that the higher education system introduced by the British has produced eminent and women, leaders in all spheres of human activity. They forget that the system has been changed drastically and several aspects completely eliminated in the very country which introduced the modern system of education in India. Change is the law of life and change we must if we want to make imoportant strides in the world of education.

Knowledge is always expanding and unless we change our rigid systems introduced long ago, we cannot bring any good to the country.

This does not mean that everything connected with Indian education right from ancient times should be discarded. The essential aspects of modern Western education could be found in the ancient Buddhist institutions that flourished in Nalanda, Takshila and Vikramshila. For example, Nalanda had a campus and a remarkable depository of information accessible to local and foreign scholars. There were three library buildings catering to 8500 resident students from India and the neighbouring countries and 1500 teachers form India; there were several dozen visiting schilars from abroad. With seven big auditoria and dozens of small halls where a hundred or more lectures were delivered every day by prominent teachers, Nalanda was the best institution of higher education in ancient South Asia (if not in the whole of Asia). Famous travellers to India form the outside world (like Huen Tsang, for example) have testified to the greatness of Nalanda. Even the modern concept of academic autonomy was prevalent in ancient Indian universities.

However, for socioeconomic and political reasons, the tradition of scholarship declined in India even among the upper castes who were custodians of learning. (The lower castes and the untouchables did not have access to education, not to speak of higher education). So when the famous (or infamous?) Minute of Macaulay (1835) led to the concretization of Englich education at the University level, the upper castes made good use of it and secured jobs in the revenue collection and law and order departments of the British government. The clamour among educated Indians was provileges equal to those of the British.

When the three universities–Calcutta, Madras and Bombay–were established in 1857, 27 colleges were already in existence and these were affijliated to the three universities. The period between 1857 and 1947 saw very slow growth in the number of universities and colleges. At the time of Independence, there were, as mentioned earlier, 20 universities and 437 colleges and five institutions offering postgraduate courses in Engineering and 22 in Medicine. Today, there are 220 universities and about 8000 colleges. This unprecedented growth in higher educaiton is the direct result of the rising expectations among people following the attainment of freedom from the foreign yoke.

The fact remains, however, that despite this phenomenal growth in higher education, all those who seek higher education cannot get it. The infrastructural facilities are not enough and those facilities that are available are not put to good use for socio-political, economic and cultural reasons. Very pertinent questions for which proper answers are yet to be found are;

- Is higher education of the kind offered noe adequate for the country?
- Should all those who pass the high school go for higher education?
- Does everyone who seek a job need a university degree? Can there not be a job-degree delking?
- Are all those who get higher education gainfully employed? If not, can we change the goals and contents of higher education?
- Should there not be a total change in the structure of courses and course designing and also in the pattern of course choice? Should there not be flexibility in course offerings to cater to the individual goals and talents of young people? Should there not be an opportunity for young and old to receive higher education at their own pace so that they can fulfil their pressing economic obligations first and then return to college?
- Can there be more opportunities for technical and vocational courses that will enable scholars not only to find employment but also to start their own business enterprises?
- Is there a need for redesigning higher education to make it helpful in national integration and nationa development?
- Does every college and University possess sufficient facilities for library and reading rooms, laboratories, computerized netwirking, physical education facilities (physical education shuld be made compulsory for all except for those who are medically advised against it) and laboratories?
- Should the affiliation system as it is practised now be revised so that college administration, teaching, course designing and evaluation become more

autonomous? Can there be genuine academic, administrative and financial decentralization in the management of universities and colleges?

- What can we do to make universities and college more relevant to society and to the solution of socio-economic and development problems faced by the nation? How can university-interactions with industry, local administration and local people be strengthened and mutual exchanges of ideas made more frequent and effective?
- Can we establish more informal and open systems of learning so that the economic burden of establishing new univestities and colleges be reduced to the maximum extent possible?
- Can the universities become real centres oflearning and leadership/so that the country benefits in a number of ways, especially in empowering women and the disadvantaged sections of the population without whose progress no real improvement in the national condition can be achieved?
- What can education do to improve conditions of living in the rural areas–health, hygiene, environment, good preservation, literacy, employment, road facilities, water-ways, sports and cultural entertainment facilities, water supply systems, transport and communication? Is higher education relevant to rural life?
- How can interactive, computerized systems of information and communication be utilized in finding solutions to all problems connected witht he above questions?
- Is there a need for re-structuring various bodies of the universities so that they will be more compact and there will be more compact and there will be higher proportion of academics in them?

Answers to these questions will pave the way towards the full utilization of the educational facilities availble at present and the establishment of newer and more effective facilities for the progress of the nation.

Quantitative growth there has been in Indian higher education; in fact, tremendous growth. But such growth is not only inadequate but patently dangerous. It has to be replaced by educational development based on national priorities, national ethos and an internationa outlook.